GENDER, VIOLENCE AND SECURITY

GENDER, VIOLENCE AND SECURITY

DISCOURSE AS PRACTICE

LAURA J. SHEPHERD

ZED BOOKS
London & New York

Gender, Violence and Security: Discourse as Practice was first published in 2008 by
Zed Books Ltd, 7 Cynthia Street, London N1 9JF, UK
and Room 400, 175 Fifth Avenue, New York, NY 10010, USA

www.zedbooks.co.uk

Designed and typeset in Monotype Garamond
by illuminati, Grosmont, www.illuminatibooks.co.uk
Cover designed by Andrew Corbett
Printed and bound in the EU by Biddles Ltd, King's Lynn

Distributed in the USA exclusively by Palgrave Macmillan,
175 Fifth Avenue, New York, NY 10010, USA

A catalogue record for this book is available from the British Library
Library of Congress Cataloguing in Publication Data available

ISBN 978 1 84277 927 9 hb
ISBN 978 1 84277 928 6 pb

CONTENTS

ACKNOWLEDGEMENTS

On beginning my Master's degree, after some time away from the academy, I found the language of International Relations almost entirely impenetrable. Struggling, I made an appointment to see the course director to tell her that I couldn't possibly continue with the programme. She told me to hang in there, that it would all become clear if I persevered. In the weeks that followed, as we began to study more critical theories of International Relations, I found my feet, and at the end of the semester the course director asked whether I had ever considered doing doctoral research. I replied that I hadn't, and she said simply, 'Well, maybe you should.' So I did, and the course director, Jutta Weldes, eventually co-supervised that research along with Judith Squires. It is no overstatement to say that without their inspiration, guidance and support, this book would not have been written. I also thank colleagues and friends from the University of Bristol, particularly Penny Griffin, Ana Jordan and Christina Rowley, for conversations about discourse theory, gender politics and shoes over pink wine, and I am grateful to Jindy Pettman and Marysia Zalewski for their enthusiasm about this project and their encouragement of its author. Finally, I would like to dedicate this book to my extended family, friends being the family that you get to choose in life, but most specifically my partner Brian and our brand new son Joe.

Laura J. Shepherd, February 2008

LIST OF ABBREVIATIONS

AI	Amnesty International
BPFA	Beijing Platform for Action
BRIDGE	Briefings on Development and Gender
CDA	Critical Discourse Analysis
CEDAW	Convention on the Elimination of All Forms of Discrimination Against Women
CoGG	Commission on Global Governance
DDR	Disarmament, Demobilization and Reintegration
DEVAW	Declaration on the Elimination of Violence Against Women
DTA	Discourse-Theoretical Analysis
ECA	Economic Commission for Africa
ECOSOC	Economic and Social Council
GA	General Assembly
HAP	Hague Appeal for Peace
HMSO	Her Majesty's Stationery Office
IA	International Alert
ICC	International Criminal Court
IDS	Institute of Development Studies
IGO	Inter-Governmental Organization
INSTRAW	United Nations International Research and Training Institute for the Advancement of Women
IR	International Relations
NGO	Non-Governmental Organization

NGO WG	Non-Governmental Organization Working Group
OPSI	Office of Public Sector Information
P5	Permanent members of the UNSC
PKO	Peacekeeping Operation
UK	United Kingdom
UN	United Nations
UNDAW	United Nations Division for the Advancement of Women
UNDP	United Nations Development Programme
UNDPKO	United Nations Department of Peacekeeping Operations
UNESC	United Nations Economic and Social Council
UNIFEM	United Nations Development Fund for Women
UNFWCW	United Nations Fourth World Conference on Women
UNSC	United Nations Security Council
UNSCR	United Nations Security Council Resolution
UNSG	United Nations Secretary-General
USA	United States of America
USSR	Union of Soviet Socialist Republics
WCRWC	Women's Commission for Refugee Women and Children
WHO	World Health Organization
WILPF	Women's International League for Peace and Freedom

1 | INTRODUCTION

Women's bodies have actually become battle grounds ... the violence is all about destroying ... the inbuilt strength of a woman to build a community.

> Ruth Ojiambo Ochieng, Uganda, 2006

We have documented ... systematic sexual violence, committed by the Burmese military as a weapon of war in the ongoing conflict ... where women are raped ... in order to terrorize the women, and the local community, morally, psychologically, and also physically.

> Nang Charm Tong, Burma, 2006

We've had reports from women ... about some very difficult situations that lesbians have been going through. There is more violence towards them because they've broken away from the gender role expected of them. This is why there is more repression.... they suffer direct repression on their bodies and their lives.

> Elisabeth Castillo, Colombia, 2006[1]

These personal narratives, provided by women reflecting on the difficulties of coordinating research on and activism against gendered violence, are disturbing to say the least. Taken from the website of Amnesty International's 'Stop Violence Against Women' campaign, the above testimonies draw attention not only to the crucial need to better the experiences of women who live under threat of violence, but also to the conceptual and practical impediments to combating

violence against women in contemporary academic and policy environments. In the academic discipline of International Relations (IR), one
of the most salient obstacles is the ways in which gendered violence
has been conventionally and conceptually precluded as an object of
study (Peterson and Runyan 1999: 115–17).

Feminist challenges to the well-defined and equally well-defended
boundaries of IR[2] have drawn attention not only to the potential
of transgressing those boundaries but also to the importance of
understanding (gendered) violence in relation to security.[3] Turning the
analytical focus of this research to *gendered* violence is motivated by
two related concerns. '[V]iolence establishes social relationships ... it
marks and makes bodies ... it constitutes subjects even as it renders
them incomplete' (D'Cruze and Rao 2004: 503). This latter understanding of violence, as constitutive of subjectivity, has historically
been absented from academic theorizing of security, where violence
is conventionally conceived of as a functional mechanism within an
anarchic international system.[4] Second, given that violence 'marks
and makes bodies', I seek to understand the types of body that
are marked and made through violence that is specifically gendered
– that is, violence that 'emerges from a profound desire to keep
the binary order of gender natural or necessary' (Butler 2004: 35).
Stemming from a desire to formulate a theorization of security in
relation to violence, I argue that studying the subjects produced
through gendered violence in the context of debates over the meaning
and content of security provides more coherent accounts of both
violence and security.

The notion that identity is central to theorizing security has been
well explicated by scholars critical of conventional, state-centric
approaches to security.[5] 'Recognising gender as a significant dimension
of identity and security opens the door to non-state-based views of
security and aptly illustrates how identity shapes individual and collective security needs' (Hoogensen and Rottem 2004: 156). However,
most of these critical voices seek to interject into academic debates on
security by broadening the accepted agenda of security – to include
the recognition of multiple phenomena, from earthquakes to economic
deprivation, as threatening to security – and proliferating the referent
objects of security discourse, such that security is no longer solely the

concern of states but also of communities, societies and individuals. While scholars of security have contested the parameters of debates about security, and feminist scholars of security have drawn attention to the importance of gender as a category of analysis, there is little work being done on the ways in which the organizational logics of security and violence are discursively constituted (see Shepherd and Weldes 2007).

CONTRIBUTIONS OF A FEMINIST POSTSTRUCTURALIST[6]

I identify myself as a feminist researcher, and recognize that this entails a curiosity about 'the concept, nature and practice of gender' (Zalewski 1995: 341). This curiosity questions the ways in which gender is made meaningful in social/political interactions and the practices – or performances – through which gender configures boundaries of subjectivity. In this book, I treat gender as a noun, a verb and a logic that is product/productive of the performances of violence and security I investigate here. I espouse a feminism that seeks to challenge conventional constructions of gendered subjectivity and political community, while acknowledging the intellectual heritage of feminisms that seek to claim rights on behalf of a stable subject and maintain fidelity to a regime of truth that constitutes the universal category of 'women' (Butler 2004: 8–11). While a feminist project that does not assume a stable ontology of gender may seem problematic, I argue, along with Judith Butler, that '[t]he deconstruction of identity is not the deconstruction of politics; rather, it establishes as political the very terms through which identity is articulated' (1999: 189).

A focus on articulation entails a further commitment to the analytical centrality of language – or, as I see it, discourse. Elizabeth Grosz argues that an integral part of feminist theory is the willingness to 'tackle the question of the language available for theoretical purposes and the constraints it places on what can be said' (1987: 479). To me, this aspect of feminist theory is definitive of my feminist politics. If 'men and women are the stories that have been told about "men" and "women"' (Sylvester 1994: 4), and the way that 'men' and 'women' both act and are acted upon, then the language used to tell those stories and describe those actions is not just worthy of analytical attention but can form the basis of an engaged critique. Furthermore, an approach that recognizes that there is more to the discursive constitution of gender – the stories that are told about 'men' and 'women' – than linguistic practices can enable thinking gender differently.

Alison Stone, reading Butler's work on feminism and political theory, argues that this type of approach constitutes a 'genealogical feminism', in which the organizational logics of feminism – historically assumed to be 'women' and/or 'gender' – are 'continually re-enacted through corporeal activities' (2005: 12). This approach allows for research that investigates the ways in which 'women' as subjects and objects act, speak, write and represent themselves, are represented, written about, spoken about and acted on. There is no singular feminine subject or feminist approach, just as, in my understanding, the notion of a singular feminist project is unsustainable. My study therefore seeks to contribute to contemporary debates in its desire to think differently the concepts of gender, violence, security and the international by investigating how these concepts are (re)presented and (re)produced in a particular discursive context.[7]

Espousing a poststructural politics is not always acknowledged to be compatible with a commitment to a feminist politics.[8] Traversing this terrain entails constructing a politics that speaks of 'undecidability' (Elam 1994: 32). With reference to the difficulties of formulating a feminist politics without a definitive subject, Diane Elam argues that 'undecidability forms part of a situation of representation, political action, or ethical judgement … We may not yet know what women can do or be, but feminism has an obligation at the very least to think about what this might mean' (Elam 1994: 32). Thus, the theory/practice[9] of feminist poststructuralisms in whatever guise does not represent 'simply another oxymoron, a new quagmire of contradiction for feminists to sink in' (Moi 1990: 368) but rather a dynamic and thorough exploration of what feminism itself 'might mean'.

This in no way suggests that other feminisms have not enabled the articulation of critiques of gender and other relations of power that are valid, vigorous and vital. My political consciousness developed through the tracing of feminist work in the discipline of anthropology that drew attention to the 'margins, silences and bottom rungs' of the discipline.[10] It was from this perspective that I learned what I meant when I called myself a feminist, and what it meant politically to pay close attention to the development of gendered subjectivities. This background gave me a strong appreciation for the particular rather than the abstract, the specific rather than the general, and most of all for the practices of power that are product/productive of ways of being in the world. The value in telling a different story is in the telling, in illustrating the ways in which these stories are constructed and could be constructed differently. The transience is best encapsulated in this quote from de Lauretis:

> This shift implies, in my opinion, a dis-placement and a self-displacement: leaving or giving up a place that is safe, that is 'home' … for another place that is unknown and risky, … a place of discourse from which speaking and thinking are at best tentative, uncertain and unguaranteed. But the leaving is not a choice: one could not live there in the first place. (cited in Brooks 1997: 211)

INTRODUCING 1325

In this study, I explore the discursive constitution of concepts of (gender) violence and (international) security in particular texts.[11] In using the texts that I do as vehicles for analysis I emphatically do not want to suggest that the documents as they stand are too problematic to serve as the foundation for academic and activist work that seeks to combat gender violence and frame such violence as an international security concern. The texts themselves are treated as vehicles for the theoretical investigation I undertake here: an exploration of the potential for reconceptualizing the concepts of (gender) violence and (international) security. However, the study undertaken here is explicitly not 'merely' theoretical, or 'academic' in the pejorative sense of the term.[12] My interest in the concepts of (international) security and (gender) violence is indeed motivated by a desire to see whether these concepts could be reconceived, in keeping with a commitment to thinking these concepts differently. However, I also consider the implications of such a reconceptualization on policy as well as academic work. I wish to provide for those undertaking such work the possibility of alternative concepts with which to proceed. Therefore, this book, despite its theoretical leaning and heritage, does indeed have an avowedly practical application.

In undertaking this study, I wish to contribute to both policy and academic debates. I offer a reconceptualization of (international) security and (gender) violence through my analysis, drawing on bodies of academic literature to establish the limits of the relevant discourses. Furthermore, I illustrate the ways in which these concepts, as they currently inform policy and academic debates, are both a product of and productive of the difficulties described above. This book uses United Nations Security Council Resolution 1325, and related documentation from the United Nations and the NGO Working Group for Women, Peace and Security, as a vehicle for the analysis of the question, 'How are the concepts of (international) security and (gender) violence discursively constituted, and with what effects?' These two institutions both claim a degree of author-ity over the Resolution,[13] the United Nations through the Security Council and the NGO Working Group through the advocacy of its members that, as they claim, successfully resulted in the adoption of the Resolution (NGO WG 2005).

UNSCR 1325 was adopted in 2000 with the aim of ensuring that all efforts towards peace-building and post-conflict reconstruction, as well as the conduct of armed conflict itself, would entail sensitivity towards gendered violence and gendered inequalities. The Resolution is an appropriate vehicle for this analysis, providing as it does an articulation of the concepts of gender, violence, security and the international with which I am concerned. The Resolution refers to 'the primary responsibility of the Security Council under the Charter for the maintenance of international peace and security' (UNSC 2000a: Preamble) and, further, to the need for the international community to 'protect women and girls from gender-based violence, particularly rape and other forms of sexual abuse' (UNSC 2000a: Article 10) in the provision of security.

Thus, I treat UNSCR 1325 as a site at which discourses of (international) security and (gender) violence are in contact, a site at which it is possible to identify different articulations of the concepts of gender, violence, security and the international that constitute different discourses of (gender) violence and (international) security. Through discourse-theoretical analysis, I explore the tensions and inconsistencies that are product/productive of the contact of these discourses.

That is, specific conceptualizations of security (as 'international') and violence (as 'gender') inform the Resolution. Through my analysis I unpick the discursive construction of these concepts and investigate the implications of the Resolution, and therefore the concepts that are product/productive of it, for policy and research in this area. I conclude that the organization of the Resolution around liberal concepts of international security and gender violence suggests that transformation of social/political community can only be achieved through processes of peace(state)building and gender mainstreaming.[14] In developing a critique of these processes, I argue that they cannot deliver the radical reforms that UNSCR 1325 purports to seek.

Academic and advocacy research that exists on UNSCR 1325 affirms the significance of the Resolution, arguing for instance that

> Resolution 1325 is a watershed political framework that makes women – and a gender perspective – relevant to negotiating peace agreements, planning refugee camps and peacekeeping operations and reconstructing war-torn societies. It makes the pursuit of gender equality relevant to every single Council action, ranging from mine clearance to elections to security sector reform. (Rehn and Sirleaf 2002: 3)

UNSCR 1325 has been lauded as 'unique' (Cohn 2004: 8–9), and has provided governments and non-government actors alike with a comprehensive set of tools with which to approach the issue of conflict resolution through a gendered lens. In a survey of civil society activity, '[o]ut of a total of 44 respondents, 38 indicated that they use 1325 in their work on women, peace and security issues' (NGO WG 2004: 5).

However, it has also been recognized that 'peace agreements, electoral and judicial reform and government restructuring are only as good as their implementation' (Rehn and Sirleaf 2002: 84). The capacities of UNSCR 1325, such as they are, while potentially enabling the redress of gendered inequalities in conflict and post-conflict situations, have largely been lost in translation in the Resolution's journey from adoption to advocacy tool. It has been argued that the implementation of policy aimed at ameliorating the situations of women can function to misrepresent the involvement of women in processes of reconstruction by sustaining the women-as-peacemaker stereotype (Pankhurst 2004: 38; see also Whitbread 2005; Wilson 2005). Also, such 'gender-sensitive' policy is easily sidelined, as a result of the widely evidenced belief that 'issues regarding women, gender and human rights are "soft" or marginal issues' (Mazurana 2005: 40) that can safely be put on a back burner while the 'hard' issues of political organization and reconstruction are dealt with.

Therefore, while UNSCR 1325 is both a remarkable document in its own right and an opportunity for the construction of more inclusive reconstruction programmes in a variety of contexts, gaps and weaknesses remain. This book proceeds on the understanding that the concepts around which the Resolution is organized are instrumental in constructing the ways in which specific policy can be implemented; without critical engagement with these concepts, efforts to understand the limited successes of the Resolution will be partial. While there has been extensive involvement with UNSCR 1325 in the research and construction of advocacy tools and evaluations in specific conflict situations, there has been little consideration of the 'productive force [of UNSCR 1325] in shaping conceptions of women and gender' (Cohn et al. 2004: 136). In identifying the Resolution as a fitting vehicle for analysis, I recognize this 'productive force', not only in the context of 'women and gender' but also in the discursive construction of violence, security and the international. The discourses that I seek to analyse in this book are both produced by and productive of the documents that I use to conduct the analysis, and UNSCR 1325, mandating as it does subsequent reports by the United Nations Secretary-General that allow for the investigation of the ways in which the articulations of these concepts change over time, is a suitable focus for this investigation.

I offer a feminist reconceptualization of international security and gender violence because the current conceptualizations are not adequate for the task of thinking gender differently in the context of violence and security. They do not allow for the development of theory or practice that is capable of addressing the complexities inherent in these issues. As Wendy Brown argues, 'What suspicion about the naturalness of gender subordination persists when feminism addresses only the wrongs done to women and not the socially produced capacity for women to be wronged, to be victims?' (2003: 11). In the context of security, investigating this capacity manifests in a curiosity about 'what Foucault would have called the overall discursive fact that security is spoken about at all' (Dillon 1996: 14) and the ways in which performances of security discourse function to (re)produce particular configurations of social/political reality. The theoretical inadequacies, relating to the ways in which current conceptualizations of international security and gender violence inform policy and practice, have grievous consequences. These consequences impact not only on future policy addressing gender in situations of armed conflict and post-conflict reconstruction, but also on the grass-roots organizations that use UNSCR 1325 to lobby for reconstruction and thus the individuals who live the impact of these policy decisions.

AIMS

The first of four related aims of this study is to illustrate the ways in which discourses of (international) security and (gender) violence are in contact in UNSCR 1325. This involves not only identifying the moments at which UNSCR 1325 explicitly mentions these two concepts, but also tracing the ways in which these concepts are situated in relation to each other. Mapping the concepts through the Resolution in this way enables me to make an argument about the 'before' of the Resolution – that is, how it came to be written in the way that it did. Furthermore, this technique allows me to identify the ways in which the conceptualizations of gender violence and international security evidenced in the Resolution are taken forward into policy discussions about the 'after' of UNSCR 1325 – or, indeed, the way that they are left unproblematized in such discussions.

The second aim of the study is to demonstrate that the discursive construction of the concepts in question determined the failure of UNSCR 1325. Although I explore the explanations given by the United Nations and the NGO Working Group on Women, Peace and Security for the failures – and successes – of the Resolution, neither the institutions nor academic research on the subject problematizes the discursive construction of the organizing concepts. Therefore, my third aim is to establish the ways in which UNSCR 1325 was constructed through, and represents, particular conceptualizations of (gender) violence and (international) security and, furthermore, to highlight that these discourses, on which the Resolution relies for textual coherence, could have been constructed differently.

Ultimately, I argue that (international) security can be reconceptualized in conjunction with (gender) violence, and to separate these concepts is to construct an analytical framework that is both partial and highly problematic. I recognize that focusing on gender in an effort to understand the particular articulations of violence and security in the documents with which I am concerned also functions to produce a partial reading, as I marginalize concerns of race, class, ethnicity and other (post)structural hierarchies of exclusion. I refer to these hierarchies as (post)structural as I see them as mutable through contextual performance, rather than as sedimented structural conditions. Moreover, this book is of relevance not only to academics working on security and violence, but also to the institutions in question, the UN Security Council and the NGO Working Group. The book evidences the ways in which academic and policy discourses are largely mutually constitutive. Policymakers and academic theorists '[b]oth use and are used by language ... that dominant powers ... always dream of fixing' (Der Derian 1990: 297), and that is 'fixed' in the authoring of documents such as UNSCR 1325.

The policy relevance of this study is the exploration of different possibilities. I do not wish to map out 'the best', or even 'a better', way that UNSCR 1325 could have been written. I wish to think gender, violence, security and the international differently through this research process, joining Butler in her desire to

> follow a double path in politics: we must use this language to assert an entitlement to conditions of life in ways that affirm the constitutive role of gender and sexuality in political life, and we must also subject our very categories to critical scrutiny. (2004: 37–8)

I do not read the use of 'must' in the above exhortation as inscribing a sense of unified agenda, with which I would not be entirely comfortable. Such usage would suggest that work that does not follow this 'double path' can be judged by some standard as lesser. Rather, I read it as an acknowledgement that I am (an assumed 'we' are) both literally and philosophically bound by the language available to discuss 'conditions of life', by the limits of the discourses. Therefore, the insistence on focusing on the words that are used to make policy, on subjecting those words to 'critical scrutiny', is certainly compatible with the approach I take in this book.

OUTLINE OF THIS STUDY

Guided by the central research question, 'How are the concepts of (international) security and (gender) violence discursively constituted, and with what effects?', this book seeks to answer a series of related questions pertaining to the discursive construction of international security and gender violence. Each chapter addresses a specific question in relation to the broader question that guides the study. In Chapter 2, I ask: What are the most appropriate analytical strategies to use in this study?[15] Arranging the chapters thus offers to the reader the sense that consideration of analytical strategies occurred prior to the consideration of extant literature on the subject with which I am concerned. This is true, but I also wish to draw attention to the ways in which the review of the literature in Chapter 3 is informed by the strategies I discuss in the previous exploration of ontology, epistemology and methodology, a linkage that is not commonly acknowledged.

Chapter 3 explores several related questions, and functions as a review of the relevant extant literature. This chapter is central to the study as a whole, asking as it does: What are the differences between thinking about 'violence against women' and thinking about 'gender violence? Similarly, what are the differences between thinking about 'national security' and thinking about 'international security'? Which approaches – and, therefore, which conceptualizations – are currently dominant?' The analysis I conduct, which begins in Chapter 4 with the Reports of the United Nations Secretary-General, both textually and intellectually develops from this review, and I bring the analytical strategies outlined in Chapter 2 to bear on the literature to identify dominant conceptualizations of gender, violence, security and the international.

Surveying two bodies of literature, one concerned with security situated firmly in the discipline of International Relations and the other more broadly sociological, addressing violence and gender, demands that careful consideration is given to the links between them. Therefore, in Chapter 3, the questions that I ask relate to the organizing concepts of these two literatures. In the discussion of the security literature, I question how different approaches to security conceive of the referent object of security, and how they conceive of threat. Similarly, in the discussion of the violence literature, I draw out the ways in which the various approaches conceptualize the referent object of their analyses, and how they too conceive of threat – in this case, violence. Finally, I draw together these discussions and relate them to more specific writings on 'gender violence' as an 'international security' issue, arguing that these conceptualizations are dominant in academic debates and policymaking.

Through a discourse-theoretical analysis of the Secretary-General's Reports, Chapter 4 asks: 'How has UNSCR 1325 affected/effected the treatment of 'gender violence' as an 'international security' issue? What are the dominant explanations offered by the United Nations Secretary-General's Reports (2004a; 2002a) regarding the lack of gender equality in relation to peace and security?'[16] This chapter refers to literatures concerning gender and peacekeeping, gender mainstreaming, sexualized violence in war, gender and conflict, gender and peace processes and the domestic–international dichotomy in the analysis of the explanatory factors offered in the Reports. The conclusions detailed in the Reports are problematized, as I question the dominant explanations offered by the Reports (2004a; 2002a) regarding the lack of gender equality in relation to peace and security. Thus, this chapter forms the basis for the analysis of UNSCR 1325. I seek to demonstrate in this chapter that, whether or not the factors offered in explanation by the Reports are convincing, it is of vital importance to interrogate the concepts around which UNSCR 1325 is organized.

Chapter 5 details the discourse-theoretical analysis of UNSCR 1325, seeking to identify and explore the conceptualizations of gender, violence, the international and security that order the document through asking: 'How did UNSCR 1325 come to be written in the way that it was? What are the discursive conditions of possibility constructed by UNSCR 1325?' It is argued that these conceptualizations construct the horizons of possibility for the successful implementation and utilization of the Resolution by UN institutions,

NGOs and independent activists. To provide a basis for the analysis of the narratives of production of the Resolution, this chapter investigates the documents and organizations to which the Resolution explicitly refers. UNSCR 1325 refers to four UNSC Resolutions in its Preamble: UNSCR 1261 (1991); UNSCR 1265 (1999); UNSCR 1296 (2000); and UNSCR 1314 (2000). These are Resolutions that refer to the experiences of civilians and children during periods of armed conflict, and are offered in UNSCR 1325 as the documentary heritage of the Resolution, alongside 'relevant statements of its [the United Nations'] President' (UNSC 2000a: Preamble).

In Chapter 6, I explore the contested narratives of production of UNSCR 1325, asking: 'Which discourses of (international) security and (gender) violence played a significant role in the construction of UNSCR 1325? Which discourses of (international) security and (gender) violence were marginalized?' Both the United Nations and the NGO Working Group on Women, Peace and Security deploy narratives that seek to explain the production of the Resolution. This chapter analyses these narratives, using documents freely available from the UN and the NGO Working Group. For each institution, I provide a conventional descriptive account of their involvement in the construction of the Resolution, and then proceed with a discourse-theoretical analysis that draws out the tensions and compatibilities in these narratives of production. In the concluding section of this chapter, I draw out various conceptualizations of, for example, global governance and global civil society that delimit the discursive terrains of the institutions in question. I then problematize the conceptualizations of international security and gender violence in relation to these organizing concepts, exploring the conditions of possibility enabled by these discourses in the treatment of (gender) violence as an (international) security issue.

Finally, in Chapter 7, I explore the different possibilities that could have been enabled through different discourses of international security and gender violence. This concluding chapter asks: 'How could different possibilities have been enabled through different discourses of (international) security and (gender) violence?' The UN Secretary-General's Report of 2004 mandates annual Reports to assess the successes and failures of UNSCR 1325. I integrate these Reports in this concluding chapter to illustrate the ways in which UNSCR 1325 has, for the most part, failed to address effectively the issues with which it is concerned, and has thus been recognized as having very limited successes even by its own standards. I argue that there is a violence done to the concepts of gender and the international through their ordering according to binary logics: the domestic/international divide and the assumption of differentiated genders. Furthermore, I problematize the articulations of gender and the international that inform and organize the dominant discourses of violence and security that are product/productive of UNSCR 1325. To draw together the preceding chapters, I consider the ways in which UNSCR 1325 was constructed and could have been constructed differently, reflecting on the conceptualizations of the violent reproduction of gender and of the international that inform my analysis and the impact of this research on the policymakers and academics with whom I seek to engage.

ENDINGS AND BEGINNINGS

It may seem that there is a tension between espousing a feminist poststructural politics and undertaking research that seeks to detail, through deconstruction, the ways in which particular discourses have failed to manifest the reforms needed to address security and violence in the context of gendered subjectivity and the constitution of political community. In keeping with the ontological position I hold, I argue that Resolution 1325 could have been constructed differently: there is nothing inherent in the concepts of (international) security and (gender) violence that necessitated their being made meaningful in the way they were. However, through the exploration of the discursive terrains of the institutions that claim author-ity over the Resolution, I show that the contextual configuration of these terrains was such that the Resolution was both produced by, and continues to be productive of, the discourses of gender violence and international security that I problematize through my review of the relevant literature. Finally, I suggest that those working on policy and advocacy in the area of security and violence can use the reconceptualization I offer 'to enable people to imagine how their being-in-the-world is not only changeable, but perhaps, ought to be changed' (Milliken 1999: 244).

As a researcher, the question I have grown most used to hearing is not 'what?' or 'how?' but 'why?' At every level of the research process, from securing funding to relating to the academic community, it is necessary to be able to construct a convincing and coherent argument as to why this research is valuable, indeed vital, to the field in which I situate myself. A discourse-theoretical approach, as detailed in Chapter 2, acknowledges that my legitimacy as a knowing subject is constructed through discursive practices that privilege some forms of being over others. In the study of security, because of the discursive power of the concept, and of violence, which can quite literally be an issue of life and death, these considerations are particularly important.

Furthermore, as a result of the invigorating and investigative research conducted by exemplary feminist scholars in the field of IR, I feel encouraged to reclaim the space to conduct research at the margins of a discipline that itself functions under a misnomer, being concerned as it is with relations inter-state rather than inter-national. As Cynthia Enloe has expressed it:

> To study the powerful is not autocratic, it is simply reasonable. Really? ... It presumes *a priori* that margins, silences and bottom rungs are so naturally marginal, silent and far from power that exactly how they are *kept* there could not possibly be of interest to the reasoning, reasonable explainer. (1996: 188, emphasis in original)

If this is the case, I am more than happy to be unreasonable, and I am in excellent company.

2 | ANALYTICAL STRATEGIES

In analysing discourses of security, violence, the international and gender through the vehicle of UNSC Resolution 1325, I make a series of implicit and explicit statements about the world as I see it and judgements about how best to go about finding out about that world. In order to give context to these judgements and expand upon these statements, I reflect here on my chosen analytical strategies in four sections. First, I discuss the conceptualization of discourse that informs the analytical approach that I use in this investigation, which leads on to the second section in which I reflect on the Foucauldian conceptualization of power as productive and, more specifically, intrinsically related to the production of meaning. In order to give focus to the analytical strategies that I employ, in the third section I attempt to define some key concepts, such as articulation, representation and text. Finally I give a full account of the three related analytical strategies that I use and reflect on the textual placement of this chapter within the book as a whole.

The attempt to construct a rigorous and useful methodology using discourse theory is made particularly demanding by the various ways in which the label 'discourse theory' is utilized by various scholars to mean different things, both in theoretical and in practical application. Discourse theory has developed over time, drawing on cultural theory, literary theory and linguistics as well as social and political theory, and there are competing theories of discourse within the broad umbrella term of 'discourse theory'. Broadly speaking it is possible to trace the divisions along ontological lines, where empiricist understandings of discourse conceptualize discourses as 'frames, ... primarily instrumental devices that can foster common perceptions and understandings for specific purposes' (Howarth 2000: 3). According to the assumptions of this approach, it is possible to measure how effectively a discourse is *used* by people. Meaning is assumed constant and identifiable through the discourse, rather than constituted by discourse. For the reasons I expand upon below, I cannot subscribe to this approach.

Ontologically compatible with the above approach is another realist understanding that conceives of discourses as 'particular objects with their own properties and powers ... and the task of discourse analysis is to unravel "the conceptual elisions and confusions by which language enjoys its power"' (Parker cited in Howarth 2000: 3). Discourses have causal effects that can be analysed and the *structures* of language and language-in-use are of analytical primacy. The development of Critical Discourse Analysis (CDA) as a distinct school of thought draws on this realist approach, integrating these foundational assumptions with an understanding of human agency such that there exists a dialectical relationship between 'discourses and the social systems in which they function' (Parker cited in Howarth 2000: 4). Scholars who associate themselves with Critical Discourse Analysis or Text-Oriented Discourse Analysis (see inter alia Fairclough 2003; Jaworski and Coupland 1999; van Dijk 1997a, 1997b) support this notion of discourse. It is predominantly this conceptualization of discourse analysis from which I wish to differentiate the type of discourse analysis that I will use.

Openly owing an intellectual debt to Bakhtin, Gramsci, Althusser and Foucault (Fairclough and Wodak 1997: 260–62), Fairclough and other proponents of CDA have explored and expanded upon the possibilities for engagement with political analysis by CDA and developed useful tools and strategies for analysis that have enabled to some extent the 'mainstreaming' of discourse analysis in social science (Howarth and Stavrakakis 2000: 1). However, there is a distinct difference between CDA and the type of discourse analysis that I employ in my research. This is evident in a close examination of the way in which Fairclough (1992), Fairclough and Wodak (1997) and Teun van Dijk (1997a, 1997b) posit a distinction between the realm of the discursive and the 'non-discursive', which, as I discuss below, I do not. As Jane Sunderland argues, 'CDA *entails* the extra-discursive: ... a "real world" where reality does not depend on what is known about it' (2004: 11, emphasis in original). While Fairclough talks of 'discursive practices' (1992: 60), the notion of language in use, and accepts that discourse can encompass more than just language, he insists that 'these [discursive] practices are constrained by the fact that they inevitably take place within a constituted, material reality' (1992: 60). Although Fairclough conceives of a dialectic relationship between the discursive realm and reality, he struggles to offer a convincing account of how exactly the 'constituted, material reality' is constituted. I find this problematic as, in linking 'material' with 'reality' so explicitly, Fairclough does not problematize the processes through which the 'reality' is constructed and the 'material' given meaning as a 'reality'.

I do not conceive of a distinction between a discursive and a 'non-discursive' realm. However, I do draw heavily on Foucault in the construction of my analytical strategies, so it is important to recognize that Foucault himself is inconsistent in his treatment of the issue of the possibility of theorizing a 'non-discursive' realm. In his early work, describing the 'the conditions necessary for the appearance of an object of discourse' (Foucault 1972: 44), Foucault identifies three realms of relations, the first of which is '*real* or *primary* relations' which, 'independently of all discourse or objects of discourse, may be described between institutions, techniques, social forms etc.' (1972: 44, emphasis in original). These can be seen to represent precisely the same kind of 'non-discursive' realm as Fairclough posits. Foucault goes on to delineate 'a system of *reflexive* or *secondary* relations, and a system of relations that might properly be call *discursive*' (1972: 44, emphasis in original). It seems, from this passage at least, that Foucault would wish to posit some extra- or non-discursive realm, which is compatible with, and insufficiently theorized in much the same way as, the 'constituted, material reality' to which Fairclough refers. However, in a later work, Foucault refers to '[d]iscursive practices' that are 'embodied in technical processes, in institutions, in patterns for general behaviour, in forms for transmission or diffusion, and in pedagogical forms which, at once, impose and maintain them' (1977: 100).

The imbrication of the discursive within the 'non-discursive' effectively collapses the 'non-discursive' as a theoretical or analytical device, as the primary relations to which Foucault refers in the earlier writing are five years later 'embodied' in the discourse at the same time as the discourse is embedded in them, rendering all 'discursive'. Furthermore, it is in this later work that Foucault theorizes the conceptualization of power that informs my research, as I will discuss below, and explicitly defines discourse as comprising more than language. According to Foucault, discourse analysis 'consists of not – of no longer – treating discourses as groups of signs (signifying elements referring to contents or representations) but as *practices* that systematically form the objects of which they speak' (1972: 49, emphasis added). Therefore, I remain unwilling to dismiss the potential of analysis that draws explicitly on Foucault, an analysis in which I might endeavour to 'show that things are not as self-evident as one believed, to see what is accepted as self-evident will no longer be accepted as such' (Foucault cited in Campbell 1998: 191).

However, Foucault does not explicitly discuss the processes of 'contents or representation' that he counterposes to discursive practice, and I wish to retain a notion of representation, as it is both conceptually useful and analytically fruitful. Therefore, in addition to Foucault I explore the analytical strategies utilized by theorists who explicitly acknowledge a debt to Foucault in their own research. Jacob Torfing suggests that the analytical approach of Ernesto Laclau and Chantal Mouffe and that of Foucault's later work 'can be viewed as two of a kind' (Torfing 1999: 91) – that is, ontologically and epistemologically compatible. Thus, drawing predominantly on Foucault (1972, 1977, 1978, 1984), Laclau and Mouffe (2001), and Roxanne Doty (1993, 1996), I have constructed the analytical strategies that I expand upon below. To draw attention to the difference between CDA and the strategies employed by Foucault and by Laclau and Mouffe, Torfing suggests the term 'discourse-theoretical analysis' (DTA) (1999: 12), and I use the same terminology to describe my methodology.

ON DISCOURSE

DTA provides me with analytical strategies that allow me to identify, problematize and challenge the ways in which 'realities' become accepted as 'real' in the practices of international relations. Defining the analytical tools with which I investigate the discourses of (international) security and (gender) violence requires that attention is given to understanding *how* I can identify the discursive practices to which Foucault refers. Devising an appropriate set of analytical strategies that will enable me to answer the research questions outlined in the previous chapter has entailed considerable time spent thinking about the ontological and epistemological positions I espouse, and the ways in which these inform my notions of methodology. When I first began to consider these issues, and attempted to construct a justification for the way in which I see the world, all I could come up with was, 'I see the world like *this* because *this* is the only way that the world makes any sense to me.' However, the very act of acknowledging that the way I see the world is perhaps different to the visions of others is a performance of an ontological position, which then has epistemological and methodological implications.

In this section, I explore and explain the conceptualization of discourse that informs my research. I consider the ways in which practices of (re)production, (re)presentation and (re)legitimization[1] are all 'discursive' practices and the ways in which these practices relate to the concept of discourse. As Doty cogently expresses it, '[a] discourse delineates the terms of intelligibility *whereby a particular reality can be "known" and acted upon*' (1996: 6, emphasis added). Discourses are therefore recognizable to me as systems of meaning-production rather than simply statements or language, systems that 'fix' meaning, however temporarily, and enable us to make sense of the world. In suggesting that discourses 'fix' meaning I do not want to imply that there is any transhistorical continuity or universality to meaning. Rather, the 'terms of intelligibility' are multiple, open and fluid. This conceptualization is explicitly poststructural, according to Alan Swingewood, as acknowledging the fluidity of discourse entails the recognition that a discursive field 'does not constitute a totality since it lacks a unifying centre but consists of fragments, perspectives, discontinuity' (2000: 198).

Laclau and Mouffe affirm this conceptualization of discourse in the context of clarifying their position on the possible existence of a 'non-discursive' realm. Their contribution is particularly useful and is worth quoting at length:

> Our analysis rejects the distinction between discursive and non-discursive practices. It affirms: a) that every object is constituted as an object of discourse, insofar as no object is given outside every discursive condition of emergence; and b) that any distinction between what are usually called the linguistic and behavioural aspects of a social practice, is either an incorrect distinction or ought to find its place within the social production of meaning, which is structured under the form of discursive totalities. (Laclau and Mouffe 2001: 107)

Using Doty's conceptualization of discourse, in which 'a discourse is inherently open-ended and incomplete … [and] [a]ny fixing of a discourse and the identities that are constructed by it can only ever be of a partial nature' (1996: 6), it is the *partial* nature of fixing that allows critical space for engagement. 'No discursive formation is ever a sutured totality' (Laclau and Mouffe 2001: 107), and each formation is contingent, relying on the articulation, as discussed below, of discursive elements to (re)produce meaning. Discursive practices maintain, construct and constitute, legitimize, resist and suspend meaning, and it is these practices that theorists can analyse using DTA.

This theoretical commitment leads to the explication of a number of analytical strategies that can be integrated into DTA with great effect, as it is possible to analyse the ways in which specific discursive practices function to position objects and subjects in relation to each other in configurations that change over time. These strategies are: double reading, analysis of rhetorical schemata/nodal points and analysis of predication/subject-positioning.[2] I discuss these strategies further in the following section. Doty (1993, 1996) influences my research in her operationalizing of a set of analytical strategies that are similar in intellectual heritage to my own[3] and encourages the asking of questions that 'examine how meanings are produced and attached to various social subjects and objects, thus constituting particular interpretive dispositions that create certain possibilities and exclude others' (1996: 4). Power is central to the creation of 'certain possibilities' and to the processes of exclusion to which Doty refers, and is therefore central to this research.

ON POWER

As I mention above, this conceptualization of discourse is consciously poststructural. Butler eloquently expresses her interpretation of what this means for political research when she suggests that

> if there is a point ... to what I ... understand as poststructuralism, it is that power pervades the very conceptual apparatus that seeks to negotiate its terms, including the subject position of the critic; and further, that this implication of the terms of criticism in the field of power is ... the very precondition of a politically engaged critique. (1994: 157)

Like Butler, I am influenced by Foucault in the construction of an appropriate set of analytical strategies with which to conduct my research. In addition to drawing on particular tools or methods in his own research, I make explicit use of Foucault's conceptualization of power in my work. I subscribe to a Foucauldian vision of '[t]he omnipresence of power: not because it has the privilege of consolidating everything under its invincible unity, but because it is produced from one moment to the next, at every point, or rather in every relation from one point to another' (Foucault 1978: 93).

Thus everything we can see or conceive of is a product of power relations.[4] This renders every decision, every representation, every aspect of the social world, political. As Enloe comments, '[o]ne of the simplest and most disturbing feminist insights in that "the personal is political". Disturbing, because is means that relationships we once imagined were private or merely social are in fact infused with power, usually unequal power' (2000: 195). Although there are distinct differences in our analytical strategies, and Enloe draws her conceptualization of power from feminist theory rather than Foucault, this explication of the ubiquity of power is both concise and useful. Furthermore, the relationship between power and politics is fundamental to the way in which I conceive of my analytical approach. Through DTA, analysis can 'reveal a body of political knowledge that is not some kind of secondary theorizing about practice, nor the application of theory.... It is inscribed, from the outset, in the field of different practices in which it finds its specificity, its functions and its networks of dependence' (Foucault 1972: 214). These 'different practices' are discursive, as described above, but power is immanent in discourse and therefore in discursive practices.

As Kathryn Woodward comments, 'signifying practices that produce meaning involve relations of power' (1997: 15). Power is understood by Foucault as 'a productive network which runs through the whole social body, much more than ... a negative instance whose function is repression' (1977: 119), and this is the conceptualization that informs my analytical strategies. Power produces conditions of meaning, instances of meaning, webs of meaning that are both locally specific and 'run through the whole social body' – or, rather, are productive of the 'social body'. If power is 'productive', as Foucault argues, and discursive – or signifying – practices are also productive, specifically of meaning, and involve 'relations of power', then it is reasonable to sustain the theoretical assumption that power is implicated in the production of meaning. That is to say, the ways in which discursive practices construct an intelligible reality that then itself acts as a referent for the construction of meaning are intrinsically related to power.

DTA, then, gives analytical primacy to this Foucauldian conceptualization of power. It is this primacy of power that makes the approach so useful, whereby 'the polymorphous techniques of power' (Foucault 1978: 11) can be identified, problematized and challenged. In understanding that discursive practices are practices of power, DTA provides theorists with the tools to question *how* meanings become fixed, however temporarily or partially, as discussed above. Stuart Hall states that 'meaning ... depends on the contingent and arbitrary stop – the necessary and temporary "break" in the infinite semiosis of language' (1997a: 54), and DTA allows for the investigation of these 'contingent and arbitrary' breaks. More specifically, it investigates 'the interrelationship of power and representational practices that elevate one truth over another' (Der Derian 1992: 7). However, in order to proceed with the formulation of specific analytical strategies, it is first necessary to theorize the relationship between representational practices, power and discourse.

ON REPRESENTATION

If discursive practices both manifest and construct discourse through (re)presentation and (re)production, then practices of (re)presentation and (re)production are the sites at which it is possible to locate power in a given discursive terrain. Thus DTA is concerned with representation as a source for the (re)production of knowledge (Hall 1997b: 43). Woodward suggests that '[r]epresentations produce meaning through which we can make sense of our experience and of who we are. We could go further and suggest that these symbolic systems create the possibilities of what we are and what we can become' (1997: 14). DTA would certainly 'go further', following Butler in her argument that representations 'are never merely descriptive, but always normative, and, as such, exclusionary' (1994: 166). Butler is specifically referring to representations of identity in this context, but drawing out the wider implications of such a position, it is possible to theorize representation not only as a repository of meaning but also connective and constitutive.[5]

In this investigation I use the concept of representation in two ways: representation as an *instance* and representation as a *practice*. Representations can be seen as instances of discursive practice. For example, taking a photograph produces a representation of a situation. However, the image in the photograph is determined by the photographer, the subject, the lighting, the notions of appropriate subject-material for a photograph, whether the photograph will be developed privately or commercially, whether the photograph is meant for a personal collection or a more formal display and so on – these are all discursively constructed. As Jutta Weldes notes, '[d]ifferent representations of the world entail different identities, which in turn carry with them different ways of functioning in the world, are located within different power relations and make possible different interests' (1996: 287). In this vision, representations are texts, where text is 'the fabric in which discourse is manifested' (Talbot cited in Sunderland 2004: 7). Text is not limited in this conceptualization to written material, but rather refers to 'utterances of any kind and in any medium, including cultural practices' (Scott 1994: 284).

The notion of text entails consideration of intertextuality. According to Julia Kristeva, 'text is "a permutation of texts, an intertextuality in the space of a given text'" (cited in Allen 2000: 35). This is evident in two ways. First, a text such as this one – or any academic work – is an intertext in that it directly refers to other texts. Extrapolating from this premiss, a photograph is an intertext as it references other texts (such as cars, bodies, buildings) through representation, a film is an intertext, as is a novel, and so on.[6] Second, the intertextuality of text is established by its social context. 'Texts do not present clear and stable meanings; they embody society's dialogic conflict over … meaning' (Allen 2000: 36). Therefore, in analysing texts as representations, DTA 'obviates the need for recourse to the interiority of a conscious, meaning-giving subject … In the Discursive Practices Approach signifiers refer only to other signifiers, hence the notion of *intertextuality*, i.e., a complex and infinitely expanding web of possible meanings' (Doty 1993: 302, emphasis in original).[7]

Conceiving of representation as practice is slightly different. It refers to the process of meaning-making immanent in the production of representations. Hall refers to these processes as 'articulations':

> The term has a nice double meaning because to 'articulate' means to utter, to speak forth, to be articulate. It carries that sense of language-ing, of expressing, etc. But we also speak of an 'articulated lorry' (truck): a lorry where the front (cab) and back (trailer) can, *but need not be* connected to one another. (cited in Weldes 1996: 285, emphasis added)[8]

The emphasis on contingency refers back to the contingency of meaning, as discussed above, and therefore the opening of analytical space to identify the practices of power that represent these contingent relations as 'natural' and seamless.

To summarize, then, discursive practices are representations, and representations can be (inter)texts or articulatory practices. Furthermore, articulatory practices are evident in (inter)texts, made possible by the analytical separation of representation into both noun and verb for the purposes of this study. The (inter)texts with which this book is concerned, the Report of the UN Secretary-General (2004a; 2002a), the United Nations Security Council Resolution 1325, the competing narratives of production issuing from the United Nations and the NGO Working Group, are all simultaneously practices of articulation, sections of a social text and products/producers of meaning.

Researching the ways in which discourses of gender, security, violence and the international are articulated, interrelated and in conflict in these textual localities of power calls for methods that engage with the production of meaning within and between the texts. The final section of this chapter explores such methods.

ANALYTICAL STRATEGIES

This research investigates the discursive construction of Resolution 1325 through the identification of practices of (re)production, (re)presentation and (re)legitimization in the document itself, with specific reference to articulations of gender, violence, security and the international. The same strategies are then applied to related documentation. In this section, therefore, I discuss the specific analytical strategies that make up the tripartite DTA that I employ in this study. The first of these is double reading. I then go on to explore the two sets of strategies that I operationalize: analysis of rhetorical schemata/nodal points, and predication/subject-positioning.

In addition to the intellectual debt owing to Doty, Foucault, and Laclau and Mouffe that I acknowledge, it is also important to engage with the theories of knowledge propounded by Jacques Derrida (2000, 1978, 1974), given that I conceive of my analytical approach as being broadly deconstructive, a description with which Derrida is closely associated (Derrida 1974: 10–18). I take 'deconstruction' to be 'a reading which is sensitive to what is irreducible in every text, allowing the text to speak before the reader, and listening to what the text imposes on the reader' (McQuillan 2000: 5). Deconstruction is not a 'method' or strategy, rather '[d]econstruction is what happens' (McQuillan 2000: 6) *as a result of* strategies of analysis employed in research – in the context of my own study, the strategies of analysing rhetorical schemata/nodal points and predication/subject-positioning, which I discuss further below.

The DTA that I employ in this investigation is compatible with a Derridean understanding of critique, in addition to drawing on the theorists mentioned above. As Kanakis Leledakis explains, Derrida's 'call is for the acceptance of "openness", of indeterminacy, of the impossibility of any full closure and determination' (2000: 176). In this study, I hope to illustrate the ways in which UNSCR 1325 and associated documentation attempts to effect 'full closure and determination' on the concepts of gender, violence, security and the international through the intrinsically political representation of these concepts as discourses of (gender) violence and (international) security. The strategies that I use to do this are not explicitly Derridean but there are significant similarities, despite differences in terminology.

Primarily, as mentioned above, compatibility exists on the meta-level of analytical approach. Derrida questions the notion of inherent rationality, or the ordering of the universe through 'metaphysics in its totality' (Derrida 1974: 13), entailed in his exploration of 'logos' and attention to the play of signification. As he argues, '[t]here is not a single signified that escapes, even if recaptured, the play of signifying references that constitute language … [t]his, strictly speaking, amounts to destroying the concept of 'sign' and its entire logic' (7). The 'destruction, not the demolition but the de-sedimentation, the de-construction, of all the significations that have their source in that of the logos' (10) draws attention to the ways in which premissing order on the divisibility of signifier and signified, and on the hier-archical organization of these two concepts, informs contemporary Western critical thought. These insights then inform the theorizing of a potentially useful notion of 'exteriority', to which I will return below. However, Derrida suggests that

> it is necessary to surround the critical concepts with a careful and thorough discourse to mark the conditions, the medium, and the limits of their effectiveness and to designate rigorously their intimate relationship to the machine whose deconstruction they permit; and, in the same process, designate the crevice through which the yet unnameable glimmer beyond the closure can be glimpsed. (1974: 14)

These analytical strategies are comparable to those I employ in this study, where the 'critical concepts' are those of gender, violence, security and the international and their articulation through specific discourses; the 'machine' refers to the regimes of truth that claim to fix their meaning; and the 'glimmer beyond closure' is illustrated through the discourse-theoretical analysis.

The second similarity is that of deconstruction and 'double reading' (Ashley 1988: 235). This primary analytical strategy shapes the research as a whole: each text is interpreted through a descriptive reading, and then subjected to a second, discourse-theoretical reading. Deconstruction illustrates the ways in which the master signifiers, or nodal points, work to (re)produce, (re)legitimize and (re)present the concepts with which I am concerned in the texts I use as vehicles for analysis. What Richard Ashley calls 'double reading' is a very similar strategy. In his analysis of 'the anarchy problematique', Ashley establishes the 'heroic practice ... the foundational presence to which this discourse endlessly returns, the totalising principle from which everything in this discourse originates' (1988: 232), which, as outlined above, is recognizable as the master signifier or nodal point of this discursive terrain. As Derrida comments, this master signifier – or Ashley's 'heroic practice' – organizes the terrain but can never fix the discourse, instead offering a semblance of fixity. The 'coherence of the system' depends on accepting the 'truth' of the master signifier or nodal point, through which the 'play' of the discursive elements is limited 'inside the total form' (Derrida 1978: 351–2).

Through his first – or 'monological' (Ashley 1988: 229) – reading, Ashley 'determine[s] indubitably what may be counted as the meaning of the text and what, by contrast, is extraneous, accidental, unintended' (1988: 232). That is, the reader in this first reading submits to the prescribed limits of the discursive terrain, accepting the hierarchical organization of the texts around the implicitly unproblematic presence of the nodal points. Following this, Ashley conducts a second (dialogical) reading in an effort to illustrate 'that the supposed fixity and "deep structuring" of a sovereign presence, and the resultant "hard core" homogeneity and continuity of meaning ascribed to a text, is always to be grasped as a problematical historical effort' (1988: 233). These two readings can then be considered, with a view to asking questions that 'do not invite certain answers. They are not oriented to the problem of disciplining an ambiguous history. They are oriented, on the contrary, to the exploration of possibilities hitherto closed off' (1988: 260). This exploration is exactly what I intend to undertake in the DTA that I employ in this study.

In the context of theorizing a politics of rape, Sharon Marcus draws on Foucault and Butler to construct the claim that 'violence ... is enabled by narratives, complexes and institutions which derive their strength not from outright, immutable, unbeatable force but rather from their power to structure our lives as imposing cultural scripts' (1992: 389). I prefer to employ the concept of discourse, congruent with Doty's conceptualization of discourse, but there are some similarities between the concept of discourse that informs my research and Marcus's notion of script, evident when she argues that a 'script should be understood as a framework, a grid of comprehensibility' (1992: 391). The notion of script is problematic in its connotations of boundedness, beginning and end, and authorship, but in order to be comprehensible, discourses must conform to the temporary boundaries of a given discursive field. Thus (inter)texts must be intelligible and more or less coherent in order for the text to be meaningful within its social context. It is possible to analyse this coherence through the investigation of the organization of the texts. Foucault describes this cohesion as 'the various rhetorical *schemata* according to which groups of statements may be *combined* (how descriptions, deductions, definitions, whose succession characterizes the architecture of the text, are linked together)' (1972: 63, emphasis in original).

Laclau and Mouffe refer to 'nodal points'. These are recognizable in Derridean theorizing as 'master signifiers', 'the so-called quilting point or *point de capiton* around which the shifting of signifiers is temporarily halted and meaning installed' (Edkins 2002: 72, emphasis in original). Despite the differences in terminology, both concepts – master signifier and nodal point – '[conceal] the lack around which the social order is constituted, the antagonism at its heart' (Edkins 2002: 72). In the context of this study, the nodal points are the concepts of gender, violence, international and security, and through analysis I explore the different ways in which these signifiers are ordered within the texts so as to inscribe a meaningful relationship between them. Analysing these nodal points allows me to disturb the coherence of these texts, to demonstrate the antagonisms, in a broadly deconstructive approach.

Therefore analysis of the rhetorical schemata of the text also entails the analysis of the emergence of 'nodal points' (Laclau and Mouffe 2001: 112). This requires a degree of flexibility, of back-and-forth within and across texts produced in a discursive terrain. That is, the nodal points emerge *as* nodal points through the organization and coherence of the text, through predication and subject positioning, but the construction and recognition of nodal points allows 'meaning' and therefore the representational practices that allow their emergence.

> The impossibility of an ultimate fixity of meaning implies that there has to be partial fixations – otherwise the very flow of differences would be impossible. Even in order to differ, to subvert meaning, there has to be *a* meaning…. Any discourse is constituted as an attempt to dominate the field of discursivity, to arrest the flow of differences, to construct a centre. We will call the privileged discursive points of this partial fixation, *nodal points*. (Laclau and Mouffe 2001: 112, emphasis in original)

The representational practices analysed in the first stage of DTA are the combination of grammatically correct statements (meaning in this context 'groups of words') into a coherent text. This will include the analysis of the rhetorical tropes used in the (inter)texts, as these figures of speech are themselves representational practices. As Laclau and Mouffe explain, '[s]ynonymy, metonymy, metaphor are not forms of thought that add a second sense to primary, constitutive literality of social relations; instead they are the primary terrain itself in which the social is constituted' (2001: 110). Thus, in the first phase of DTA, I look for the 'forms of thought' or linguistic structures that provide a sense of order in the texts, thus constructing the meaning of the concepts with which I am concerned. In the identification of representational practices specific to gender, for example, I look for instances of gendered identities described 'as' or 'like', statements about gendered identities that can be problematized and emphasis on aspects of gender provided by placement within the text and/or repetition.

The second stage of discourse analysis investigates the articulation of subjects and objects, what Doty terms predication, which 'affirms a quality, attribute, or property of a person or a thing' (1993: 306), and the positioning of these subjects and objects in relation to each other in the texts. As Doty explains, '[t]he production of subjects and objects is always vis-à-vis other subjects and objects' (1993: 306). For example, I look at the multiple ways in which violence is represented, as legitimate, as gendered, as threatening to civil society and so on, and investigate how these predicates affirm the properties of violence within these narratives. These representational practices are 'articulatory' as they establish a 'relational complex' (Laclau and Mouffe 2001: 93). These articulatory practices manifest and (re)produce the discourses with which I am concerned, and the representations in the text of violence, for example, illustrate the ways in which attempts are being made to transform the discursive elements (for example, 'violence' and 'legitimate') into a relationary moment ('there are times when violence is legitimate'), so that the identity of the discursive elements are modified ('so not all violence is bad') (Laclau and Mouffe 2001: 105).

As mentioned above, the analytical strategies that I employ can be broadly considered deconstructive, and therefore I need to acknowledge a debt to the theorizing of Derrida. However, another of Derrida's most renowned contributions to political theorizing also influences my research project and design. The considerations of method, the exploration of concepts of discourse, power and representation that inform my analytical strategies must own to the intellectual influence of Derrida and his assertion that '[t]here is nothing outside of the text' (1974: 158, emphasis in original). This recognition affirms the legitimacy of analytical strategies that prioritize the textual (re)production, (re)presentation and (re)legitimization of meaning, and use text as the vehicle for this analysis. It is not to say that the social world is reducible to textual 'truth', but rather that textual 'truths' should be problematized – or deconstructed – in order to illustrate the contingency and fragility of that which is taken as empirically, verifiably, solidly, real.

It is not the overall aim of this book to juxtapose the different readings with a view to dismissing one or another of the narratives as 'untrue'. Looking for the origin or root of meaning, the reality to which a representation purports to relate is not the task of DTA. Rather, I offer these readings in an effort to draw out and comment on the 'regimes of truth' operant in this discursive terrain. 'Truth is a thing of this world.... Each society has its regime of truth ..., the type of discourses which it accepts and makes function as true'. This has profound implications for political research, in that a search for the 'truth' of the matter/'reality' becomes in this mode of investigation a search for the 'systems of power which produce and sustain it [truth], and the effects of power which it induces and which extend it' (Foucault 1980: 131, 133). Through this study, I hope to encourage critical interpretations of and reflections on the policy documents that order the lives of individuals everywhere, employing as they do concepts that, like all concepts, are inherently value-laden. As Dvora Yanow points out, '[i]nterpretations ... are more powerful than "facts". That makes the policy process, in all its phases, a struggle for the determination of meanings' (1996: 19).

DTA as I have described it above would be recognizable to David Howarth as what he terms a 'strategy of problematization [that] carries with it an intrinsically ethical connotation, as it seeks to show that dominant discursive constructions are contingent and political rather than necessary' (2000: 135). This definition appeals to me, congruent with what I have outlined above as the primary aims of DTA: to identify, problematize and challenge. The processes of identification are themselves problematic, as such processes can only ever be interpretation – to take meaning from a given text and write a convincing story about that meaning. In my own study, then, I reflect on the ways in which the meanings that I make of the texts with which I work are themselves challengeable, asserting as they do a truth claim about the text under consideration. John Tomlinson expresses these concerns with great eloquence and his appeal to continued reflexive awareness is extremely convincing. 'For not only will I, through ignorance, "silence" voices in the discussion, I will also organize and "discipline" the discourse via my discursive categories' (1991: 28). However, reflecting on the analytical strategies I choose to employ in this book, as well as reflecting on the motivations I have for undertaking this study at this time, and continuing this reflexivity throughout the work, at least ensures that I am conscious of my 'privileged discursive position' (Tomlinson 1991: 28).

The analytical strategies I develop in this chapter impact on the critiques that I undertake in the following chapter, and, given my belief that research is inherently political, this would be the case whether or not I were explicit about it. It therefore makes sense to me that the reader of my study is equipped with as much information as possible concerning my ontological and epistemological assumptions and how these inform my analytical strategies before I apply these strategies to a critical review. Giving primacy to the analytical strategies I use allows me to make a textual statement about the value I attach to the work I produce. The strategies that enable this work are developed from an intellectual heritage that considers the value to be in problematizing rather than establishing truth claims. That is, I proceed with the awareness that the claims that I make are contingent and are themselves open to challenge. In exploring the most appropriate analytical strategies, above, I am also making a claim as to the validity of the study as a whole: these strategies will enable me to 'get at' what I want to analyse and therefore produce valuable and interesting work.

It is necessary to reflect on the issues of textual representation, power and discourse throughout the research process, and to evaluate the ways in which it is possible to engage critically with naturalized knowledge, the ways in which cultural and historical specificity is key to understanding, and that knowledge is inseparably related to power and practice (Foucault 1972: 48–9). Identifying the discursive practices through which identities are temporarily fixed in specific historical and cultural locations, and investigating how these identities enable certain behaviours and performances for lived individuals, conceive of 'politics [not] as a means to truth but as the activity of contesting truths' (Aladjem 1991: 280). Refusing to accept that there is any 'natural fact' that cannot be contested, any essence to the identity of subject or object, allows for multiple interrogations of truth claims that can expose the very political processes that are naturalized through practices of power. Recourse to the insistence that this or that is 'natural' effects closure on reflective politics, and it is this closure that I seek to resist.

3 | THE STATE OF THE DISCIPLINE(S)

Having established the analytical strategies that guide this study, in this chapter I undertake a critical review of the literatures to which I owe an intellectual debt and to which I wish to contribute. This chapter is divided into two sections, drawing on a wide range of literature from various disciplinary homes. The first section explores dominant academic conceptualizations of gendered violence. This section has three subsections in which I map out the contours of each of the three approaches I have identified: 'violence against women', 'gender violence' and 'the violent reproduction of gender'. I offer six critiques of each of the first two approaches, before outlining the approach I find most persuasive.

The analysis of the literature on international security proceeds in the same way in the second section of this chapter, and is divided up similarly, with three subsections addressing 'national security', 'international security' and 'the violent reproduction of the international'. In the last subsection, I demonstrate that security can be conceptualized as a set of discourses that function to reproduce 'the international' in various ways. Comparisons are drawn across the two bodies of literature regarding the ontological and epistemological assumptions that inform each conceptualization and I argue that the different approaches have more common ontological and epistemological ground across the two literatures than the approaches within each literature do with each other.

Treating two literatures – one concerned with gender violence, the other with international security – that are assumed to be analytically and theoretically separable as an analytical whole for the purposes of critical review is not only legitimate but also instructive. I want to investigate the ways in which gendered violence has been articulated as a security issue with specific reference to UNSCR 1325. Thus, the review of literature I offer in this chapter does more than provide an overview of the relevant academic work on the subject. It provides an insight into dominant discourses of (gender) violence and (international) security. I argue that the literatures, despite their differences, can be mapped according to their analytical foci, their underlying assumptions, and the types of subjects produced through each discourse, and I provide a tabular representation of this argument at the end of this chapter. I do not seek to represent fixed definitions of the concepts with which I am concerned. Rather, in both cases, I wish to explore how discourses of violence and security function in the literatures under discussion, and how they are product/productive of policy and advocacy concerning (gender) violence and (international) security.

(GENDER) VIOLENCE

In the various histories of the development of feminist theory/practice, some consensus has developed concerning the division of feminist work into first, second and, potentially, third 'waves'. Within 'second wave' feminism in the 1970s and 1980s in both the UK and the USA, divisions between so-called 'liberal feminism' and its 'others' – more radical feminist projects based on critiques of liberalism from a variety of theoretical positions – led to serious internal conflict over the formulation and implementation of 'a/the' feminist emancipatory project (see Nicholson 1997: 1–5). Given the issues with which this chapter is concerned, it is noteworthy that '[t]he conflicts were as much over the perspectives and priorities of feminism itself [as they were] over whether we saw the sphere of the sexual and the problem of male violence as the root of women's oppression' (Segal 1987: 208).

Continued debate over the issue of feminism and its place, not only in academic circles but also as part of wider social discourse, has constructed fragmented feminist movements attempting to create paths forward for feminisms which are no longer necessarily congruent or even mutually acceptable. In the 1980s, the recognition of difference among women questioned the legitimacy of an emancipatory politics that had taken the unity of its subject as a given. The influence of postmodernist/poststructuralist thought became apparent as feminist academics struggled with the concept of feminism 'without women'. As Butler writes, '[w]ithout a unified concept of woman ... it appears that feminist politics has lost the categorical basis of its own normative claims' (Butler 2001: 327). These debates, as mentioned above, are not 'merely' academic; they go to the heart of what it means to espouse a feminist politics, however that politics is conceived, and of what it means to construct feminist theory/practice and the issues with which this theory/practice should be concerned.

The development of distinct but related bodies of literature that, as mentioned above, are founded on different assumptions about gender and violence has affected the language with which those concerned with these issues can speak of them. The literatures are related to different conceptions of feminist theory/practice through their foundational assumptions, without necessarily mapping directly to these broad 'strands'. Thus, it is possible to speak of issues of gender and violence with a variety of feminist voices. I do not wish to inscribe rigid boundaries on the categories I discuss, nor do I assume that positioning a given author in a particular literature at a certain time entails her/his permanent placement there. Furthermore, I am uncomfortable with the imposition of a suggested chronology of feminist theory/practice: it is simply not the case that these are linear teleological developments. With this in mind, it is possible to sketch in the links between radical feminisms and the discourses of 'violence against women', between liberal feminisms and discourses of 'gender violence', and finally between poststructural feminisms and discourses concerning the violent reproduction of gender.

The foundational assumptions of each of the bodies of literature I discuss in the first half of this chapter, that which addresses 'violence against women' and that which addresses 'gender violence', are often implicit, or taken to be unproblematic. Each literature speaks to a specific manifestation of violence and is informed by a particular theory of gender. On its own terms, each literature is internally both coherent and consistent, and there are significant differences between the ways in which this coherence and consistency is constructed. However, there is a third mode of thinking about the issues of violence, gender and power that I expand upon in the third subsection below. This position, which I have labelled the 'violent reproduction of gender', is premissed on the idea that it is the reproduction of gender difference that is analytically interesting.

VIOLENCE AGAINST WOMEN

Jill Radford, Liz Kelly and Marianne Hester are prominent activist-researchers concerned with 'violence against women'. They situate their work in a context of the debates within wider feminist theorizing, stating that 'throughout the 1980s a series of separations occurred: of women's studies from feminism; of theoretical writing from women's lived experiences; of knowledge creation from activism' (1996: 8). Their implicit placement within these dualities is on the side of an activist feminism concerned with 'women's lived experiences' (see also Bograd 1988). Researching and writing about 'violence against women' has a particular, albeit internally differentiated, politics that differs in several key ways from researching and writing about 'gender violence', and one aspect of this is the location articulated by Radford, Kelly and Hester above.

Researching 'violence against women' was an explicit and vital challenge to the self-proclaimed objectivist and value-free research programmes of mainstream social science. This was a political under-taking in two main ways: research was conducted 'with the aim of achieving a description as well as a comprehensive understanding of the problem' (Dobash and Dobash 1992: 283). The importance of being able to talk about 'women' and the violences they experience as part of their oppression in a patriarchal society is central to this understanding, as '[v]iolence against women has been termed one of six "structures of patriarchy", which control women and consolidate men's political, economic and social dominance' (Walby cited in Pickup et al. 2001: 19). Thus, from this perspective, the claims of some feminists regarding the illusory nature of the notions of 'subject', 'truth' and 'knowledge' have been vigorously refuted if not dismissed out of hand. Researchers who work on 'violence against women' situate themselves firmly in opposition to the 'insidious and unhelpful ... critique ... [that] includes the suggestion that work on sexual violence is "essentialist" and that it constructs and positions women as inevitable "victims"' (Radford et al. 1996: 9).

Based on an 'interpretive analytic' (Dobash and Dobash 1992: 282), the language employed to describe the issue of violence against women in society, aimed at drawing public attention to the gravity of the situations faced by many women in different communities, was largely related to the descriptions given by participants in research as well as the language used by the researchers themselves. In this way, the connection to the grassroots level remained central to the politics of theorizing 'violence against women' and the women in question were able to set their own threat agenda relevant to their own experiences: the ownership and authority of this knowledge was firmly rooted in these experiential accounts. Thus, research into 'violence against women' sustains an empiricist epistemology.

Qualitative reports of violence against women are relatively well documented, especially by the IGOs and NGOs working to combat such violence, and, as mentioned above, the representational categories used in these documentations are taken to be unproblematic. Within this approach, the violences that are addressed are those perpetrated against individuals who are socially identified as women, perpetrated as a result of this identity. The position of women, treated within this discourse as a group that shares more cross-cultural similarities than it has differences when it comes to experiences of violence, is seen as one of marginality.

Raising the profile of women's experiences of violence, and seeking to bring these experiences from the margins to the centre of the political agenda, the documentation of violence against women can be seen as an effort to overcome this 'silence', and also to go some way towards constructing a better, safer world. This is an ongoing project, drawing critical attention to the ways in which various knowledges and practices have been subjugated. The empowering of women to tell their own stories of life experiences, including those that are violent, has impacted on the ways in which violence against women is researched, and is also a function of the ways in which knowledge is understood within this conceptualization. To say that 'sexual violence was discovered: unearthed from layers of historical disbelief and denial' (Kelly et al. 1996: 84) privileges a focus on the *reclamation* of knowledge. Just as 'women' exist as the subjects of this discourse, the knowledge they possess concerning their lived experiences is conceived of as reflecting an objective reality that can be communicated without paying analytical attention to the ways in which 'reclaiming' this knowledge relies upon its interpretation.

An alternative conceptualization of knowledge and meaning would emphasize the ways in which knowledge is *constructed* rather than reclaimed. To speak of construction is in no way to suggest that the accounts are somehow fabricated. Rather, it draws attention to the processes of representation involved in the telling and retelling of these accounts. While the violences reported by those who have experienced them are in no way 'untrue' and it is vital to raise awareness of these issues, it is also important to problematize the politics of constructing these accounts and the ways in which processes of interpretation and representation are implicated in the 'reclamation' of knowledge that is perceived as unproblematic within this conceptualization. This is the first of six critiques I offer of an approach that seeks to theorize 'violence against women': the suggestion that in claiming a truth based in experience, whatever the strategic gains, literature that addresses 'violence against women' is largely insensitive to the ways in which these claims appeal to the existence of an objective reality that is difficult to sustain.

Articles that aim to raise the profile of violence against women also construct the profile of violence against women, who are vulnerable and often infantilized. Elizabeth Stanko encapsulates this idea when she writes that 'women *know*, consciously or unconsciously, what it means to be vulnerable to sexual and/or physical male violence' (Stanko 1985: 1, emphasis in original). This construction of women-as-victim has negative consequences noted even by those who work on violence against women using the same referents. Liz Kelly, Sheila Burton and Linda Regan give an example of an exercise they use when working with women who have experienced violence in which the group are asked to free-associate using 'victim' as the point of departure. Words that are frequently mentioned include: 'Passive Helpless Weak Vulnerable Shame Small Hurt Powerless Confused Controlled Guilty' (1996: 91).

A second critique of this literature is this: in suggesting that 'men' hold and exercise power, this approach is founded on a certain conceptualization of power that is never fully explicated as male power *over* women. Kelly discusses sexual violence, defined as 'a collective noun to encompass all forms of male violence against women and girls' (Kelly 1988 cited in Kelly 2000: 62), conceiving of it as 'one of the most extreme and effective forms of patriarchal control' (Kelly 2000: 45). Kelly argues that violence against women is a means by which men gain and retain power; the perpetrators are 'men who presume power refusing to give up one iota of historical privilege' (45) and the victims are women.

Thus, this approach, thinking about 'violence against women', is congruent with existing gender narratives, which tell of 'men' as being empowered, controlling, and active, as well as aggressive. The discourses of gender through which this conceptualization constructs the notions of what it means to be a woman or a man, to be a victim or a perpetrator of violence, relate male bodies to action rather than passivity, and to aggressive and controlling behaviours rather than defensive and controlled.

My third critique of this conceptualization challenges the ways in which theorizing 'violence against women' denies women agency as a result of these processes of representation. Jill Radford suggests that 'while men are murdered more frequently then women, men are rarely murdered simply because they are men.... Most murders by women are in self-defense or represent a desperate attempt at self-preservation' (1992: 10). In disallowing women the potential to be actors in violent situations, these constructions are inherently political and serve to define violence as the preserve of masculinity, which 'naturally' maps to male bodies. 'The agency which women exhibit ... in resisting and coping ... through collective opposition' (Kelly 2000: 46) is not critically examined, although it represents a thoroughly feminized sense of agency, congruent with dominant traditionalized narratives of gender.

A fourth critique challenges the way in which a chapter that addresses 'Wars Against Women: Sexual Violence, Sexual Politics and the Militarized State' (Kelly 2000) explicitly links 'sexual violence' with women, thereby precluding the possibility that men may be victims of such violence. As noted above, Radford argues that 'men are rarely murdered simply because they are men', but this construction arguably sustains a link between sexual violence and women that may not be helpful in securing effective prevention of and treatment for male victims of violence. There is very limited space for the expression of positive masculine agency, in terms of explaining why the majority of men do not perpetrate violence against women, resulting in the rendering of a one-size-fits-all masculinity in which '[m]en affirm one another as men through the exclusion, humiliation and objectification of women' (Kelly 2000: 57).

Kelly also introduces a discussion of the violences done to children without commenting on the ways in which making the link between women and children in this manner has important consequences for the meaning made of women through this discourse. This forms the fifth critique. Using words such as 'vulnerable' and 'exploitation', and continually running together the two collective nouns 'women and children' (58–62) serve to associate women with children and thereby bracket the two together conceptually, constructing what Cynthia Enloe calls 'womenandchildren' (1990). Given that children are not fully mature, are depicted as not fully capable of rational thought and are also seen to be in need of care and protection, this association is inevitably problematic.

Finally, I argue that the 'violence against women' literature tends to pathologize relations between gendered individuals, supported by the unproblematic linkages presumed to exist between 'men' and power and 'women' as victims. This tendency is a result of other assumptions sustained by this approach, namely the gendered dichotomy of power that sees power as always-already a male *possession* and the preclusion of positive male agency. Gender, on this view, is a differential relationship to be negotiated, managed and, in the last instance, overcome.

Research that focuses on 'violence against women' posits women as coherent and stable subjects whose life experiences can be ameliorated

---

BOX 3.1 SIX CRITIQUES OF 'VIOLENCE AGAINST WOMEN'
LITERATURE

- Claims that truth is experiential
- Power is conceptualized as (men's) 'power over' (women)
- Women are denied agency
- Men are precluded from being victims of violence
- Women(andchildren) are represented as eternal victims
- Gender is pathologized

---

by appropriate policy practice. This approach identifies materially determined gendered individuals as a result of its empirical approach to the study of politics and social life. The notion of sovereignty is central here, and provides an important link to the literature on international security, an issue to which I return in the final section of this chapter. The subject constructed through the discourse of 'violence against women' is assumed to be sovereign; the 'women' affected by violence have sovereign rights over their own material forms and should not therefore be subjected to violence. Moreover, this sovereignty is preconstituted and taken to be an empirical 'reality'. In the following section I illustrate how research that focuses on 'gender violence' problematizes this assumption of a stable sovereign subject, as well as the implications that this assumption has for the development of a political project addressing gendered violence.

GENDER VIOLENCE

As a conceptualization, 'violence against women' prioritizes practice over theory and activism over academia; similarly, the conceptualization of 'gender violence' has its own politics of location. However, the location articulated within this discourse is one of multiple and fluid sites of study and perspectives from which to study. Work on 'gender violence' can be located within the academy affiliated with the disciplines of sociology, criminology, development, law and politics. The sites of study may be domestic, international, contemporary or historical, and the context also diverse, with theories of gender violence concerned with the experiences of individuals and societies at every stage of life in every possible social context.

Laura O'Toole and Jessica Schiffman argue explicitly that the theorizing of 'gender violence' is qualitatively different from the theorizing of 'violence against women'. 'By widening our analytical lens, we are able to incorporate important connections among violence against heterosexual women and men, lesbians and gay men, and children and suggest important questions about structural and interpersonal violence for future analysis' (1997a: xiii). Thus theorizing 'gender violence' becomes possible partly due to the increasing recognition of the critiques mentioned above that have been raised and integrated into academic study, research and activism related to gender and violence.

Challenging the focus of studies addressing 'violence against women' has resulted in a broader multifaceted analytic and a recognition that '[t]he complexity of the nature of violence means that the necessary social changes should also be diverse and wide-ranging' (Alder 1997: 442). However, the first of six critiques I offer of 'gender violence' challenges the ways in which 'gender violence' is assumed to be 'knowable'. I acknowledge that it is vital to understand the various effects and implications of violence on gender relations and the lives of individuals globally. However, research on 'gender violence' tends to assume that the collection of case study evidence (to draw attention to the context-specific social construction of gender relations, see Moser and Clark 2001: 4) and its analysis, using appropriate frames and devices (see Moser 2001), will enable the eradication of such violence (see Moser and McIlwaine 2001). While research on 'gender violence' differs importantly from research on 'violence against women', in that it espouses a constructivist rather than an empiricist epistemology, it still makes claims based on 'giving voice' to survivors of gendered violence (see Ibáñez 2001) and constructs policy suggestions based on this knowledge.

Some theorists, such as Veena Das and Arthur Kleinman, who comment that 'it would ... be perilous to ignore the larger political environment which addresses the hurts that have been incurred in acts of violence' (2001: 19), explicitly make the connection between the organizational notions of violence, gender and power that are implicated in the study of 'gender violence'.[1] Theorists working within this conceptualization suggest that thinking about 'gender violence' enables a different approach to thinking about 'violence against women'. This approach is based on an understanding that 'the "language" of a violent act, the way the violence manifests itself, can only be understood within a certain social experience' (Kaufman 1997: 33) and that this 'social experience' also impacts upon the construction of gender. Thinking about 'gender violence' centralizes the narratives of gender that are subjected to a partial or limited critique using an approach that takes 'violence against women' as its analytical focus. In doing so, theorizing 'gender violence' takes a particular conceptualization of power as the point of analytical departure where power is seen as integral both to the conceptualization of gender and to the conceptualization of violence.

Within the discourse of 'violence against women', power is conceived of as male 'power over' women, in that men hold the power that enables them to oppress women through acts of violence. Power as conceived in theorizing 'gender violence' is reconfigured as 'power to', a conceptualization that envisions power as affirmative and capacity-building, as well as oppressive. This creates the space to conceive of violences as regulatory and themselves contributing to the very normalizing practices through which they are sustained. 'Wheresoever power orients practice – and that is everywhere – there is violence' (Kleinman 2000: 238). This vision of power is more compatible with what Steven Lukes called 'the radical conception of power' (cited in Digeser 1992: 979) in which structures of power are implicated in the construction of experiences, interests and social interactions. However, the productive power of violence is undertheorized in this account, despite analytical attention being paid to different cultural and historical contexts in which such violence occurs. 'Gender violence' offers 'a close examination of structured inequalities and the ability to devise a framework to transform unequal power relations' (Sharoni 2001: 90). This is my second point of critical engagement with this approach, as I argue that inequalities – and the exercise of power – cannot be so easily identified. Given the theory of power I outline in Chapter 2, the 'transformation' of power relations is difficult, if not impossible, as power is omnipresent and not by definition repressive (Foucault 1978, 1980).

A third critique relates to the ways in which violence is theorized within the account of 'gender violence'. Single acts of violence are impossible (see Moser 2001). Rather, the societal, the communal, the interpersonal and the individual levels function together to produce violences, which regulate and are regulated by existing social norms and practices. In much the same way as discourses of 'violence against women' can be said to homogenize women as a social group regardless of their socio-historic and cultural location, this approach could be seen to homogenize acts of violence as power. 'This entanglement of the larger political environment in ... the acts of violence' (Das and Kleinman 2001: 19) must be established and adequately theorized. Using this conceptualization, an explanation of honour killings in Pakistan, for example, implicates not only the direct perpetrator/s of the act of violence, but also the community which implicitly or explicitly condones the murder to appease family honour of a woman who has transgressed the boundaries of her 'proper' place, and the legal structure which supports it.

It is important to note that the power structures that support gender violences are in no way absent from Western society; it is not the case that they represent a 'traditional' means of conflict resolution or are a product of a peculiar (read 'Other') 'religious' culture. The normalization of violence in particular historical and cultural settings is evident, although notions of legitimate and illegitimate violence vary with these settings, and the sensitivity of representing these cases through existing value-systems attached to the physical and symbolic spaces they inhabit should be noted. Vivian Fox notes that 'the law in the west ... played a significant role in articulating and re-enforcing male superiority and domination' (2002: 19) through the normalization of violent relations between spouses[2] and the principles of non-intervention in cases of such violence adhered to by the majority of police forces in the UK and the USA until relatively recently. 'Ten years ago, when asked why the US Senate was not holding hearings on wife abuse, as it did for child abuse, a senator replied sarcastically that eliminating wife abuse "would take all the fun out of marriage"' (Gelles 1997: 71). Legislation that regulates gender is a global phenomenon, taking culturally specific forms.

Within this conceptualization, gender violence can occur at every level of social interaction, not just the interpersonal.[3] As Cynthia Cockburn notes, '[g]ender links violence at different points on a scale reaching from the personal to the international' (2004: 41; see also Giles and Hyndman 2004). Although researchers working on 'violence against women' would identify the (patriarchal) power structures that facilitate the continuation of violence against women, thinking about 'gender violence' enables a more sensitive understanding of the representation of women as simultaneously 'victims, perpetrators [and] ... actors' (Moser and Clark 2001) and the different conceptualization of power that this representation entails. The conceptualization of power that underpins work on 'gender violence' is implicated in the conceptualization of violence. Caroline Moser suggests that there is a 'gendered continuum of conflict and violence' (2001: 31), and, moreover, that this continuum is a result of the ways in which 'gender is embedded in relations of power/powerlessness' (2001: 37). This forms my fourth critique of this literature, as, while I sustain the challenge to a unidirectional power–violence relationship as offered by work on 'violence against women', the 'embedded' nature of gender in power as suggested by Moser and others does not fully problematize the links between masculinity and violence that are assumed by the previous literature. Moser offers Robert Connell's theory of 'hegemonic masculinity' as a potentially more useful analytical device than patriarchy but nonetheless continues to associate power 'with male authority and dominance' (2001: 37).

The power involved in making meanings of gender and of violence is, however, placed under scrutiny in accounts of 'gender violence'. Lillian Artz argues that the telling of an incidence of gender violence is made intelligible through structures of masculinized power. 'A woman's story of abuse ... is "organized" for her ... Anything that appears "inconsistent" ... erodes her legal position as a victim of a violent crime' (2001: 14). Thus challenging the representation of gender violence is as much concerned with exploring the boundaries of legitimate and illegitimate behaviour as it is concerned with the inscription of these boundaries. Violence is normalized in a vast number of social settings, and images and representations of violence are common in literature, in film, in news media. 'Community acquiescence to gender violence certainly varies ... yet analysts continue to show the ways in which the larger social contexts shape and reproduce the meanings and practices that hold sway in the most basic relationships we form' (O'Toole and Schiffman 1997b: 69).

However, metaphor and imagery used to describe 'gender violence' are often similar in conceptual make-up to the language used to talk about 'violence against women'. This is the fifth of six critiques I offer of this conceptualization, related to the critiques laid out above of the theorizing of 'violence against women'. Primarily, while attention is paid to the specificities of situational manifestations of violence, issues of cultural 'difference' and relativism have required the negotiation of critical issues of representation and discursive privilege. Artz constructs a strong argument for the importance of paying serious attention to the culturally specific regulatory practices that organize gender and sexuality when theorizing violence, but in both the title and the body of the article itself, the women with whom she is working to stop gender violence are referred to as 'the weather watchers', and no critical attention is given to this self-identification or the consequences of reproducing it. Thus the fifth critique concerns the way in which literature discussing 'gender violence' can still act to inscribe a crude rendering of masculinity that marginalizes the lived and often violent experiences of 'men'. Describing violent acts perpetrated by particular male individuals as 'like a storm ... the storming thunder that bangs down upon you' (participant in research cited in Artz 2001: 8) reinscribes the natural-ized link between masculinity and violence that should be examined as part of any theorizing of gender and of violence (see also Moser 2001; Cockburn 2004).

The final critique I suggest is that 'gender violence' literature has not successfully overcome the tendency within analysis to pathologize gender. In an attempt to move beyond what she terms 'gender traditionalism', in which gender is readable from sex and differences between genders are thus biological, and 'gender liberalism', which stresses the equality of the genders despite differences between them, both of which 'can combine in unfortunate ways ... to prevent gender from being seen as significant or explanatory' (Cockburn 2001: 14), Cynthia Cockburn develops a subtle and thoughtful account of gender violence with specific reference to situations of armed conflict. Centralizing the power inherent in gender relations enables the 'uncovering [of] the differentiation and asymmetry of masculine and feminine as governing principles, idealized qualities, practices or symbols' (2001: 16).

However, Cockburn 'calls, first, for a sensitivity to *gender difference*' (2001: 28, emphasis in original) that I believe may undermine the utility of this approach. It does, in a way, put the empirical cart before the theoretical horse, in much the same way as the framework employed by Kelly described above. If difference between the genders is taken as a starting point for the analysis of gender, then the (re)production of this difference is obscured from critical attention. This potentially allows for a third conceptualization that differs slightly from the notions of 'violence against women' and 'gender violence'. It is specifically the discursive practices through which gender is (re)produced that I seek to analyse in this project, and, while the conceptualization of 'gender violence' can constitute a particular form of critical engagement, assuming that gender has a stable ontology of difference does not allow for the type of investigation I wish to undertake.

The approach I discuss in this section, which focuses on 'gender violence', in contrast to research addressing 'violence against women', does not assume sovereignty of a stable subject. Attention is paid to the ways in which individuals are both product and productive of their social environments, positing a socially constructed individual within a similarly socially constructed matrix of gender relations. Gender is therefore not assumed to be a transhistorical or universal system of identity production, nor is it assumed that individuals experience gender in the same way, even within a particular social/political context. This emphasizes the ontological difference between research on 'violence against women' and 'gender violence'. The former assumes a material reality, and in the context of theorizing identity insists that gender can thus be read unproblematically from sexed bodies. The latter approach focuses on gender as a social construct, where sexed bodies are gendered in accordance with variable matrices of gender norms. The approach I outline below offers an alternative to both these approaches, investigating the ways in which

---

BOX 3.2 SIX CRITIQUES OF 'GENDER VIOLENCE' LITERATURE

- Sustains truth claims based on experiential accounts
- Power is related to inequality, conceived of as structural
- Violence is omnipresent and related to structural inequalities
- Gender relations are sedimented into structural inequality
- Insufficient attention is paid to politics of representation
- Analytical focus on gender difference obscures (re)production of difference

---

gender violence can be conceptualized as the performance of gender through instances of violence.

THE VIOLENT REPRODUCTION OF GENDER

While thinking about 'violence against women' can be seen as politically located in feminist activism, the approach to which I now turn is more broadly conceived of, by both its proponents and its critics, as based in the academy (Evans 1982: 17; Jeffries 1999). The bifurcation of feminist work into two strands, alluded to by Radford, Kelly and Hester as noted above, one of which became academically disciplined and the other which focused on activism as conventionally conceived, has allowed for the proliferation of feminist theorizing about the concepts of gender, violence and power, and also for the continued theorizing about theory/practice. Undoubtedly influenced by postmodern, poststructuralist and postcolonial literatures and theorizing, this approach, which investigates 'the violent reproduction of gender', works from the premiss 'that there is no necessary difference between reported, subjective experience and theoretical and analytical work' (Evans 1997: 18). Language, representation and the construction of meaning are central to both and thus the distinction between theory and practice should be collapsed.

As mentioned above, in the literature addressing 'violence against women' the women in question are identified unproblematically *as* women; as Sylvia Walby asserts, in a possibly unintended witticism, that 'the concept of 'woman' [is] essential to grasp the gendered nature of the social world' (1992: 48). Those advocating caution as regards these notions have been variously characterized as nihilistic, apolitical, traitorous and elitist (see Francis 2002: 15–17; Stanley 1997: 276–7 inter alia). While it may overstate the case a little, Brown's statement that 'postmodern deconstruction of the subject incites palpable feminist panic' (1995: 39) has particular resonance in this discussion.

Against claims that poststructural feminism is unsustainable, that feminism is inherently modernist in its claim to rights on behalf of a stable subject and the eventual emancipation of this subject, I would suggest that being *suspicious* of the truth claims of such grand narratives is not only desirable but also necessary, and that this suspicion does not preclude political action. Where thinking about 'violence against women' does not problematize the categories around which it is organized, and thinking about 'gender violence' does not fully explore the possibilities that problematizing these categories offers, a discourse-theoretical approach in which thinking about 'the violent reproduction of gender' directly addresses these concepts as a vehicle for the construction of a feminist politics of uncertainty, of instability and fluidity holds, for me, far greater appeal.

Gender can be understood as a form of identity for the ordering of society, one that is culturally specific but globally recognized. Putting the analytical category of gender under critical scrutiny allows for a theory of gender that questions the reproduction of difference rather than assuming difference and progressing from there. As Butler writes, 'this is the occasion in which we come to understand that what we take to be "real", what we invoke as the naturalized knowledge of gender is, in fact, a changeable and revisable reality' (1999: xxiii). Just as power is central to the process of maintaining the fictions of gender as a reality, the relations that define gender are power relations. However, the most important aspect of gender for the purposes of this analysis is that social understandings of gender are never *fixed*, meaning that gender needs to be reproduced through any means, violent if necessary.

This approach draws heavily on Butler's theorizing of gender as performative. Rather than proceeding from a preconceived notion of difference, this approach investigates the ways in which 'gender is an identity tenuously constituted in time, instituted in an exterior space through *a stylised repetition of acts*' (Butler 1999: 179, emphasis in original). To argue that gender is performative is not to deny the materiality of gendered bodies, it is to acknowledge that this materiality, what Butler refers to as 'the "I"', emerges 'within and as the matrix of gender relations themselves'. These 'gender relations' are 'the differentiating relations by which speaking subjects come into being' (1993: 7). Gendered violence, on this view, is conceivable as a physical manifestation of 'differentiating relations'.

I find it far more persuasive to conceptualize gender violence, of which violence against women is a part, as violences that are both gendered and gendering. Power is conceived of within this mode of analysis as productive, a conceptualization that Peter Digeser has called 'the fourth face of power' (1992: 980). Thinking about 'the violent reproduction of gender' allows for the consideration of the ways in which culturally and historically specific narratives or discourses produce particular understandings of notions of violence, gender and power, thus enabling the emergence of gendered subjects. By analysing the ways in which these subjects are temporarily 'fixed' through discursive practice, through their *performance*, it is possible to investigate 'the discursive practice by which matter is rendered irreducible' – that is, how it comes to be accepted that subjects embody a pregiven materiality – and to refuse the conceptual bracketing of the 'problematic gendered matrix' that organizes the logic of this materiality (Butler 1993: 29).

Instances of violence are one of the sites at which gender identities are reproduced. Thus, gendered violence is the violent reproduction of gender. This conceptualization of gendered violence can include such instances as homophobic 'queer-bashing' and other forms of discrimination which discipline gender (McGinnis 2001; Tatchell 2002). These examples, and all of the examples given in the two sections above, serve to (re)produce specific gender orders by dividing and controlling gendered identity groups through violence. 'Forms of violence against women, from rape and domestic violence to sexual harassment and sexual abuse, are perhaps the most oppressive by-products of what Foucault calls "technologies of sex"' (cited in Lees 1997: 86).

Gender myths serve to naturalize a configuration of the gender order particular to a given space and time. Furthermore, this naturalized gender order is performed daily, through bodily acts of obedience to and transgression of gender norms, in culturally specific ways, across the world, and notions of the 'natural' regulate this performance. Transgressants, or those who deviate from this norm, may be punished, and this is where the theorizing of violence begins to take shape. An account of the masculinization of 'men' in a township in Cape Town, South Africa, eloquently encapsulates this notion. Ramphele comments on the existence of 'repeated stories of the men and women they ought to become. Forms of storytelling are varied: Gentle cuddles, coaxing whispers … firm drawing of boundaries, harsh words for non-conformists, or even *physically imposed pain* all find a place' (Ramphele 2000: 102, emphasis added).

To illustrate this perspective, I investigate the ways in which it is possible to make meaning of rape as an instance of the violent reproduction of gender. When I describe the discursive construction of rape, I wish to make it clear that I am not disputing the 'reality' of rape as a crime; rather, I follow Sharon Marcus when she asserts that 'rape is a question of language, interpretation and subjectivity' (1992: 387). Along with Marcus, I am working towards the formulation of a politics of rape, which conceives of the act itself, the circumstances which 'allow' for the act, the immediate and long-term legal procedures following the act and associated reportage and documentation as equally implicated and important in the theorizing of rape, arguing 'against the political efficacy of seeing rape as the fixed reality of women's lives, against an identity politics which defines women by our violability' (Marcus 1992: 387).

The legal definition of rape was amended under Section 1 of the UK Sexual Offences Act 2003. Section 1 of the Sexual Offences Act 1956 stated that '[i]t is an offence for a man to rape a woman or another man'; the relevant legislation now rules that 'A person (A) commits an offence if – a) he intentionally penetrates the vagina, anus or mouth of another person (B) with his penis; b) B does not consent to the penetration; and c) A does not reasonably believe that B consents' (OPSI 2003). This legal definition of rape is interesting on many levels, but for the purposes of this analysis I would like to consider the implications of closing off the discursive space for women to be agents of rape. While 'men' have been added to the construction of potential victims of rape, 'women' are legally precluded from the list of aggressors. 'Male rape victims often feel stigmatised as female or homosexual, whatever their sexual orientation. This was a major reason why men [in the study] did not report the offences to the police. When asked why he didn't tell the police, one man replied "Only women are raped"' (Lees 1997: 95). This is partly a product of the ways in which rape is (re)presented in society as something done *by* men *to* women (and children). In dominant social constructions of gender, masculine behaviours are associated with aggression, control and action, femininities with their antonyms. Current theories of rape perpetuate this linkage, thereby reinforcing these gender stereotypes. Preserving the masculinity of rape is fundamental to its discursive construction, and therefore must be exposed and challenged as a base for the formulation of a politics of rape.

Rape can be seen as a culturally sanctioned masculine realm; although the legislation talks of 'men' the assumption is that masculinities will map on to socially defined 'male' bodies, following the myths of a 'natural' gender order. In the UK, rape is discursively constructed as a resource of gender violence, a violent means of inscribing the boundaries between masculinities and femininities, apparent from the outset once the legal definition of rape has been examined. '[R]ape is predominantly carried out by men whose sexual orientation is heterosexual ... and [is] related to the control of homosexuality and the hegemonic heterosexuality' (Lees 1997: 106). The cultural conditions that sustain gender violence are pervasive and deeply internalized. Not only does violence rely on these cultural conditions, but, to an extent, these cultural conditions also rely on violence for their (re)production.

To summarize, this section has investigated the dominant conceptualizations of gender violence that are evident in academic and policy work on this subject. Each of the three approaches I identify above is organized around specific ontological, epistemological and methodological commitments, which produce different understandings of gendered subjects and the social/political realms that these gendered subjects inhabit. For clarity, I have outlined the three approaches in Table 3.1.

There must be no tolerance of violence against women, but addressing violence against women in isolation will not reduce the

TABLE 3.1 CRITICAL REVIEW OF GENDER VIOLENCE LITERATURE

Approach	Focus	What kinds of subjects are being produced?
'Violence against women'	Empirically identifiable gendered entities and the violences they experience	Sovereign individuals
'Gender violence'	Constructed gendered entities and the violences they experience	Constructed individuals
'Violent reproduction of gender'	Discursively constituted gendered entities and the function that violence performs in (re)producing these discourses	Performative individuals

incidences of the violent reproduction of gender as I conceptualize it. I would suggest that any gains made would be temporary; it is likely that resources would be directed towards shelters, counselling and treatment of 'victims' – all of which are both worthy and necessary but none of which challenges the underlying problem. Enabling the security of people to live free from gendered violence necessitates an exploration of the ways in which security has been conceptualized, as well as an exploration of the ways in which attempts have been made to frame gendered violence as a security issue. Thus, in the second section of this chapter, I conduct a critical review of the literature on security.

(INTERNATIONAL) SECURITY

It has been suggested that security is 'what W.B. Gallie has called "an essentially contested concept"' (Buzan 1991: 7), and that the degree of debate over the precise meaning, application and utility of security as a concept within the discipline is partly a result of this contestedness. Others have pointed to the 'ambiguous' nature of security as a concept (Wolfers 1952), to the fact that analysts 'have not found it intellectually easy' (Ullman 1983: 129) to develop a pertinent and useful definition of the concept, and to the complexities inherent in recognizing and theorizing the proliferation of 'diverse terms (common, cooperative, collective, comprehensive) as modifiers to "security'" (Krause and Williams 1997: 230). In this analysis I intend to address these concerns through the mapping of security literature in a different way. The division into 'national security' and 'international security' is one that I have made for the purposes of analysis, the reasons for which will become clear as I expand on these approaches.

I begin by assessing the assumptions and normative implications of considering security with the modifier 'national', which supports an empiricist epistemology. Within this approach I consider literature produced by those working predominantly within classical and neorealist theoretical frameworks. Through the analysis of a selection of this literature, I investigate the ways in which the concept of security offered by those working within this approach is problematic. Those who work with a conceptualization that takes 'international' as a modifier for security have offered some cogent critiques of the former approach, and these will be integrated into my analysis of the assumptions and implications of studying 'international security', which is built on a constructivist epistemology.

The literature on 'international security' incorporates work on 'human security', 'critical security' and 'common security'.[4] The literature represents a variety of different theoretical frameworks, and draws heavily on representations of, and arguments concerning, 'global civil society' and cosmopolitanism, as I discuss further below. However, in this analysis I treat these works as minimally unitary, and label them 'international security' for three interconnected reasons.[5] Primarily, the term 'international' easily differentiates this approach from the literature on 'national security'. Second, the use of the modifier 'international' denotes the association of this approach with global, or universal, values. Third, the term resonates with the discipline in which this literature is situated – International Relations.

In the final section of this analysis I offer a third, discourse-theoretical conceptualization of security, building on the insights of the first two conceptualizations, which conceives of the study and politics of security as performative. The assumptions and implications of this third approach, which speaks of the violent reproduction of 'the international', will be opened to critical scrutiny. This alternative is a conscious effort to avoid producing a contribution to an already predetermined field of security studies, an unsettling of disciplinary boundaries as indicated by the remapping of the literature that I undertake. Challenging the conceptual and theoretical boundaries of the literature in an effort to define security such that both the concept and the literature, which I understand as intimately related, are reconfigured is an integral part of this analysis.

The conceptualizations that I outline here map to those presented in the previous sections concerning the differences in thinking about 'violence against women' and thinking about 'gender violence'. In the same way that those working within the approach broadly conceived as 'violence against women' take as unproblematic the identification of violence and women, there are certain assumptions either implicit or explicit in the theorizing of 'national security' that relate to the 'realities' of the organizational concepts. Similarly, while 'gender violence' literature problematizes gender as relational and conceives of violence more broadly, the literature that addresses 'international security' is largely built on critiques of literature that addresses 'national security'. In the exploration of the possibilities for a third conceptualization concerning security, just as in the formulation of a conceptualization that addresses the 'violent reproduction of gender', I will build on a critical review of the existing literature and offer some suggestions as to how security could be usefully reconceptualized.

NATIONAL SECURITY

According to Keohane, '[i]t is important to understand realism and neorealism because of their widespread acceptance in contemporary scholarship and in policy circles. Political realism is deeply embedded in Western thought' (1986: 4). The different strains of realism benefit from these claims to legitimacy and authority; realist theories are given credence through their relation to philosophers and social theorists throughout history.[6] The most regularly cited are Machiavelli, Thucydides and Hobbes, who are represented as the forefathers of International Relations in a highly effective genealogical sleight of hand.[7] Every time a view such as this one is expressed, it (re)presents realism as the orthodoxy that it professes to be, thereby increasing its status *as* the orthodoxy.

While the discipline of IR proclaims itself to be concerned with Inter*national* Relations, it would be more appropriate within a realist framework to refer to the study of relations between *states*. The assumption that guides this act of boundary inscription is that the 'national' will always be congruent with the 'state', as discussed further below. Thus, the primary object of analysis for realisms is the state, assumed to be unitary and cohesive, that acts on behalf of its population in a system of states functioning with no higher authority than the state itself. Thus both internal and external sovereignty are central to the conception of the state, and the logical corollary of this conception constructs the state system as anarchic. Realist IR theory 'sees' the state as its object of analysis and therefore '[s]tates are the principle referent objects of security because they are both the framework of order and the highest sources of governing authority' (Buzan 1991: 22).

The initial point of critical engagement with this approach to security is the way in which the state is conceptualized. Within both classical (or 'political') realism and neorealism (or 'structural' realism), the state is represented as a unitary actor.[8] Both variants proceed according to the assumption that all human existence is bounded by states, according to the assertion that states are the primary object of analysis. If, as Kenneth Waltz claims, '[s]tatesmen and military leaders are responsible for the security of their states ... no one at all is responsible for humanity' (1959: 416), then states are further assumed to be the object to which security policy and practice refers and humans can only be secured to the extent that they are citizens of a given state.

Given the foundational assumption of anarchy, discussed in more detail below, states are only able to achieve security, and thus survival, through self-help aimed at self-preservation. This is where the formulation of a concept of security as 'national security' begins to take shape, as the internal logic of a realist framework demands that security refers to the 'national', that is assumed to be congruent with the state. The state is what exists to be secured, thus '[t]he main focus of security studies is easy to identify ... conflict between states is always a possibility ... Accordingly, security studies may be defined as *the study of the threat, use and control of military force*', where military force is assumed to be within the control of the state as a component of sovereignty; 'conflict between states is always a possibility' (Nye and Lynn-Jones cited in Walt 1991: 212, emphasis in original); thus, conflict is, by definition, *between states*.

Containing human existence within the boundaries of the state and assuming that individuals are defined in relation to the state that is in turn assumed to have ultimate authority, seen as domination, over its peoples, is problematic. In studying the peace camps at Greenham Common, for example, feminist IR scholars also challenged this interpretation of identity and experience as being contained by the state. The individuals at Greenham, who were exercising agency through the use of their bodies in protest against the fact that nuclear 'security' didn't make them feel secure, 'subverted the security-based strategic vision of international relations by showing ... acts of everyday insecurity' (Sylvester 1994: 193). The very articulation of these 'acts of everyday insecurity' challenges conventional logic as represented within this conceptualization of 'national security', and demands that the relationship between individuals and the state be examined and problematized.[9]

The second critique concerns the construction of the state in classical realist theories on 'national security'. In classical realist theory, representations of state behaviours draw heavily on ideas relating to 'human nature' (Morgenthau 1952: 963). As mentioned above, classical realism claims as its antecedents theorists of 'human nature' such as Thucydides, Machiavelli and Hobbes, and appeals to logics of 'human nature' to explain self-interest and rationality as 'evidenced' by the unitary state. As Gilpin argues, 'political realism itself ... is best viewed as an attitude regarding the human condition' (1984a: 290). With no higher authority to whom to appeal for justice or protection, according to this literature on 'national security', the anthropomorphized state must act on its own behalf. 'As Thomas Hobbes told his patron ... "it's a jungle out there". Anarchy is the rule, justice and morality are the exceptions' (1984a: 290; see also Carr 1939: 80–81).

The construction of 'human nature' that is seen to define the behaviour of states is untenable (see Hoffman 2001; Grant 1991), but enjoys considerable discursive privilege in academic and policy discussions of 'national security'.[10] The 'human nature' under discussion is, on closer inspection, the nature of 'man' (see Morgenthau 1973: 15–16), and is thus problematic in its partiality as well as its pessimism. John Herz's conception of the 'security dilemma' is explicitly premissed on these assumptions regarding the potential of human nature, and therefore state behaviour, to provide circumstances of collaboration and cooperation. '[I]t stems from a fundamental social constellation ... where groups live alongside each other without being organized into a higher unity ... Since none can ever feel entirely secure in such a world ... power competition ensues and the vicious circle of security and power accumulation is on' (Herz 1950: 157). The 'fundamental social constellation' posited by classical realists is a population of rational, unitary, masculine entities that will, and can, never be otherwise.

The third critique challenges neorealist theories of state behaviour in the literature on 'national security'. Neorealist theories of 'national security' prioritize structural logic, rather than relying on the logics of 'human nature' as discussed above. While classical realist assumptions are informed by an explicit link between 'human nature' and state behaviour, neorealist assumptions concerning the construction of security in an anarchic system appeal to a structural logic of uncertainty. 'Uncertainty is a synonym for life, and nowhere is uncertainty greater than in international politics' (Waltz 1993: 58). These arguments are still underpinned by an assumption of systemic anarchy.[11] Anarchy 'will exist so long as independent states endure' (Waltz 1959: 417), and is represented as the permissive cause of violence. It is the organization of the realm external to the state – the domain of the international – or rather the lack of organization in this realm that governs the quest for security, according to neorealist work on 'national security'. 'In anarchy,' Waltz has stated, 'security is the highest end' (1979: 126). This allows for the conceptualization of 'national security' as necessary in response to certain objectively identifiable security threats. As states are not organized into a social hierarchy of states in the external domain, it may become 'necessary to undertake war ... out of apprehension for one's own security ... [This] *amounts to doing what necessity dictates*' (Waltz 1967: 206, emphasis added).

John Mearsheimer develops a critique of alternative approaches to security premissed on neorealist assumptions again concerning 'the basic nature of states' (1990: 55). The suggestion that a bipolar balance of power during the Cold War afforded greater stability and therefore security to the world is similarly premissed on these realist assumptions: 'there is little room for trust among states ... each state must guarantee its own survival since no other actor will provide its security ... States seek to survive under anarchy by maximising their power relative to other states' (Mearsheimer 1990: 12). Thus the state is assumed to be a rational actor with regard to its international relations, seeking both to accumulate knowledge concerning the activities of other states and to gear all statecraft towards the essential survival of the state as a territorial and political unit.

However, despite the reductive logic of neorealism that upholds claims to abstraction, the conceptualizations of states and state behaviour that inform these abstractions remain thoroughly masculinist. International Relations as a discipline and relations international remain, on this view, the preserve of 'men' (Waltz 1993, 2000; Mearsheimer 1990, 1995) and behaviours of the state are premissed on masculinist understandings of subjectivity. Mearsheimer insists that '[s]tates ... look for opportunities to take advantage of each other' (1990: 53) while weighing up the advantages and disadvantages of their behaviours in a purely self-interested manner. While Mearsheimer suggests that this behaviour is a product of the anarchic system, this conceptualization of the cooperative impulses exhibited by states, or lack thereof, rests on a masculinist understanding of international politics.

A fourth critique relates to the conceptualization of violence within this approach to security. If security threats are eternal and external, then security 'is nothing but the absence of the evil of insecurity, a negative value so to speak' (Wolfers 1952: 488). The construction of a non-society of states, each rationally seeking to maximize their gains and preserve their territorial and political integrity, in which threats are reducible to the hostile use of force by other states leads to the assertion that it is a '*fact*' that security is being sought against external violence' (Wolfers 1952: 490, emphasis added). While some theorists working within this conceptualization have admitted the possibility that threats may equally arise from internal unrest and civil violence,[12] the predominant vision is one of threat as objectively identifiable and external to the state. This also functions to exclude the possibility that states may be the actors that threaten their own populations,[13] through the inscription of the state as the referent object of security policy and practice.

Mearsheimer's analysis of security during the Cold War period, in which he argues that the bipolarity of power provided a more secure system than the ensuing multipolarity in the post-Cold War period, affirms this conceptualization of violence. However, the argument that, '*ceteris paribus*, war is more likely in a multipolar system than a bipolar one' (Mearsheimer 1990: 14) is problematic. Furthermore, in admitting that '[i]n a bipolar system ... major powers generally demand allegiance from lesser states' (1990: 14) Mearsheimer alludes to a weakness in this conceptualization of violence. Allegiance may be coerced, or achieved through interventions that lead to 'lesser states' feeling less than secure by any realist definition of the term, and these violences seem to fall outside of an analysis that not only equates violence with war, but with war between 'major powers'. While the logic of 'conflict dyads' and 'miscalculations' appears convincing, it is unreasonable to assume that *ceteris* is ever *paribus* in the practice or study of IR. The complexities of lived experience do not easily lend themselves to such abstraction.

This leads me to the fifth point of critical engagement. As states can only ever achieve relative security, the quest for security is a never-ending search for research and development that leads to better policy and practice. This secures the future prospects of those who work within this conceptualization, as long as they are not 'diverted into a prolix and self-indulgent discourse that is divorced from the real world' (Walt 1991: 223). The diversion warned against by Stephen Walt is an effort to secure the disciplinary boundaries against the incursion of critical theories. 'If participants observe the norms that have guided the field in recent years ... prospects for continued advance are good' (1991: 232).[14] As long as it is as it has always been, the study of 'national security' will continue to be as it has always been – and the world will be perpetually *in*secure.

The concept of security driving these prescriptions is premised on a particular vision of the social relations between states, and furthermore constructs a particular notion of what is considered to be a security threat within this conceptualization, as eternal and external to the state. The necessity of security behaviours is derived from the anarchic system and 'rests on the argument that the distribution and character of military power are the root causes of war and peace' (Mearsheimer 1990: 6). Thus threats, reduced to external violences and ultimately war between states, are perpetual, a theoretical move that serves to perpetuate the understanding of security as reducible to military force. This functions to blind those working within a conceptualization of 'national security' to the possibility that threats are variously constructed depending on context. Moreover, the assumption context of anarchy that is taken to be a foundational reality within this conceptualization prescribes and proscribes certain behaviours that are then never opened to critical scrutiny.

The implications of insisting that 'the world can be used as laboratory to decide which theories best explain international politics' (Mearsheimer 1990: 9) are not addressed by theorists working within this conceptualization. However, in raising this as a focus for critical interjection, I draw attention to the impossibility of constructing a concept of security that is *not* founded on value-laden theoretical assumptions. Deconstructing the 'scientific', detached observer of the realist theoretical tradition enables IR scholars to reflect on their position as thoroughly embedded subjects within their research, complete with the internal conflicts and inconsistencies of selfhood that are part of social identity.

The cumulative impact of the five critiques detailed above is 'that military force, not security, has been the central concern of security studies' (Baldwin 1997: 9). This is the sixth, and final, critique of the literature on 'national security'. The militarization of the study of 'national security' has affected the ways in which it is studied, the policy prescriptions offered by the experts in the field and the funding afforded to research programs that attend to this central issue in the discipline of IR. It allows for the construction of research addressing 'national security' to speak of 'the real world' while maintaining '[t]he hygienic order of neo-realism [as] one manifestation of the "escape from the real"' (Booth 1995: 105). The 'real' world constructed through the representations of those who work on 'national security' is one

---

BOX 3.3 SIX CRITIQUES OF 'NATIONAL SECURITY'
LITERATURE

- All human existence is assumed to be bound by the state
- Classical realism assumes state behaviour derives from human nature
- Neorealism assumes state behaviour derives from anarchic system
- Violence is eternal and external to the state
- Security can never be achieved
- Adherence to this approach increases militarization

---

in which 'relative harmony can, and sometimes does, prevail among nations, but always precariously so' (Waltz 1993: 76), a world that is indeed, as Hobbes would have it, 'poore, nasty, brutish and short'. The inhabitants of this world are thus justified in taking up arms to ensure their own survival.

Research on 'national security' takes as unproblematic the existence of the sovereign state, as described above, and the protection of the territorial integrity of this sovereign state is – or should be – the focus of security studies. The approach described above 'fits comfortably within the familiar realist paradigm' (Walt 1991: 212), and the academic conceptualization of security *as* national fits comfortably with the ontological assumptions of research addressing 'violence against women'. Those engaged in both forms of research posit the empirical reality of the subjects that they study, and the social/political realities in which these subjects function. In the case of research on 'national security', the explicit 'outside' of the sovereign state is the anarchic international system, which is an issue to which I return below.

New approaches to the study of security and new challenges to the existing literature are disciplined in such as way as to reaffirm the primacy of 'national security' as a conceptualization for considering security concerns. Despite claims that 'it is no longer helpful or reasonable to define the field in dualistic terms: with the realist, state-centric military-minded approach at the core' (Paris 2001: 101), the very articulation of a core of security studies reproduces the dominance of this literature. While work on 'national security' admits a proliferation of alternative approaches to security (see Baldwin 1997), the military defence of state interests is constituted as the baseline of security to which other understandings can be added. However, those working on 'international security' conceive of the referent object(s) of security, and the threats posed to it/them, very differently, as I discuss below.

INTERNATIONAL SECURITY

It is vital to recognize that the concept of 'national security' has developed in a specific cultural context (Haftendorn 1991: 5), the context of predominantly Anglo-American positivist-oriented and science-dominated IR scholarship within which realism is the self-proclaimed orthodoxy. Thus, 'national security' is premised on particular assumptions that need to be made explicit for the purposes of critical analysis, and this recognition has encouraged the development of a second approach. An awareness of 'national security' as partial and problematic, much as 'violence against women' can be critically rethought, and the interaction with those who write to a different conceptualization of security, has led to the formulation of an alternative conceptualization, that of 'international security'. As mentioned in the introduction to this chapter, the literature on 'international security' encompasses work on security from a variety of perspectives, bound by its adherence to assumptions concerning security, community and emancipation, as I discuss below.[15]

The arguments presented within the framework of 'international security' are more loosely bound by their theoretical assumptions and research priorities. Just as the literature addressing 'gender violence' encompasses a more diverse and eclectic approach to the issues with which it is concerned, the literature within this conceptualization of security is not necessarily built on an integration of the six points of critique outlined above. However, the foundations of this literature are built on engagements with 'national security' as a concept and research programme. Broadly speaking, these literatures respond to those who write within a conceptualization of 'national security' in an effort to challenge the boundaries that the latter construct around the concept of security within the scholarship of IR. The perspectives from which they engage with the concept of 'national security' are varied, but, as I will discuss below, they are minimally unitary in their desire to reconceptualize security and demand a qualitatively and quantitively better concept with which to proceed in their analyses.

Often tracing its heritage back to the 1994 UNDP *Human Development Report*,[16] which includes a chapter entitled 'New Dimensions of Human Security', work on 'international security' seeks to reconceptualize security such that the referent object is no longer conceived, as in 'national security', as the sovereign state (see Newman 2001: 240; Booth 2004: 5). As McDonald explains, this reconceptualization is 'a potential response to the growing insecurity of security' (2002: 277) and incorporates several of the critiques discussed above. Roland Paris argues that this 'paradigm shift' does not necessarily represent a coherent research agenda, but recognizes that this work comprises 'a distinct branch of security studies that explores the particular conditions that affect the survival of individuals, groups and societies' (2001: 92–3, 102). Broadly, the analytical focus of 'international security' is 'we, the peoples' (Dunne and Wheeler 2004) and research within this conceptualization requires the recognition of 'both the indivisibility of human rights and security, and the concomitant responsibility to rescue those trapped in situations of violence, poverty and ill-health' (Dunne and Wheeler 2004: 20).

In my discussion of the literature on 'gender violence', above, I engage critically with the literature while wanting to acknowledge that it represents positive critical engagement on its own terms with the literature on 'violence against women'. I proceed with the analysis of work on 'international security' in the same way. That is, the works cited in this section are all 'critical', in that they are founded on critiques of the literature on 'national security' and on an active desire to find a 'better' conceptualization of security with which to proceed (see Sheehan 2005: 4). However, I share with Matt McDonald a concern that such an undertaking necessitates a certain wariness 'of imposing an alternative structure of power in ways that may simply replace one power structure with another' (2002: 293).

The first point of critical engagement with the literature on 'international security' concerns the assumptions that underpin the arguments for the recognition of the 'international' as a domain of cooperation rather than conflict. The 'international' is still represented as always already external to the state (see Dunne and Wheeler 2004: 10; Newman 2001: 241), as in the 'national security' approach, but is premissed on ideas of collectivity and connectivity that are comparable with the realist insistence on seeing the world as an inherently aggressive and hostile environment. Work on 'international security' gives primacy to 'human beings and their complex social and economic relations' (Thomas 2001: 161) over state behaviours, but in the last instance it is the cooperative 'world community' (Booth 1991: 318) to which this approach appeals. It could be that articulating a vision of world politics in which 'the international community' plays a central role actually serves to absent the state from discussions of democracy, agency and politics. Locating these values in the domain of the 'international' could prove dangerous, in that there is nothing inherent in this domain that necessitates the 'better' provisions of security that work on 'international security' seeks.

If 'anarchy is what states make of it' (Wendt 1992: 395) and states are not constructed as the unproblematic unitary rational actors pursuing defensive policies, as assumed by theorists of 'national security', then cooperation is as likely as hostility in the domain of international relations. In fact, it is argued, conceiving of security as 'international' highlights the importance of relations between states and the salience of the construction of an 'international community' (McRae 2001: 19). However, just as the state is asserted as autonomous with the conceptualization of 'national security', as I have described above, in this conceptualization 'international security' is similarly asserted as relational. These assumptions are in opposition but are equally problematic, as both assumptions treat the state and the international as predetermined objective realities, which impacts on the ways in which it is possible to conceptualize security.

The second critique I make of the 'international security' literature derives from the first: 'global civil society' is implicitly and explicitly the locus of agency in the 'international community' assumed by this approach. In place of the state of nature/systemic uncertainty posited by theorists working within the conceptualization of 'national security', Booth suggests that 'the embryonic global civil society'

(1991: 326) can function cooperatively and with compassion for their fellow citizens to construct a safer world (see also Dunne and Wheeler 2004: 10; Paris 2001: 88). In contrast to the assertion of a system populated by sovereign states, those researching 'international security' see cooperative collectives as the desired mode of political organization. The institutionalization of compassion is an inherently political process and I argue that, within this conceptualization, insufficient attention is paid to the ways in which the violences experienced in the construction of community and cooperation are glossed over and fall outside the parameters of discussion.

Richard McRae, for example, argues that 'global civil society' needs to address the issues of insecurity facing those 'citizens of … noncountries' (2001: 20, 19) whose governments are unable to provide adequate security measures. Tim Dunne and Nick Wheeler also cite the cooperation of 'an alliance of states and transnational civil society' needed to 'rescue those trapped in situations of poverty and violence' (2004: 10, 20). Recognizing the 'structural inequalities generated by global capitalism' (16) goes some way towards challenging the assumptions of 'national security' literature, in the same way as work on 'gender violence' offers sustainable critiques of the literature on 'violence against women'. However, theories of 'international security' do not take into account the implications of their representations of a 'global civil society' versus citizens of 'noncountries' who need rescuing.

The concept of 'global civil society' is ideologically and normatively loaded with implications of its global reach, its civilized nature and its social form. All of these characteristics are constituted in opposition to their relevant 'others': the local/parochial, the uncivilized, and the forms of behaviour associated with states and international institutions, all of which are conceived of as negative. Despite this, the construction of 'global civil society' is undertheorized, represented unproblematically in the literature on 'international security' and assumed to confer authority and legitimacy in the realms of morality, efficacy, democracy and social cohesion (see Scholte 2002: 159–64; Hopgood 2000).

Just as the referent object of security is multilevel and complex, violences and threats are conceived of more broadly within this approach. This forms the third critique that I identify of this literature. The narrow military focus of those addressing 'national security' is critiqued, on this view, as a wider variety of threats are recognized (see Smith 2005: 40–46; McDonald 2002: 277). Threats are not necessarily eternal and external, as a function of the anarchic international system. Threats and violences are still objectively identifiable, but within this conceptualization they are many and various, ranging from the interpersonal to the systemic level and encompassing gender violences and global warming, earthquakes and economic deprivation.[17] Representing threats in this way assumes that such events, or acts of violence, affect all individuals in the same way. In addition, through listing threats in this way, theories of 'international security' inscribes a division between inhabitants of 'noncountries' and the 'international', as theories of 'international security' are most often concerned with providing security for 'the oppressed, women, poor, middle powers and so on … rather than focusing only on the hopes and fears of the greatest *power* in the world' (Booth 2004: 5, emphasis in original).

Furthermore, 'international security', in both broadening and deepening the concept of threat (Booth 2005: 14–15), implicitly conveys the urgency and priority built into the concept of security propounded by work on 'national security', in which security is, as discussed above, 'the highest end'. 'An implicit assumption … is that the elevation of issues of human rights, economic inequality and environmental change, for example, to the realm of security will allow greater priority to these issues' (McDonald 2002: 277). Even as it problematizes the conceptualization of security evidenced in the conceptualization of 'national security', literature on 'international security' tends to naturalize it, constructing security as a 'single continuum … protected and enhanced by a series of interlocking instruments and policies' (McRae 2001: 22). This suggests that the approach to 'national security' is broadly valid, needing only supplementary analysis to fill in the gaps rather than a thorough reconceptualization of its basic organizational concepts.

The fourth critical interjection I offer concerns the conceptualization of security as not necessarily relative, as assumed by 'national security', but potentially absolute. Within the conceptualization of 'international security', it is argued, 'the study of security … is finally beginning to engage comprehensively with the real' (Booth 2004: 8). This engagement, in addition to inscribing the appropriate interpretation of 'the real', can – and should – 'have a real impact' (Newman 2001: 250) and 'prevent, or halt, threats' (McRae 2001: 26). The suggestion is that the objectively identifiable and multiple threats faced by citizens of 'noncountries' and those at the sharp end of structural inequality can be dealt with. The conceptualization of 'international security' is firmly embedded within a normative and problem-solving framework, arguing that security for all is the future of 'the real' so long as security providers work with 'global civil society' towards 'the reduction of global poverty, the reduction of inequality between states and between human beings; and the harnessing of scientific advancement for the benefit of the majority of humanity' (Thomas 2001: 166–7). I am not arguing that 'international security' should retain a commitment to objectivity and shy away from critical engagement with security problematiques (cf. Smith 2005: 46). Rather, I challenge the assumption that absolute security can be achieved, which not only ignores the way in which discourses of security function in world politics but also is modelled on a foundational commitment to human emancipation that is difficult to sustain.

The conceptualization of security as emancipation forms the fifth point of critical engagement with literature on 'international security'. If 'national security' is concerned with security defined in terms of power, then 'international security' views security as 'freedom from' (Ullman 1983: 152–3). This is the central thesis in theories of 'international security': 'Emancipation should logically be given precedence in our thinking about security over the mainstream themes of order and power' (Booth 1991: 319).[18] Therefore, as opposed to the relative gains of 'national security', security within this conceptualization can be achieved as absolute because threats can be adequately neutralized and security is reducible to freedom. 'Emancipation from oppressive power structures, be they global, national or local in origin and scope, is necessary for security' (Thomas 2001: 162). This is an intuitively positive formulation of the concept of security, but there remain some serious issues to be addressed in this fifth section of critique. Focusing on freedom without adequately addressing the ways in which this freedom is to be conceptualized or achieved renders the concept of security within this optic as partial in application and utility as the concept outlined above, in the treatment of 'national security'.

Conceptualizing security as freedom carries with it implicit judgements regarding the provision of freedom from exclusive political practices, enabling all to enjoy a minimal standard of life experience. In the face of the huge disparities in access to such freedom, the suggestion that security can be achieved as absolute remains a hollow promise and security itself a hollow concept. Moreover, work on 'international security' does not recognize that security policy premised on a notion of 'freedom from fear' (McRae 2001: 15) assumes that the benefits and promise of freedom are universally applicable and achievable, paying scant attention to social/political context.

Finally, I argue that the conscious universalism of the 'international security' approach (Booth 2005: 1) and the solution it offers to the problems it tries to solve – global emancipation – is deeply problematic. Those working within this approach delimit the boundaries of 'the real' as much as those working with the conceptualization of 'national security' discussed above. 'International security' recognizes an ever-proliferating range of threats but argues that transnational cooperation can effectively provide security for all, which is premised on this notion of security as emancipation. 'Emancipation is the freeing of people (as individuals and groups) from those physical and human constraints which stop them carrying out what they would freely choose to do' (Booth 1991: 319). This philosophical underpinning is entirely devoid of any suggestion that freedom is an idea most closely associated with liberalism. Thomas argues that '[h]uman security is far removed from liberal notions of competitive and possessive individualism' (2001: 161). However, the centrality of freedom to the organizational logic of 'international security' suggests that this approach derives more from liberalism than it would like to admit.

The assumptions underpinning literature on 'international security' lead to policy prescriptions premised on the triumph of liberal values, implemented by 'a progressive alliance between … cosmopolitan transnational civil society and enlightened state leaders' (Booth 2004: 6). The formation of an informed and activist global civil society, with

---

BOX 3.4 SIX CRITIQUES OF 'INTERNATIONAL SECURITY'
LITERATURE

- States are cooperative rather than conflicting
- Assumes existence of benign 'global civil society'
- Violences and threats need to be broadly conceptualized
- Security can be achieved in absolute terms
- Security is conceptualized in terms of emancipation
- Adherence to this approach would construct a 'better' (liberal) world

---

all the problems inherent within that concept, is seen as a necessary step to the provision of security. Well-established international institutions and collectives capable of providing security and guaranteeing freedoms are also vital on this view. Ultimately, the critique I offer is concerned that the conceptualization of 'international security' I discuss here 'constitutes a Western project, predicated on the values of the developed world' (McDonald 2002: 293). In the articulation of this conceptualization of 'international security', the values upon which the prescriptions are founded are not opened to critical scrutiny, and effect closure on the ways in which it is possible to think not only about security but also about international relations more broadly.

The six points of critical engagement outlined in Box 3.4 are themselves critiques of the literatures within the conceptualization of 'national security'. However, reconceptualizing security with the modifier 'international', even suggesting as it does a more holistic and complex approach to the concept of security, is not sufficient. As Ole Waever states: 'The traditional progressive approach is: 1) to accept ... that security is a reality prior to language ... and the more security the better; and 2) to argue why security should encompass *more* than is currently the case' (1995: 46–7; emphasis in original). While this approach does engage with the boundaries of 'national security' literature, the boundaries are then reinscribed elsewhere; though conceived of as more complex, more multilevel, more permeable, these boundaries are still constructed through the representation of security as 'international'.

The ontological assumptions of this approach differentiate it from work on 'national security', as this approach posits the international as a socially constructed zone of cooperation rather than assuming the existence of a conflictual international domain. Violence and threat are still ever-present in this conceptualization, but thoughtful security policy and practice can ameliorate the situations of individuals, societies, communities, states...[19] These subjects are recognized as constructs of their social/political milieu on this view. Just as research on 'gender violence' does not see a universal stability to matrices of gender norms, research on 'international security' investigates the ways in which norms and ideas function in international relations to construct the subjects of enquiry – states. In the final subsection of this review, I attempt to formulate a third conceptualization of security that understands discourses of security as productive and performative of these subjects.

THE VIOLENT REPRODUCTION OF THE INTERNATIONAL

The basis of the tensions between the two former approaches to security are cogently summarized by Lene Hansen thus: 'whether to understand security as a matter of national security only, or to open up the concept' (2000: 56). The six critiques of each conceptualization enable those who would wish to overcome these tensions to begin the reconceptualization of security through critical engagement with the foundational assumptions and constructs that guide approaches either to 'national' or to 'international' security, thus overcoming the dichotomy to which Hansen refers. Research that addresses the 'violent reproduction of the international' conceives of security as a set of discourses rather than as something that can be achieved either in absolute or in relative terms. Engaging with research that works within this conceptualization can explore how these discourses function to reproduce, through various strategies, domains of the international with which IR is self-consciously concerned. Thus the violences and the threats, as much as the states and security itself, are interpreted through the practices that enable individuals as social beings to make sense of their social location and identity.

Literature that addresses 'the violent reproduction of gender' conceives of violence as a site at which genders are reproduced;

literature that addresses the 'violence reproduction of the international' conceives of violence, of which security practice and policy is an integral part, as sites at which the international is reproduced. Including not just acts of interstate war, but also instances of civil conflict and oppressive practices within and between states, expanding further to problematize the legal structures, policy practices and the research that guides these, theorists are enabled to investigate the ways in which these acts of violence articulated through discourses of security function to perpetuate 'the international' as various spatial and conceptual realms. Thus, within this conceptualization it is possible to say that states, acting as unitary authoritative entities, perform violences, but also that violences, in the name of security, perform states. Undertaking research within this conceptualization allows for a holistic perspective on the ways in which discourses of security reproduce grammatically correct narratives of identity and being-in-the-world, of which in international relations the 'international' is a key organizing concept.

This conceptualization goes beyond even the critical theorizing of those who work within an optic of 'international security'. Booth suggests that 'the post-modern tendency in the study of international politics … can obscure that meaning is not everything' (1991: 316). Theorizing the 'violent reproduction of the international' takes the opposing view: meaning is everything. It is not that this approach conceives of security as somehow less 'real' than the former approaches, or that there is some gap of misperception that can be righted with careful analysis. Rather, in this reconceptualization it becomes possible to ask how that which occurs became possible and is made meaningful both in theory and in practice. This approach allows for the analysis of the processes through which meaning is made and therefore 'reality' is (re)produced. Reconceptualizing security discourses in this way allows for detailed investigation of the ways in which they function to construct through representation the international as a spatial and conceptual domain. Along with David Campbell, among others, 'I embrace a logic of interpretation that acknowledges the improbability of cataloguing, calculating and specifying the "real causes" and concerns itself instead with considering the manifest political consequences of adopting one mode of representation over another' (Campbell 1998: 4).

If it is not possible to define or to achieve security, but security instead functions in particular ways in particular contexts with related effects and differential impacts, all integrated into the wider reproduction of 'the international' as a separate domain, then security policy and practice must be analysed differently. One aspect of the ways in which discourses of security, and the violences legitimized by these discourses, function within international relations is simultaneously to delimit the state as boundary between the domestic and the international realms. States are assumed to be unitary and authoritative, to maintain both internal and external sovereignty, and, furthermore, it is assumed that the internal organization of the state is undertaken in the best interests of citizenry – to protect and serve the population. Unsettling 'the international' as an *a priori* unsafe/safe domain (in the discourses of 'national security' and 'international security' respectively) challenges this truth of security as propounded by the two conceptualizations outlined above.

Considering the ways in which this domain is (re)produced is vital to understanding how security functions as a discourse. Der Derian addresses the 'new technological practice' of simulation as a means of identifying 'the reality principle that international relations theory in general seeks to save' (1990: 300). The reality principle of the international as a conceptual domain is undermined by the intertextuality of simulation and policy procedure. Discourses of security help to reassert the primacy of the international in the ways described above: through the identification of objective threats, the construction of international order and the perpetuation of the myth of the state. The processes of securitization and desecuritization (Waever 1995) that speak to an issue's discursive purchase on the reproduction of the international, and the processes through which threats and insecurities are socially constructed (Weldes et al. 1999) are all central to this conceptualization of security.

Those working within a conceptualization that addresses 'the violent reproduction of the international' explicitly challenge the assumptions concerning the objective reality of threats. '[O]bjects and events do not present themselves unproblematically to the observer ... Rather than being self-evident ... threats ... are fundamentally matters of interpretation' (Weldes 1996: 279). The same is true of states and violences within this conceptualization, and discourses of security reproduce dominant representations of threats, violences and states. Der Derian analyses processes of surveillance to illustrate this point, in which the domain of the international is conceived of as a panopticon and surveillance as a security measure functions to breed insecurities. In this way, the uncertainties and instabilities inherent in the dominant construction of the international are perpetuated: 'the superpowers have created a cybernetic system that displays the classic symptoms of advanced paranoia' (1990: 305), through which discourses of security then reproduce insecurity through interpretation.

Simultaneously, these technologies not only function to reconfigure the meanings of and give meaning to security, they also reproduce the contours of the international. The spatial arrangement of IR relies on these conceptualizations of security for its perpetuation, and through shifts in security discourse this arrangement can be reconfigured. Security arrangements between states simultaneously act to posit states as unitary entities, to reproduce the identities of these states, to reaffirm security as the concern of states and to reproduce a particular configuration of 'the international' in opposition to the domestic realm.

The discursive privilege of IR scholars who speak of security as the concern of the state imbue the state with the powers to construct in/security and to carry out actions that further entrench this privilege. As Enloe reminds us, 'it has become almost a cliché to say that the world is shrinking, that state boundaries are porous. We persist, nonetheless, in discussing personal power relationships as if they were contained by sovereign states' (2000: 196). The conceptualization of 'the violent reproduction of the international' interprets this form of discursive violence as appropriate a focus for analysis as instances of physical violence. Furthermore, the practices of power that construct the authority and the legitimacy of the state and its ability to speak on behalf of its grateful population must also be problematized (see Enloe 1996). Borrowing from Butler's theorizing of the violence done to bodies in the context of theorizing gender, 'I would like to suggest that this kind of categorisation can be called a violent one, a forceful one, and that this discursive ordering ... is itself a material violence' (Butler 1994: 168).

TABLE 3.2 CRITICAL REVIEW OF INTERNATIONAL SECURITY
LITERATURE

Approach	Focus	What kinds of subjects are being produced?
'National security'	Empirically identifiable (state) entities and the violences they experience due to the anarchic international system	Sovereign states
'International security'	Constructed (state) entities and the violences they can prevent due to the cooperative international system	Constructed states
'Violent reproduction of the international'	Discursively constituted entities and the function that violence performs in (re)producing various international systems	Performative states

The gendered dimensions of understanding security as discourse are
an integral part of analyses that work within this conceptualization.
Any understanding premised on a notion of security as existing
outside of the power relations through which discourses operate is
both inadequate and incomplete. Furthermore, gender, as a discursively
constituted identity, informs interpretation and the construction of
conceptual organization and logics. The links between the two bodies
of literature, discussed further below, become clear when the critical
review of the literature undertaken in this section is represented in
tabular form (Table 3.2).

Discussed in the table are examples of academic research that draw
together the concepts of gender, violence, security and the international, and so are part of the literature that forms the heritage of
this study. As I work through the investigation, I engage with various
secondary literatures in the process of analysis, but it has been useful
to map, however broadly, the conceptualizations of gendered violence
and international security that inform this project. The potential for
critical engagement with gender, violence and security is both limited
and enabled by the literature that already exists on these subjects.
Furthermore, without a clear understanding of the ways in which
existing academic approaches to security have precluded the study

of gender, articulating gender violence as an international security issue is extremely problematic.

Table 3.3 summarizes the findings from the critical review conducted in this Chapter. From this table, it is clear that the empiricist, constructivist and discourse-theoretical conceptualizations of gendered violence and global security share more in common with each other than they do with the competing approaches. In the chapters that follow, I demonstrate that the dominant conceptualizations of (gender) violence and (international) security that are represented in the documents I analyse are, indeed, 'gender violence' and 'international security', the constructivist approaches described above. However, the discourse-theoretical conceptualization in each case offers different potentialities for articulating gendered violence as a security issue. Although it is not the task I undertake here, for persuasive and effective policy reform the concepts that are used are due careful analytical attention. Thus, in the following chapter, I begin the exploration of the ways in which the concepts of (international) security and (gender) violence are discursively constituted through the analysis of United Nations Security Council Resolution 1325. First, I undertake analysis of the Secretary-General's Reports (UNSC 2004a, 2002a), with a view to illustrating that gender in conflict situations cannot be sufficiently theorized through an evaluation of 'the impact of armed conflict on women and girls' (UNSC 2002a: Preamble).

TABLE 3.3 TOWARDS A FEMINIST RECONCEPTUALIZATION OF (INTERNATIONAL) SECURITY AND (GENDER) VIOLENCE

	Gender Violence			International Security	
Approach	Focus	Subjects	Subjects	Focus	Approach
Violence against women	Empirically identifiable gendered entities and the violences they experience	Sovereign individuals	Sovereign states	Empirically identifiable (state) entities and the violences they experience due to the anarchic international system	National security
Gender violence	Constructed gendered entities and the violences they experience	Constructed individuals	Constructed states	Constructed (state) entities and the violences they can prevent due to the cooperative international system	International security
Violent reproduction of gender	Discursively constituted gendered entities and the function that violence performs in (re)producing these discourses	Performative individuals	Performative states	Discursively constituted entities and the function that violence performs in (re)producing various international systems	Violent reproduction of the international

4 | THE SECRETARY-GENERAL'S REPORTS

Resolution 1325, adopted by the United Nations Security Council (UNSC) in 2000, addressed 'the impact of armed conflict on women and girls' and the ways in which the full participation of women and girls in peace processes 'can significantly contribute to the maintenance and promotion of international peace and security' (UNSC 2000a: Preamble). In the following chapters I discuss the construction of the resolution itself and the narratives of its production. However, before I undertake the analysis of UNSCR 1325, in this chapter I conduct an analysis of the Secretary-General's Reports (UNSC 2004a, 2002a) that were mandated by UNSCR 1325. The Resolution required 'the Secretary General to carry out a study on the impact of armed conflict on women and girls' (UNSC 2000a: Article 16–17), and this Report, produced in 2002, offers explanations for the failures to implement UNSCR 1325 in conflict and post-conflict zones. A subsequent Report, produced in 2004, contains more detailed evidence of particular successes and failures. In order to provide contextual foundations for a research project that investigates the discursive construction of UNSCR 1325, it is crucial to explore the explanatory factors offered by the United Nations Security Council itself.

The Secretary-General's Reports offer explanations for the ways in which UNSCR 1325 has failed, and, in doing so, attempt to delimit discursively the boundaries of the Resolution's failures. That is, this chapter conceives of the Reports as discursive practices, and, in doing so, recognizes that they are also practices of power. As this study is concerned with demonstrating that the discursive construction of the Resolution determined the failures to implement UNSCR 1325 successfully, it is necessary to begin by establishing the explanations against which I intend to argue. Thus, in the first section I interpret the Reports, providing a descriptive reading of the texts. A second, discourse-theoretical, reading of the Secretary-General's Reports allows me to illustrate the ways in which concepts of the international, security, gender and violence that were articulated in UNSCR 1325 continue to inform and produce policy at the highest levels, further illustrating the importance of problematizing the concepts around which the Resolution is organized.

ABOUT THE REPORT:
REPORTING ON UNSCR 1325

The first Secretary-General's Report of 2002 articulates a specific goal: to focus 'on the challenges that must be addressed if progress is to be made in the achievement of the goal of gender equality in relation to peace and security' (UNSC 2002a: 4). This representation evidences an organizational scheme that prioritizes this aspect of the Report: gender equality in the context of peace and security. The 2004 Report is contextualized slightly differently, being pursuant to the 2002 Report and drawing on information from a number of other UN studies and reports. The 2004 Report 'provides illustrative examples of the progress achieved thus far and identifies gaps and challenges in the implementation of Resolution 1325', with particular reference to 'sexual and gender-based violence' as this violence is seen as a 'critical issue' (UNSC 2004a: 3, 4). The 'critical' importance of addressing gendered violence in conflict situations reflects another element of the rhetorical schemata that order the text. This is of particular interest as I am concerned with the priority given to representations of (gender) violence by institutions concerned with (international) security.

In terms of the actions mandated within the two Reports regarding the successful implementation of UNSCR 1325, the responses demanded by the 2004 Report are more concrete than those contained in the Report of 2002. I have divided the actions into five broad categories, which represent the actions mandated in the two Reports that are given priority within the texts, and this section details the actions in the order in which they are represented in the texts. This issue of textual priority is related to the way in which the texts are ordered and made coherent. The organization of the texts around these five groups of actions demonstrates the relative importance of these actions to the implementation of UNSCR 1325 according to the Secretary-General's Reports. These actions, mandated by the Reports, can then be interpreted as necessary for the successful implementation of the Resolution. Therefore, if these actions are not undertaken, UNSCR 1325 is doomed to fail. The actions mandated by the Reports, then, or rather the failures to undertake them, are the explanations given in the Secretary-General's Reports for the failures of the Resolution.

The first of these actions relates directly to the role and responsibilities of the United Nations and associated organizations in conflict prevention and resolution, although most of the actions mandated indict these actors in some way. While the 2002 Report makes abstract commitments to facilitating gender sensitivity in conflict resolution, including gender experts on UN missions to conflict zones and the development of 'action plans' with regard to gender mainstreaming post-conflict reconstruction (UNSC 2002a: 25, 36, 60), the 2004 Report demands more specific measures. These include the development of a 'comprehensive system-wide strategy' for mainstreaming gender perspectives, the systematic review of 'recent peace processes [to] analyse the obstacles to and missed opportunities for women's full participation' and the operationalizing of the Convention on the Elimination of all Forms of Discrimination Against Women as a guiding framework for reconstruction programmes (UNSC 2004a: 20, 30, 63). Both Reports articulate the importance of prioritizing gender perspectives at the budgetary level of conflict and post-conflict management (UNSC 2004a: 63; 2002a: 46) to ensure there are resources available for gender mainstreaming. In addition, both Reports insist on the gender sensitivity of economic, social, legal and judicial reform (UNSC 2004a: 63; 2002a: 60) to 'increase the participation of women and girls [and] fully utilize their capacities' (UNSC 2002a: 53), a very liberal notion of 'gender issues', as I discuss below. Similarly, the 2004 Report articulates a commitment to setting 'indicators and benchmarks for women's equal participation in all aspects of elections process' (UNSC 2004a: 65).

The second action I identify relates to the experiences of women and girls in conflict. The Reports recognize that the participation of women and girls in post-conflict resolution is dependent on their surviving the period of armed conflict and thus focus a significant amount of their recommendations on this issue of survival. The language in the 2002 Report is tentative, calling for the recognition of 'the extent of the violations of the human rights of women and girls during armed conflict' and the condemnation of these violations, although it does provide some detail regarding the 'important difference in the experience of women and girls', as opposed to men and boys, during armed conflict (UNSC 2002a: 15, 25, 5–15).

The 2004 Report focuses more explicitly on the responsibilities of parties to armed conflict to 'cease all violations of the human rights of women and girls, including sexual and gender-based violence' (UNSC 2004a: 87). This shifts emphasis from condemning the violations to condemning the perpetrators of the violations. The responsibility of 'Member States, intergovernmental and regional organizations, international and national aid and civil society organizations' to ensure that their operatives are not engaging in such violations, exploitations or abuse, and to ensure punitive measures are taken where such practices occur, is also explicitly recognized in the 2004 Report (103). This is alluded to in the 2002 Report in vague terms: missions are to 'investigate any allegations of sexual exploitation or assault by any peacekeeping personnel and to ensure that offenders are duly disciplined' (UNSC 2002a: 45). Giving textual priority to demanding that 'Member States' and other actors take responsibility for cessation of violences experienced by women and girls during times of conflict and post-conflict reconstruction illustrates two key discursive elements. First, women and girls are frequent victims of violence in these situations, and second, there is a sense of the liability of the 'Member States' and other organizations. It is they who must ensure that this violence is stopped.

Both Reports highlight the importance of mainstreaming gender perspectives 'explicitly into the mandates of all peacekeeping mandates' and 'into peacekeeping activities at Headquarters' (UNSC 2004a: 46, 40), which forms the third action mandated in the Reports. The issue of gender mainstreaming is frequently and unproblematically represented within the Reports, and emerges as a central explanation for the failure of UNSCR 1325. The United Nations Economic and Social Council defined gender mainstreaming as

> the process of assessing the implications for women and men of any planned action, including legislation, policies or programmes, in all areas and at all levels. It is a strategy for making women's as well as men's concerns and experiences an integral dimension of the design, implementation, monitoring and evaluation of policies and programmes in all political, economic and societal spheres so that women and men benefit equally and inequality is not perpetuated. (cited in UNDAW 2000: 2)

This is the definition that informs the practices of the UN system and therefore is the focus of analysis for this project.

The 2004 Report offers several examples of good practice, including missions in East Timor, Sierra Leone, Afghanistan and Côte d'Ivoire (UNSC 2004a: 31, 42) and draws attention to the existence of the Department of Peacekeeping Operations' 'Gender Resource Package for Peacekeeping Operations' (2004), suggesting that the concept of gender mainstreaming has been taken up by various institutions in the United Nations system. The details of gender training programmes in Canada and the UK for military and civilian personnel involved in PKOs are also documented in the 2004 Report, although these achievements are tempered by the comment that only 1 per cent of military and 5 per cent of civilian police personnel assigned by states to serve in PKOs in as June 2004 were women (UNSC 2004a: 34, 91).

The fourth action relates to the issue of participation. It is highlighted in both Reports, particularly with reference to 'contacts with women's groups and networks' (UNSC 2002a: 15). In the 2004 Report, the Secretary-General 'urge[s] Member States, United Nations entities, NGOs and other relevant actors to work collaboratively to ensure the full participation of women ... and to strengthen interaction with women's organizations' (UNSC 2004a: 21). The participation is deemed important as women and girls 'facilitate the achievement of greater equality' and make 'a critical difference in the promotion of peace' (UNSC 2002a: 26, 27). Collaboration with local and regional women's organizations has had positive effects in West Africa, the Democratic Republic of Congo and Afghanistan, and women have cooperated across 'ethnic and religious lines to make valuable contributions to peace processes' in Azerbaijan, Liberia and Northern Ireland (UNSC 2004a: 7, 27). The 2004 Report pays particular attention to the involvement of women in Truth and Reconciliation Programmes, mandating a 'review [of] the extent to which women have participated and their concerns met in truth and reconciliation processes'. Safe access to these processes for women is also demanded (UNSC 2004a: 64, 52).

Finally, the fundamental importance of the physical safety of women and girls in situations of armed conflict and post-conflict resolution is well documented in both Reports. 'During conflict, women and girls are vulnerable to all forms of violence, in particular sexual violence and exploitation' (UNSC 2002a: 7). The specific reference to gender-based violence in UNSCR 1325 'has contributed to increased recognition of the escalation in scope and intensity of sexual and gender-based violence as one of the most visible and insidious impacts of armed conflict of women and girls' (UNSC 2004a: 73). The only action mandated by the 2002 Report in relation to gender-based violence referred to the development of 'programmes on the prevention of domestic violence'; elsewhere in the Report, gender-based violence is articulated as a violation of human rights and protection needs are articulated through a human rights framework (UNSC 2002a: 65, 11, 15, 25).

All five actions mandated in the Reports are aimed at redressing 'cultures of violence and discrimination against women and girls' (UNSC 2002a: 5) to ensure 'the full implementation of Resolution 1325' (UNSC 2004a: 1). Within this remit, gender-based violence is represented in both Reports as having 'political and symbolic significance' (UNSC 2002a: 7), a strategic weapon within wider structures of discrimination during periods of armed conflict (UNSC 2004a: 9).

The 2004 Report calls for 'adequate human and financial support to programmes that provide care and support ... to survivors of gender-based violence' that occurred during armed conflict, giving examples of such programmes functioning in Rwanda and Haiti (UNSC 2004a: 88, 83). However, it recognizes that there is 'unacceptable violence against women and girls in peacetime' and that the response to this violence 'remains inadequate' (UNSC 2004a: 76). The Report insists that states must 'recognize their responsibility and ... enforce law, end impunity, prosecute perpetrators of violence and provide redress and compensation to survivors of gender-based violence' (2004a: 81).

The wide-ranging mandates in the two Reports reflect the difficulties that have been experienced in the implementation of UNSCR 1325. 'Despite significant achievements, major gaps and challenges remain in all areas' of conflict and post-conflict resolution (UNSC 2004a: 4). The partial or total failure to undertake the actions outlined in the 2002 Report is the implicit explanation given for the failure of UNSCR 1325 to ameliorate the situations of women and girls in conflict and post-conflict zones as UNSCR 1325 suggests. 'In order to effectively respond to the needs and priorities of women and girls during armed conflict, gender perspectives have to be integrated into all peace-building, peacekeeping and peacemaking efforts and during humanitarian operations and reconstruction processes' (UNSC 2002a: 66). Thus, ineffective response is based on the failures to integrate such 'gender perspectives'. The 2004 Report identifies many areas in which UNSCR 1325 was successfully implemented by various actors in many conflict and post-conflict zones. However, the Report concludes that 'in no area of peace and security work are gender perspectives systematically incorporated in planning, implementation, monitoring and reporting' (UNSC 2004a: 118). The lack of 'political will, concerted action and accountability on the part of the entire international community' accounts for the failures to successfully implement UNSCR 1325 (UNSC 2004a: 121), which is a damning indictment of the international system.

This section has considered the actions mandated in the two Secretary-General's Reports; the failure to undertake the required actions forms the explanation for the deficiencies in implementation of UNSCR 1325. Ultimately, despite the persuasiveness of this explanation, my study is premissed on the suggestion that there are important issues relating to the discursive construction of the Resolution that enable a different understanding of how and why UNSCR 1325 has failed. In the following section I offer a discourse-theoretical reading, investigating the representational practices of predication and subject-positioning alongside analysis of the rhetorical schemata of the texts. I do not undertake this analysis with a view to establishing the 'truth' of the Reports, but rather to demonstrate that the Reports themselves, and the explanations offered within them, are a product of particular discourses of international security and gender violence that are in contact in UNSCR 1325. That is, the Reports evaluate the successes and failures of UNSCR 1325 according to the standards of the Resolution itself, standards which are set with reference to concepts of security, violence, gender and the international.

ANALYSING THE REPORT: PROBLEMATIZING THE SECRETARY-GENERAL'S REPORTS

The Secretary-General's Reports of 2002 and 2004 suggest that there are objectively identifiable issues of 'political will, action and accountability' that have contributed to the failure of UNSCR 1325. However, even given the persuasiveness and relevance of one or more of these factors, I intend to demonstrate that the discursive construction of UNSCR 1325 ultimately influences the processes of its implementation. That is, the concepts around which it is organized, the meanings (re)produced within the document and the tensions and inconsistencies within it have also contributed to its failure. Before proceeding with analysis of the Resolution, it is vital to explore the representations of gender, violence, the international and security contained in the two Secretary-General's Reports, to illustrate the ways in which these Reports further entrench conventional conceptualizations of gendered violence and security in the international domain. Therefore, this section analyses each of these concepts in turn to enable a more detailed analysis of the discursive construction of UNSCR 1325. Furthermore, it also provides concrete examples, from specific conflict situations, of the ways in which the concepts of international security and gender violence around which UNSCR 1325 is organized affect the lived experiences of individuals across the world.

GENDER

UNSCR 1325 and the two Secretary-General's Reports employ a conceptualization of gender that is broadly compatible with that employed in the literature on 'gender violence'. Textual priority is given to the predication of 'women' as always different from, and positioned as inferior to, 'men': 'Women do not enjoy equal status with men in any society' (UNSC 2000a: 5). Similarly, the experience of women and girls is represented as qualitatively different to that of men and boys (UNSC 2002a: 7). This unequal relationship is 'grounded in biological difference' (2002a: 8), which leads to 'specific constraints facing women and girls' (UNSC 2004a: 48). However, as Cockburn points out, '[e]ssentialism is not merely an interesting theoretical concept … It is a dangerous political force, designed to shore up differences and inequalities, to sustain dominations' (Cockburn 1998: 13). Not only do women have 'knowledge and experiences' specific to their gendered identity (UNSC 2004a: 19), they also have 'specific needs' (UNSC 2002a: 3) because part of this 'experience' is vulnerability: 'During conflict, women and girls are vulnerable to all forms of violence'; women and girls have 'specific protection needs' (UNSC 2002a: 7, 48). The representational strategies in the Reports suggest that it would be valid to reduce these articulations to their simplest form: 'women and girls are vulnerable' (UNSC 2002a: 7). Girls are represented as doubly burdened 'owing to their low status as female adolescents' (2002a: 10) – that is, their low status as females, and their low status as adolescents. Thus the universal subordination of women is affirmed through the predication of femininity as vulnerability and the positioning of femininity as 'low'.

In the 2002 Report, 'the role of women' is discussed in detail. Women are 'providers and caregivers'. They have responsibility for the 'provision of water and energy for household use and … health care', and these responsibilities increase when households experience the 'loss of men and boys'. The representation of women in this Report minimizes female agency, articulating a feminine subject position that in times of conflict is either 'forced out' or 'pushed into' dangerous situations. Women lack: they suffer from 'lack of land … lack of access to, or control over, resources' (UNSC 2002a: 9). The Report seeks to ameliorate the situations of 'populations in need, especially women and girls' (2002a: 53) but in doing so it seems to suggest that within any given population, women and girls are always more in need. This construction precludes the notion that women can display agency or strength in a positive role, as leaders or organizers. Feminist scholarship on the construction of 'women as victim' has forcefully protested and rigorously problematized this association, arguing that 'viewing women as homogeneously powerless and as implicit victims does not allow us to theorize women as the benefactors of oppression, or the perpetrators of catastrophes' (Lentin 1997: 12).

Even in the context of armed conflict, women who are active combatants are represented as having been 'driven' to it (UNSC 2002a: 13). In Liberia, 'women and girls [were] associated with fighting forces' rather than actively involved (UNSC 2004a: 24). Both Reports do articulate a female combatant – in two sentences in the 2002 Report, and barely more than that in 2004. The 2002 Report acknowledges that 'males above the age of 18 ... fit the international definition of soldiers' but insists that '[c]ombatants are not only men, but also women, girls and boys' (UNSC 2002a: 62). In reproducing the conventional discursive links of masculinized soldier in opposition to feminized peacemaker, which I discuss further below, the Reports reaffirm a very narrow and traditional narrative of gender that rests on 'assertions around an *essential* link between women, motherhood and non-violence' (Jacobs et al. 2000: 13, emphasis in original). Both the 2002 and the 2004 Reports focus in great detail on the involvement of women in peacemaking. According to the Department of Public Information, 'the issue of women as peacemakers [is] one of the top 10 unreported stories' (UNSC 2004a: 117). Quite apart from the methodological issues concerning how one would go about measuring the frequency of an unreported story, the discursive link between women and peace is systematically and unproblematically reproduced in both the Reports with systemic yet problematic implications. These implications are wide-ranging, from denying legitimacy to female combatants and therefore failing to account for their needs in demobilization and disarmament programmes, to assuming that women who act outside of their subject position of peacemaker are somehow lesser women than their counterparts who are obedient to these discursive regimes.

The peace processes and reconstruction programmes undertaken in post-conflict zones are the only sphere in which women and girls are articulated as unproblematically agential. '[W]omen play an active role in informal peace processes' (UNSC 2002a: 13); this construction strengthens the discursive construction of feminized peacemaker mentioned above. Women are represented as 'victims of armed conflict' but women can also be 'actors in early warning, reconciliation, peace-building or post-conflict resolution' (UNSC 2004a: 112). Thus readers of the document are told in no uncertain terms what women are and can be in the context of conflict and post-conflict zones; the space for transgression or reversal – that is, for women to be actors in armed conflict or victims of peace-building or post-conflict resolution – is limited. This discursive disciplining reflects feminist concerns about the recognition of women as perpetrators of violence.[1] The Reports are organized around a conceptualization of gender that assumes women are more likely than their male peers to support peace movements. Whether women and girls are 'combatants, abductees, supporters of armed groups, wives or dependants of male combatants', it is assumed that 'women and women's groups' should be involved 'in all aspects of disarmament, demobilization and reintegration' (UNSC 2004a: 66, 7). If the women and girls concerned are deeply committed to the political cause for which they bear arms, it is unlikely that by virtue of their femininity they will seek to provide assistance unless the outcome to the conflict is one they feel is just. There is significant literature concerning women's involvement with violence and oppression; 'feminists in the North and South [have] challenged the so-called peaceful nature of women by examining their involvement in national liberation struggles, their direct and/or indirect support of armed conflicts and their contributions to war and militarism generally' (El Jack 2003: 12).

Loosely defined 'women's groups' are cited in both Reports as a space for female agency, a construction that is articulated in UNSCR 1325 where 'all actors involved, when negotiating and implementing peace agreements' are called on to include '[m]easures that support local women's peace initiatives' (UNSC 2000a: Article 8). Two aspects of this construction are particularly noteworthy. The first involves the assumption that women and girls who are active in local peace initiatives have a common agenda. 'There are many positive examples of women making a critical difference in the promotion of peace, particularly in preserving social order and educating for peace' (UNSC 2002a: 27). This may be empirically verifiable, but the exclusion of the examples of women and girls making a critical difference in the promotion of conflict is a political move that serves to strengthen a specific construction of female identity. As Carol Cohn, Helen Kinsella and Sheri Gibbings argue, 'it remains important to ask *which* women are included and are we expecting more from women (super heroines) than we expect of men?' (2004: 136, emphasis in original). Furthermore, drawing attention to women's organizing for peace across 'party and ethnic lines', as mentioned in both Reports (UNSC 2004a: 27; 2002a: 27), suggests, problematically, that it can be expected that femininity will take precedence as a political identity.

Furthermore, the specific skills that women and girls bring to post-conflict reconstruction are those associated with a feminine subject position articulated within an essentialist narrative of gender, as described above. The emphasis on 'preserving the social order' (UNSC 2002a: 27) is constructed through a narrative of gender that sees women as tied to the private sphere, impacting on the public only through expanding care of the household to care of the community at large. Thus the emphasis put on '[w]omen's contributions to ... "people to people diplomacy"' (UNSC 2004a: 12) seems premissed on an understanding of gender that is ordered along conventional dichotomous lines. Disrupting these dichotomies draws attention to 'the coerced nature of dichotomous gender systems, [and] their effect on the individual's propensity for aggression and passivity' (O'Toole and Schiffman 1997c: 424). In these Reports, while the privileging is reversed – the feminine/peaceful/private/emotional is held in higher regard than the masculine/aggressive/public/rational – the organizing principle is still founded on a very conventional dichotomous and essentialist conceptualization of gender.

The second aspect of the construction that is of interest relates to the conflation of gender and women in the Reports. Despite the assertion that 'promoting gender equality is not women's responsibility alone', both Reports address 'the gender dimensions of peace processes' (UNSC 2002a: 44, 1) as if these dimensions can be adequately theorized through detailed documentation of 'women's equal participation with men and their full involvement in all efforts for the maintenance and promotion of peace and security' (UNSC 2004a: 2). Article 4 of the 2002 Report makes this link explicit: 'the study on women, peace and security ... focuses on the challenges that must be addressed if progress is to be made in the achievement of the goal of gender equality' (UNSC 2002a: 4). The specific example of peacekeeping operations, represented in both Reports (UNSC 2004a: 31–40; UNSC 2002a: 37–46), reproduce the discursive construction of gender as binary and, moreover, as *about* women. Making 'explicit reference to women and girls, or to the different impact of armed conflict or post-conflict recovery on women and girls' would demonstrate 'a commitment to gender equality' (UNSC 2002a: 38). In the 2004 Report, men are mentioned: 'Training on gender issues should be provided to all staff at decision-making levels, men as well as women' (UNSC 2004a: 97). However, in articulating the suggestion that 'gender issues' are relevant to 'men as well as women' the Report allows for the suggestion that readers might be forgiven for thinking that gender is just about women. As Terrell Carver (1996) has succinctly remarked, 'gender is not a synonym for women', but nevertheless 'we slip from gender to women and women to gender but have yet to slip from gender to men' (Cohn et al. 2004: 136). This (re)produces a concept of gender in which 'gender describes everything that is weak (old people, women and children) and is in need of protection' (cited in Puechguirbal 2003: 113).

The different needs of women and girls, discussed above, also affects these issues of participation and gender mainstreaming. The foundational assumption guiding the policy prescriptions in the Reports relates to 'the proactive role women can play in peace-building' (UNSC 2004a: 13) as a result of their essential femininity. While the Reports pay lip service to the anti-essentialist position – 'the presence of women does not guarantee attention to gender issues' – the Reports systematically undermine this position through their insistence that '[s]ustainable and durable peace requires the participation of women and girls' (UNSC 2002a: 29, 54). In the final paragraph of the 2004 Report, this articulation is reproduced at length:

> Resolution 1325 (2000) holds out a promise to women across the globe that their rights will be protected and that barriers to their equal participation and full involvement in the maintenance and promotion of sustainable peace will be removed. We must uphold this promise. (UNSC 2004a: 121)

However, to encourage the participation that the Reports are so keen to facilitate, both reproduce a female subject whose life experiences are curtailed by virtue of her femininity. There are 'concerns specific to women'; these concerns, and women themselves, are currently marginalized (UNSC 2002a: 29, 28). The Reports state that this marginalization can be overcome by the institutionalizing of '[s]pecial measures' (UNSC 2002a: 56). Women 'need to receive early support and training in order to facilitate their active participation' and in the context of electoral participation, 'women running for office need skills building and support' (UNSC 2004a: 27, 58). Access to resources in specific locations have resulted in women's participation according to the Reports, for example in Afghanistan, which is held as an example of good practice, where women hold 20 per cent of the seats in the Loya Jirga, and in Rwanda and Iraq (UNSC 2004a: 54, 55–6).

However, in representing women as needing 'support', 'training' and 'skills building', the Reports construct women as a problem to be overcome, as opposed to problematizing the complexity of gender. Women are entitled to 'equal participation and full involvement', but in suggesting that in order to achieve this they need special training, the Reports continue to provide those who would wish to maintain the status quo of gender inequality and devaluation of the feminine with ammunition to do precisely that. Furthermore, the Reports fail to mention that many men need similar interventions on their behalf as they are marginalized on account of their class, race, politics, sexuality and so on. This may not be surprising in Reports explicitly addressing 'women, peace and security', but it is important to remember that men do feature in the Reports – just not in this particular exercise in boundary delimitation.

VIOLENCE

Having articulated a dichotomous, broadly essentialist, narrative of gender, the Reports can only articulate a particular understanding of gendered violence. 'Gender violence' is explicitly recognized as an issue for the attention of the Security Council by virtue of its inclusion in Resolutions and Reports, but it is necessary to further investigate with which conceptualization of gendered violence these Resolutions and Reports work. Building on UNSCR 1325, which 'calls on all parties to armed conflict to take special measures to protect women and girls from gender-based violence' (UNSC 2000a: 10), both Reports represent the concept of violence, experienced by women during conflict, as inherently gendered. The assertion in 2002 that '[d]uring conflict women and girls are vulnerable to all forms of violence, in particular sexual violence and exploitation' (UNSC 2002a: 7) led in 2004 to the treatment of 'sexual and gender-based violence' as a 'critical issue' (UNSC 2004a: 4). Thus the Reports are organized around a concept of violence that is inherently gendered in very specific ways. Moreover, violence is predicated as 'a strategic and tactical weapon' that is used *against* not *by* women and girls (UNSC 2002a: 8; 2004a: 73–88).

The elision of 'sexual' and 'gender-based' violence is not surprising given the elision of sex and gender in the conceptualization of identity evident in the Reports. No attempt is made to differentiate between sex and gender in the two Reports: 'sex' is only represented as the first three letters of 'sexual', which is used to preface 'violence'. This is because the Reports articulate a concept of gender that is 'loosely synonymous with "sex" and lazily synonymous with "women"' (Carver 1996: 18). No attempt is made to differentiate between violence based on sex and violence based on gender, although both are used in the Reports. However, the suggestion of difference is minimized, if not completely elided, through the representation of the interchangeability of the two terms in the two Reports. What is 'gender-based and sexual violence' in the 2002 Report (UNSC 2002a: 8) is 'sexual and gender-based violence' in 2004 (UNSC 2004a: 73).

This construction is compatible with the understanding of violence evident in the conceptualization of 'gender violence' discussed in Chapter 3, where 'gender violence is often explained as a natural and universal consequence of the biological difference between men and women' (O'Toole and Schiffman 1997d: 3).[2] The actions mandated in response to gendered violence, as discussed above, are predicated on the understanding that 'sexual and gender-based violence … impacts … on women and girls'; the Reports document the 'widespread use of sexual violence against women and children' (UNSC 2004a: 73, 9). The repetition of these constructions serves to remind the reader not only that sex and gender are intimately related but that women are subjected to violence in ways that men are not. Articulating 'women victims of violence' as the focus of policy aimed at 'preventing such violence and protecting women and girls' (UNSC 2004a: 86, 76) again predicates 'women victims' as the problem, rather than acknowledging that women could be perpetrators of such violence or part of the solutions to such violence, and is heedless of the need for such solutions or any position in between. Furthermore, this construction precludes the notion that men can be victims of gendered violence, which is patently false.

Gendered violence is the only form of violence that is named in both Reports. Thus the Reports are organized around a notion of violence as 'gender violence', at the same time as they (re)produce the gendering of this notion of violence. In keeping with the element of violence articulated in the discourse of 'gender violence', violence in the Reports is 'named after its victims' (Kappeler 1995: 1), in that gender is assumed synonymous with 'womenandchildren'. The centrality of violence to the relational complexity of gender is thus affirmed, but the premiss that gendered violence affects only women and girls is unsustainable. This articulation is made by omission in the Reports, but the politics of what is *not* contained is as important an analytical focus as that which is. Theorizing the various violences that impact on the lives of individuals requires that discursive space is carved out for the recognition *of* violences *as* violences. For example, state-sponsored corporate violence 'has not been responded to with the same level of gravity of sanction that is reserved for the violent acts committed by less powerful members of our society' (Alder 1997: 440). Violence is articulated in the two Reports using the predicate 'gender', and positioned as outside of the remit of appropriate behaviours. That is, it is represented throughout the Reports as illegitimate, as always requiring first prevention (inter alia UNSC 2004a: 19) and then intervention to ensure its cessation (inter alia UNSC 2002a: 17).

The Reports perpetuate a conceptualization of violence that reifies and pathologizes gender as dichotomous and essential through their representations of gender violence. Violence, on this view, serves an ordering function (see Jabri 1996: 7–10). The Reports do not explicitly articulate a definition of violence, instead appealing to a broad range of threats including 'torture, rape, mass rape, forced pregnancy, sexual slavery, enforced prostitution and trafficking' (UNSC 2002a: 7). Gender violence is represented as 'a form of discrimination' and acts of violence as 'violations of *women's* human rights' (UNSC 2004a: 76, emphasis added). Such representations are product/productive of assumptions concerning the necessary materiality of violence. It is not that violence must be *physical* in this conceptualization of gender violence, rather that it must have visible material effects. There is no space for the suggestion that violence constitutes subjectivity, as I discuss in later chapters, as the Reports assume predetermined subjects that are constrained/enabled by acts of violence.

Men feature in the policy prescriptions relevant to gendered violence as empowered in a way that women are not: 'Gender-based violence ... seriously inhibits the ability of women to enjoy their rights and freedoms on a basis of equality with men' (UNSC 2004a: 76). Men also need assistance in overcoming their (natural?) violent tendencies: there is a need to 'develop programmes on the prevention of domestic violence, targeting ... especially male combatants' (UNSC 2002a: 65). These positionings fix gender as a pathological relationship based on sexed bodies, an eternal hierarchy in which men enjoy the privileges of their masculinity through their power over women and girls, an articulation that is deeply problematic. The Reports delimit gender violence according to these assumptions, and do not consider the ways in which the violences of which they speak actually function to reproduce gender as a lived experience in a multiplicity of locations.

INTERNATIONAL

The dominant articulation of space within the Reports counterposes the local with the international. UNSCR 1325 explicitly connects the UN Charter and the existence of the Security Council with 'the maintenance of international peace and security' (UNSC 2000a: Preamble) and this construction is reproduced throughout the two Secretary-General's Reports. Both Reports comment on the responsibilities of 'the international community' (UNSC 2004a: 121; UNSC 2002a: 3) without specifically delineating the components of this 'community' or exploring the connections across values and truth claims that enable the 'community' to name itself as such. The assertion of 'community' entails the construction of the international as both a spatial domain and also a quality reflecting common interests and ideals. There are marked differences between these articulations of the international in the two Reports that need investigating further. As Gillian Youngs comments, 'To think spatially is to take spatial dimensions of social relations seriously, to recognize that political, economic and cultural exchanges take place in different forms of social space and ... [to] contribute to how that space is framed and perceived' (1999: 97).

Within the 2002 Report, the existence of the international is asserted as a separate domain from the domestic, which is implicitly the site of the armed conflict that the Report seeks to address. Armed conflict affects 'civilian women and girls' in their 'households and communities' (UNSC 2002a: 7, 9) and therefore, according to the Reports, it is necessary 'to increase community commitment to conflict prevention' (UNSC 2004a: 14). In this representation, the 'community' of the domestic realm is positioned differently to the 'community' of the international, with the domestic represented as a zone of conflict and the international (community) represented as a mediator in such conflict. This is in opposition to the logic of the security discourse on 'national security' explored in Chapter 3, but entirely in keeping with the discourse on 'international security' that posits 'the international' as a domain of cooperation rather than conflict. The separation between the two realms is maintained in both conceptualizations, however, and can legitimately be challenged. Taking 'the international' *a priori* to be a benign locus of positive action is every bit as problematic as asserting that 'the international' is by definition anarchic. However, the positive articulation of 'the international' in the Reports leads to more specific critical issues.

The United Nations is repeatedly articulated as the organizer of knowledge concerning the 'impact of armed conflict on women and girls': 'The study ... builds on existing research and inputs of the

United Nations, its programmes, funds and specialized agencies'. The knowledges owned by 'scholars and local and international non-governmental organizations' is accredited but through placement in the text implicitly secondary to that of the UN and associated bodies. The 'international community' has 'responsibilities ... to provide effective responses' and, presumably, to respond to the 'recommendations for action' contained in the Report (UNSC 2002a: 1–4). This is a form of discursive violence, a kind of 'trickle-down' theory of expertise. The implication is that the knowledge accumulated by the UN system will guide conflict resolution and post-conflict reconstruction. '[L]ocal sources of information on the impact of armed conflict' are to be 'identified' and 'utilized' by the international community to better their understanding of gendered dynamics. Insisting that 'consultations with women's groups and networks can provide important information' (2002a: 15, 27) strengthens the assumption that constructing the UN as a repository for knowledge is unproblematic, that all actors can gain access to and benefit from this knowledge equally, and does a violence to those involved in the production of context-specific strategies for change.

Furthermore, this construction allows for the suggestion that gender equality can be achieved in all locations for all time through the same policy practices. Constructing the organization of knowledge in this way is problematic, as it is predicated on a fixed and essentialist concept of gender, seen as a fixed and hierarchical variable. The 2004 Report states that 'UNIFEM has created a web portal as a centralized repository of information on women, peace and security' (UNSC 2004: 117), suggesting that these issues can be contained within the immutable boundaries of the categories of 'women', 'peace' and 'security', and, moreover, that locating such a repository in cyberspace allows access to those who seek information. I contest both of these assumptions. I do not wish to dismiss entirely the benefits of increased attention to matters of gendered violence and security. However, the representation of 'women' as a homogenous category and the implied ability of the 'centralized repository' to address adequately all issues pertaining to these 'women' is deeply problematic as it reinscribes two of the conventional dichotomies I seek to challenge here: woman/man and domestic/international.

The representations of the domestic in the 2002 Report predominantly serve two functions: to illustrate cases in which gender 'issues' have been insufficiently addressed in situations of conflict and post-conflict reconstruction as is the case 'in the former Yugoslavia and in Rwanda ... [and] ... Sierra Leone'; and to celebrate those interventions of the 'international community', through its emissary the UN, which have had 'positive' effects, for example the 'missions to the Democratic Republic of the Congo, Kosovo and Sierra Leone' (UNSC 2002a: 19, 30). In making this division, the Report further entrenches the conceptual separation of the 'international' and the 'domestic' and affirms the power of the 'international' as a mediator for 'peace and security'. However, critical feminist scholarship has not only problematized the international–domestic dichotomy[3] but also drawn attention to the fact that 'national/civil conflicts are not only internal but transnational in nature, as they take place within a particular international context' (El Jack 2003: 9). These interjections render the representation of the international (re)produced within the Reports extremely problematic. Continuing to represent the international in the reified terms used in the Reports obscures the 'international context' of armed conflict as well as the involvement of members of the 'international community' in the perpetration of violence, gender or otherwise.

In its concluding observations, the 2002 Report recognizes that UNSCR 1325 has 'galvanized the Member States, the United Nations system and civil society, including at the grass roots level' (UNSC 2002a: 66). As I discuss in Chapter 5, it is claimed that it was activism at the 'grass roots level' that initially enabled the production of UNSCR 1325. To position the actors within the text in such a way as to privilege the actions of 'Member States' and devalue those of 'civil society' is therefore somewhat disingenuous. Furthermore, the conflict that the Reports address occurs 'at the grassroots level', so it is completely unsurprising that actors involved seek any means they can to ameliorate their situations. It is claimed that '[i]nternational law and existing strategies and guidelines within United Nations entities provide a strong framework for addressing gender perspectives within the context of armed conflict and its aftermath' (UNSC 2002a: 67). However, having explored the conceptualization of gender operant within these 'strategies and guidelines' it seems problematic to impose these policies without attending to the ways in which they might further entrench existing inequalities or construct new yet similarly pathological power relations.

The 2004 Report still subscribes to the notion that the UN, and in particular the Security Council, can and should act as gatekeeper to the issues of peace-building and security. The Report itself 'is based on contributions from Member States and entities of the United Nations system' (UNSC 2004a: 3). Achievements made thus far in the mainstreaming of gender perspectives into issues of peace and security are lauded in the Report. For example, attention is paid to 'women or gender concerns' in 15.6 per cent of all Security Council Resolutions in the period 2000–2004, and '[t]wo presidential statements were issued calling on Member States, entities of the United Nations system, civil society and other relevant actors to develop clear strategies and action plans' (UNSC 2004a: 6, 5). The second section of the Report, encompassing paragraphs 4 to 72 inclusive, is entitled 'Progress in Implementation', and begins with a discussion of the many and various ways that UNSCR 1325 has made life better, enabling the development of

> policies, actions plans, guidelines and indicators; increasing access to gender expertise; providing training; promoting consultation with and participation of women; increasing attention to human rights and supporting the initiative of women's groups. (UNSCR 2004: 4)

Note that 'the initiative of women's groups' is singular, suggesting that women – regardless of their socio-cultural, racial or ethnic and/or sexual identities – have a single agenda. This assumption was problematized by feminist political theorists several decades ago.[4] Where these critiques have been noted, recognition of the difference among 'women', however 'women' are conceived, has enabled the production of policy predicated on those differences, rather than merely reproducing a singular difference – that assumed to exist between 'women' and 'men'.

However, the 2004 Report explores more fully the responsibilities of the 'international' and suggests some ways in which these responsibilities demand action. The 'international' is repeatedly articulated as a 'community', moreover a community of 'Member States', and 'States ... have the primary responsibility for the protection of women and children' (UNSC 2004a: 77). While the document offers prescriptions for the behaviour of states, it does not explore the ways in which governments or elites within states might actively engage in the perpetration and perpetuation of gendered violences as part of their strategies to power. The Report does state that 'Member States need to send stronger signals to parties to conflict that gender-based violence will be investigated and perpetrators will be prosecuted', but these indictments are hollow in the face of the inability of the UN to impose sanctions in the case of violations. 'The involvement of United Nations personnel ... in sexual exploitation and sexual abuse of local populations is particularly abhorrent and unacceptable' and is something that the UN can actively punish, but the reality principle of the 'international community' – as a group of states – undermines the insistence that the United Nations has the power to '[a]pply increased pressure on parties to armed conflict ... to cease all violations of the human rights of women and girls' (2004a: 84, 99, 87).

The Reports insist that the 'International Criminal Court holds promise for meaningful accountability for gender-based crimes against women in armed conflict' (UNSC 2004a: 79), but fail to point out that such accountability is only possible if 'Member States' accept the jurisdiction of the Court. The examples given in the Report are the successes in referrals from Uganda and the Democratic Republic of the Congo; no mention is made of the states that refuse to recognize the Court and the challenge that this presents to the efficacy of the Court as a tool of retribution. States that have not ratified the Rome Statute include Zimbabwe, Haiti, Iran, Israel and the United States of America. The support that individual states do or do not give to the United Nations and associated organizations is noted in the Report, alongside representations of the ways in which individual states foster grassroots activism in various locations. The example of Afghanistan is used to represent the ways in which states are involved with increasing the participation of women and 'promoting gender equality ... [S]everal Member States have funded projects for women and girls ... The United States has allocated funding for projects that assist women with democratic organization and advocacy' (UNSC 2004a: 61). Considering the extensive involvement of the USA with domestic Afghan politics dating back to CIA-sponsored anti-Soviet militia and the more recent attacks of 2001, it is somewhat ironic that the Report praises the USA in this way.[5]

Both Reports articulate 'the changed nature of conflict' in recent times (UNSC 2002a: 24), where '[b]oth State and non-State actors are responsible' (UNSC 2004a: 76). This construction is in itself problematic, as conflict has never been the preserve of the state alone; civil conflict is part of the history of world politics. Furthermore,

> war can surely never be said to start and end at a clearly defined moment. Rather, it seems part of a continuum of conflict, expressed now in armed force, now in economic sanctions or political pressure. A time of supposed peace may come later to be called 'the pre-war period'. During the fighting of a war, unseen by the foot soldiers under fire, peace processes are often already at work. A time of postwar reconstruction, later, may be re-designated as an *inter bellum* – a mere pause between wars. (Cockburn and Zarkov, cited in El Jack 2003: 9)

In attempting to delineate boundaries of responsibility containing only groups of states – the 'international community' – the Reports disable engagement with the ways in which some conflicts may be waged against the state by non-state actors, including women and girls, and vice versa. The very existence of UNSCR 1325 and the pursuant Reports claim authority on behalf of the 'international' in the context of the provision of peace and security, at the same time as 'the peace and security arena' is represented as 'the 'hard core' of international politics (Reanda 1999: 58). The Reports reproduce the 'international' according to conventional narratives of state behaviours, leaving little conceptual space for the radical reforms that the rhetoric demands. Even if all of the actions mandated in the Reports were undertaken tomorrow, it is highly unlikely that the utopian vision of 'peace and security' represented in the Reports would be made manifest, given the problematic conceptualizations of gender, violence and the international that are represented in the texts. The Reports constitute gender as a pathological relationship that positions 'men' as oppressors and 'women' as oppressed, gender violence as a tool of this oppression and the international as a realm apart from the conflicted and battle-scarred locations where such violence occurs.

SECURITY

The concept of security represented within the Reports delimits the security for which the 'international' strives, and it is thus important to interrogate it. The first noteworthy aspect of the concept of security in the Reports is the authorship of the Reports by the Security Council. Both Reports open with a statement by the Secretary-General concerning their institutional heritage:

> The Security Council, by paragraph 16 of its resolution 1325 (2000) of 31 October, invited me to carry out a study on the impact of armed conflict on women and girls. (UNSC 2002a: 1)

> On 31 October 2002, the Security Council adopted the statement of the President (S/PRST/2002/32), in which it requested the preparation of a follow-up report on the full implementation of resolution 1325 (2000) on women and peace and security. (UNSC 2004a): 1)

Organizing the documents in this way emphasizes two aspects of their production. First, the existence of the document, in both cases, is attributed to UNSCR 1325. Not only does this reaffirm the need to investigate the documents fully to form the foundations of a project that seeks to analyse the formulation and implementation of the Resolution, but it also suggests that the Secretary-General, on behalf of the Security Council, acknowledges the unique nature of UNSCR 1325 and the ways in which the Resolution speaks to issues of 'women and peace and security'.

Second, introducing both documents with a statement articulating their author-ity represents a claim to legitimacy that affects both the Reports and the Security Council as an institution. The Reports are afforded the authority conferred upon them by the discursive association with, and rhetorical prioritizing of, the Security Council. The United Nations Charter states that '[i]n order to ensure prompt and effective action by the United Nations, its Members confer on the Security Council primary responsibility for the maintenance of international peace and security, and agree that in carrying out its duties under this responsibility the Security Council acts on their behalf' (UN 1945: Article 24.1). Signatories of the Charter agree to be bound by the principles and procedures therein; therefore, in reminding readers of the institutional heritage of the Reports, their legitimacy is (re)produced.

Furthermore, this process of (re)production simultaneously constitutes the Security Council as a legitimate body. This has important ramifications for the organization of global security. In asserting the discursive privilege of the Security Council to speak about issues of security in the international domain, the Reports further entrench this privilege, performing the identity of the Security Council as legitimate and responsible. Thus through their organizational form, the Reports contribute to the discursive linking of the concept of security with 'international', which impacts on the ability of actors to claim to speak about security and the authenticity afforded to their claims. This is in accordance with the reality principle of the United Nations as an organization of states, and is potentially disempowering for non-state actors, which may have negative implications for those who wish to organize for peace outside of or indeed against a state structure.

The repeated discursive link between 'peace' and 'security', evident in the titles of the Reports and throughout the document texts, is also important. This is at odds with the conventional Realist conceptualization of security, which sees perpetual insecurity as the organizing principle of interstate relationships.[6] Furthermore, the security of the individual is conceptually precluded by this understanding, in which security is the preserve of states. The Reports appeal to the 'international community' to act as a provider of security, which constructs this 'community' as the harbinger of global peace from which all individuals can benefit. However, a critical conceptualization of security in which security is seen as a discourse that reproduces the international as a spatial and conceptual domain, as discussed in Chapter 3, challenges this construction. The concept of security (re)produced in the Reports functions to bring into being the nation-state as the referent object of the security policies and practices detailed in the Reports but only in so far as the states are peaceable members of an 'international community'. This representation impacts on the ways in which states, as functioning imaginaries, can, and are expected to, behave, disciplining state behaviours in the international realm. It also further entrenches the conceptual divisions between 'domestic' and 'international' discussed above.

Peacekeeping operations are one means by which 'the international' 'establish[es] security', but according to the Reports there are '[d]ifferences in men's and women's security priorities and needs' in these operations (UNSC 2002a: 39). This articulation is discursively allowable given the conceptualization of gender and gendered violence through which the Reports are organized, as discussed above. That is, if gender is pathological and gendered violence is violence against women, then women do have specific 'security priorities and needs'. Therefore the Reports (re)produce a concept of security that affirms the conceptualizations of gender and violence around which it is organized, which is unsurprising. The internal coherence of the concept of security represented in the Reports is closely related to the existence of individuals as sexed bodies, where the fiction of sex is assumed to have a binary and transhistorical materiality, and furthermore to the concept of violence as violence towards and experienced by 'women'. However, in representing security in this way, the Reports delegitimize claims made by those who wish to unsettle the constructions of gender and violence that the Reports articulate.

There is a discursive link between the 'participation of women, the incorporation of gender perspectives and the protection of civilians' (UNSC 2004a: 8), suggesting that security can only be achieved with 'the full and equal participation of women and men' (UNSC 2002a: 68). However, it is possible to recognize the strategic gains made over recent years with the articulation of gendered violence as a security issue, and still be sceptical of the ways in which issues of central importance to the 'international' at this particular historical moment are articulated as 'security' issues. This study seeks to problematize the associations made within UNSCR 1325 regarding security as freedom from violence, sought for women by the international (community) and the ways in which these conceptualizations have been (re)produced in the Reports of the Secretary-General. Theorists of international relations need to give due consideration to the kinds of political orders that are constructed through these discourses of security. Without this consideration, 'security' as a concept becomes theoretically and analytically bankrupt, a term employed to justify any action, any policy or practice. Without this consideration, the theorists and politicians who invoke the concept of 'security' are reproducing a political order that manifestly does not provide security for the individuals at the sharp end of these actions, policies or practices, the very 'women and girls' to whom these Reports purport to speak.

CHALLENGING THE REPORTS:
THE IMPLEMENTATION OF UNSCR 1325

This book is concerned with a reconceptualization of international security and gender violence, which proceeds from an investigation into the ways in which security and violence become international-ized and gendered. This chapter is central to this project, provid-ing as it does an insight into the (re)production of these concepts through documentation associated with UNSCR 1325. The Reports refer explicitly to UNSCR 1325 in the context of establishing their authenticity and author-ity; before beginning analysis of the Resolution itself and seeking to explain its failure with regard to the concepts of security, violence, the international and gender that it both constitutes and is constituted through, the explanations given for its failure by the institution that claims ownership of the Resolution should be investigated.

The explanatory factors offered by the Reports are, as mentioned above, assumed to be objectively identifiable. The 2004 Report notes that '[i]n the four years since the adoption of resolution 1325 (2000), there has been a positive shift in international understanding of the impact of armed conflict on women and girls ... Member States, United Nations entities and civil society actors have made significant strides in implementing the resolution' (UNSC 2004a: 118). Despite these 'significant strides', however, 'political will, concerted action and accountability on the part of the entire international community are required' (2004a: 121). Therefore it is assumed that the lack of 'political will, concerted action and accountability' explains the failures to implement UNSCR 1325 successfully. As the Report articulates, 'important gaps and challenges remain' (UNSC 2004a: 4).

However, through the DTA of the Reports conducted in this chapter, it has been possible to identify the concepts of gender, violence, the international and security around which the Reports are organized and from there to suggest that it is precisely this discursive organization that has undermined the implementation of UNSCR 1325. The reports evaluate UNSCR 1325 according to the standards and concepts represented in the Resolution itself. They offer an opportunity to problematize these concepts, and, when read against the dominant explanation for the failures of UNSCR 1325, the critical interjections regarding the (re)production of gender violence and international security in the Reports indicate that it is both possible and necessary to challenge the representations in these documents.

Regarding 'political will [and] concerted action', the Reports (re)produce a construction of the international (community) that is reified and valorized as the provider of 'peace and security'. Discursive disciplining of the boundaries of behaviours appropriate to members of this 'community' further strengthens this construction, without problematizing the ways in which these claims impinge on the legitimacy of actors who transgress the boundaries – either of behaviour or of the community itself. The question of 'accountability' can be read as a discursive mechanism to counter this disciplining tendency, but it can also be read as affirming it, through the association of 'the international' with a domain organized around a reified notion of the state. The issues raised above, concerning the organization of the Reports around concepts of gender, violence and security that fix bodies in relation to a biologically determined narrative of sex difference, recognize that the Reports universally subordinate the feminine subject and require that female is equal to weak. Women therefore need to be secured against the violences they will experience by virtue of their femininity, thus rendering the question of accountability thinkable only in relation to this conceptual framework. That is, these discursive practices preclude the notion that the Reports, and UNSCR 1325 itself, are accountable for the violent reproduction of gender through discursive violence and the international through evocation of discourses of security.

5 | UNITED NATIONS SECURITY COUNCIL

RESOLUTION 1325

The preceding chapter illustrates the ways in which concepts of the international, security, gender and violence have become sedimented into the evaluative frame used to appraise the efficacy of UNSCR 1325 as a tool for improving the situation of women in armed conflict. The analysis of the Secretary-General's reports of 2002 and 2004 shows how the reports work with the concepts around which UNSCR 1325 is organized and therefore offers a useful insight into the ways in which these concepts function to (re)produce particular social realities. This chapter seeks to problematize these organizing concepts further through a discourse-theoretical analysis of UNSCR 1325, which in turn leads to an analysis of the competing narratives concerning the production of the Resolution in Chapter 6.

I use UNSCR 1325 as a vehicle for analysis because the Resolution is a site at which discourses of gender violence and international security come into contact. This chapter explores these moments of contact more fully and investigates the ways in which the Resolution is produced through and is productive of these discourses. Through the descriptive reading I offer, I explore the meaning of UNSCR 1325 according to the 'heroic practice' (Ashley 1988: 232) to which the reader must submit to make sense of the document. That is to say, the descriptive reading offers an interpretation of UNSCR 1325 as if the meanings of the concepts it employs – and (re)produces – are stable. The discourse-theoretical reading that follows offers a reconceptualization of these concepts and the discourses into which they are interpellated drawing on evidence from the document itself. Finally, I argue that the continuities and ruptures in the organizational logics of the document are best illuminated through the discourse-theoretical reading that I offer. The conclusions that I draw from this analysis can then be considered in the context of the reconceptualization of security and violence that this study seeks to offer.

ABOUT UNSCR 1325

When reading UNSCR 1325, it is evident that the Resolution appeals to existing documentation to provide the foundations for the actions it mandates. The first three paragraphs of the Resolution outline the previous Security Council Resolutions, UN Declarations and Reports that are presented as instrumental to UNSCR 1325 (UNSC 2000a: Preamble). The Preamble and Articles 9 and 12 also mention 'the Windhoek Declaration and the Namibia Plan of Action' (Preamble), various international conventions (Article 9) and previous UNSC Resolutions (Article 12). The documentary heritage claimed by UNSCR 1325 is represented as central to the Resolution in the text of the Resolution itself, and provides useful insights into the ways in which UNSCR 1325 draws together disparate documentation in an effort to provide a systematic overview of the issue of 'women, peace and security'. For the purposes of this section, the documentation on which UNSCR 1325 draws is divided into three groups: UNSC Resolutions; international conventions and declarations; and statements, statutes and Reports.

The UNSC Resolutions referred to in UNSCR 1325 include 'resolutions 1261 (1999) ... 1265 (1999) ... 1296 (2000) ... and 1314 (2000)' (UNSC 2000a: Preamble), as well as UNSCR 1208 (1998) (2000a: Article 12). These Resolutions relate, respectively, to children and armed conflict, the protection of civilians in armed conflict, children in armed conflict and the need to assist African states in maintaining the peace and security of refugee camps with particular reference to the 'security needs of women, children and the elderly, who are the most vulnerable groups' (UNSC 1998: Preamble). Claiming these Resolutions as the foundations on which to build UNSCR 1325 'make[s] it clear that the Council considers the protection of civilians, particularly women and children, to fall within its competence' (Otto 2004: 8).

UNSCR 1296, in particular, expresses 'concern at the hardships borne by civilians during armed conflict, in particular as a result of acts of violence directed against them, especially women, children and other vulnerable groups' (UNSC 2000b: Preamble). In articulating a direct commitment to these previous Resolutions, UNSCR 1325 both draws on the support for the issues contained within these Resolutions and further legitimizes these concerns as pertinent to 'the maintenance of international peace and security' (UNSC 2000a: Preamble). Diane Otto persuasively argues that 'these resolutions [are] an attempt by the Council to ... [develop] protections for some of those who have suffered as a result of the spread of militarism' (Otto 2004: 8), and it is true that UNSCR 1265 emphasizes 'the importance of preventing conflicts that could endanger international peace and security' in the context of a Resolution addressing 'the protection of civilians in armed conflict' (UNSC 1999: Preamble). However, these earlier Resolutions 'seem[ed] to foreclose the possibility that the Council might recognize women's agency in their own protection and in the resolution of armed conflict' (Otto 2004: 8–9), and it is this shortcoming that UNSCR 1325 seeks to redress.

The conventions and declarations cited in UNSCR 1325 also offer an insight into the formation of the Resolution. The historic conventions to which the Resolution refers in Article 9 are 'the Geneva Conventions of 1949 ... the Refugee Convention of 1951 ... the Convention on the Elimination of All Forms of Discrimination Against Women of 1979 ... and the United Nations Convention on the Rights of the Child of 1989' (UNSC 2000a: Article 9). Taken together, these conventions form a strong platform from which UNSCR 1325 can challenge current provisions for 'women, peace and security'. For example,

> article 27 of the Fourth Geneva Convention provides that: 'women shall be especially protected against any attack on their honour, in particular against rape, enforced prostitution, or any form of indecent

assault'. The Convention contains no corresponding obligation to investigate or punish individuals in the event that women are not protected. (UNIFEM 2005)

CEDAW and the Optional Protocol of 1999, however, can be seen to redress this lack, as the Convention demands that 'States commit themselves ... to establish[ing] tribunals and other public institutions to ensure the effective protection of women' (UN Division for the Advancement of Women 2005).

The Beijing Declaration and Platform for Action (BPFA) are mentioned in the second paragraph of the Preamble of UNSCR 1325, following on from the listings of the UNSC Resolutions upon which UNSCR 1325 builds. The Declaration explicitly commits to 'enhancing further the advancement and empowerment of women all over the world, and agree[s] that this requires urgent action' (UNDAW 2005), and the Platform for Action lists six strategic objectives in relation to women and armed conflict.[1] The objectives relate closely to the actions mandated in UNSCR 1325, which are discussed further below, focusing on representation of women at decision-making levels in post-conflict reconstruction, participation of women in conflict resolution and the protection of women during periods of armed conflict (UNDAW 2008).

A further set of documents that UNSCR 1325 mentions is the Windhoek Declaration and the Namibia Plan of Action (UNSC 2000a: Preamble). The Windhoek Declaration states that '[i]n order to ensure the effectiveness of peace support operations, the principles of gender equality must permeate the entire mission ... from peacekeeping, reconciliation and peace-building, towards a situation of political stability' (UNGA 2000), and the Plan of Action addresses 'Mainstreaming a Gender Perspective in Multidimensional Peace Support Operations'.[2] The 'useful, concrete recommendations' (UNIFEM 2005) made in the Plan of Action clearly relate to the mandate of UNSCR 1325 and the stated importance of 'mainstreaming a gender perspective into peacekeeping operations' (UNSC 2000a: Preamble).

Two remaining documents to which UNSCR 1325 refers are the Rome Statute of the International Criminal Court (UNSC 2000a: Article 9) and Article 41 of the Charter of the United Nations (UNSC 2000a: Article 14). According to UNIFEM, '[t]he Rome Statute of the International Criminal Court is historic with respect to violence against women in armed conflict as well as during peacetime in that it includes a series of core crimes of sexual and gender violence' (2005).[3] Including reference to the Rome Statute in UNSCR 1325 indicates the recognition that crimes of 'rape, sexual slavery, enforced prostitution, forced pregnancy, enforced sterilization, or any other form of sexual violence of comparable gravity' (ICC 1998) impact negatively on efforts to provide for 'women, peace and security' and must therefore be addressed. UNSCR 1325 also appeals to the president of the Security Council as well as the Charter of the United Nations for institutional legitimacy, recalling the statement 'on the occasion of the United Nations Day for Women's Rights and International Peace (International Women's Day) of 8 March 2000' in which the president emphasizes 'the importance of promoting an active and visible policy of mainstreaming a gender perspective into all policies and programmes while addressing armed or other conflicts' (UNSC 2000c).

As is evident from this exploration, UNSCR 1325 recognizes an influential documentary heritage and also enjoys a significant degree of legitimacy conferred through reference to the historic documents mentioned above. The ways in which the documents mentioned in this section have been drawn together to provide the foundation for a UN Security Council Resolution that addresses 'women, peace and security' is the focus of the following section. I provide a descriptive reading before proceeding to conduct an alternative discourse-theoretical reading in the third section. Further analysis of the ways in which UNSCR 1325 got to be written in the way that it was, including analysis of the discursive terrains of the institutions that claim influence over the Resolution, is the focus of Chapter 6.

UNDERSTANDING UNSCR 1325: A DESCRIPTIVE READING

UNSCR 1325 is available in seventy-seven different languages (Peace-Women 2007) and is acknowledged as 'a historic statement, with significant implications' (Naraghi-Anderlini 2000). The United Nations Development Fund for Women (UNIFEM) published a document entitled 'Security Council Resolution 1325 Annotated and Explained'[4] to assist with the reading of the Resolution and its uses as an advocacy and policy tool. The Preamble to UNSCR 1325 is extensive, not only detailing the documentary heritage of the Resolution, but also contextualizing the Resolution and providing a strong foundation for the mandates contained within it. The Preamble outlines a commitment to '*Reaffirming* the important role of women in the prevention and resolution of conflicts and in peace-building' (UNSC 2000a: Preamble, emphasis in original), which Otto argues 'has provided important new leverage for local women's groups to claim a role in peace negotiations and post-conflict decision-making' (2004: 1). Paying particular attention to the need to 'mainstream a gender perspective' into peacekeeping and conflict resolutions, the text of the Resolution makes an explicit statement about the importance of putting in place 'effective institutional arrangements to guarantee [the] protection and full participation in … peace processes' of women and girls (UNSC 2000a: Preamble).

In addition to the information contained in the Preamble, UNSCR 1325 mandates certain actions to be undertaken by 'Member States' (UNSC 2000a: Article 1) that are deemed necessary in order to address the issues raised when the question of 'Women and peace and security' is considered.[5] The first recommendation in 1325 relates directly to the issue of representation, stating that there is a need 'to ensure increased representation of women at all decision-making levels in national, regional and international institutions' (2000a: Article 1). The actions mandated in Articles 1 and 3 relate to the representation of women, suggesting that this is a priority of UNSCR 1325. This emphasis is in keeping with the Resolution claiming the Beijing Platform for Action as part of its heritage, as 'the Fourth UN World Conference on Women in Beijing in 1995 and the Beijing +5 virtual conference in 2000 made women's political representation a priority' (Jaquette 2003: 332).

It is, however, recognized that sufficient representation will be severely impeded by a lack of institutional support for women's access to decision-making mechanisms, as the Resolution calls for an increase in 'voluntary financial, technical and logistical support for gender-sensitive training efforts' (UNSC 2000a: Article 7). The call for institutional support mirrors a concern in UNSCR 1325 about the structural issues of gendered discrimination and oppression that 'impact ... on durable peace and reconciliation' (UNSC 2000a: Preamble), although the emphasis in the Resolution is on achieving representation, presumably with a view to achieving a 'critical mass' and thus transforming the institutional structures. 'Generally, the figure set for critical mass of women is about 30% of a legislature; ... that was the threshold set by the United Nations in 1995 as the necessary minimum of women representatives needed for women to be fairly represented' (Lovenduski 2001: 744).

The focus of Articles 2 and 4 is participation of women, differenti-ated from representation by the emphasis on 'role and contribution' (UNSC 2000a: Article 4). The importance of gender mainstreaming – or 'incorporat[ing] a gender perspective' (Article 5) is also mentioned; it is suggested that providing 'training guidelines and materials on the protection, rights and the particular needs of women' (Article 6) will help facilitate both representation and participation. Recent research suggests that this assumption is sustainable, as

> a critical mass of women in peacekeeping missions fosters confidence in local populations, enhances peace negotiations and breaks down traditional views of women in local communities, thus affecting the participation of local women in decision-making positions in the post-conflict phase. (United Nations Department of Peace Keeping Operations cited in True 2003: 373; see also Bhatta 2001: 22–5)

UNSCR 1325 also focuses on issues of protection (UNSC 2000a: Articles 8–10), both in terms of human rights and in terms of '[t]he special needs of women and girls' (UNSC 2000a: Article 8a). In situ-ations of armed conflict, UNSCR 1325 '[c]alls on all parties to armed conflict to take special measures to protect women and girls from gender-based violence' (Article 10), and, in doing so, builds on the mandates concerning gendered violence laid out in the Resolutions claimed as its documentary heritage, as described above. These recom-mendations draw on a particular vision of security that negotiates 'the Hobbesian premise that security and human rights must be traded off against each other' (Bahdi 2003: 44), and specifically implicate states in the provision of security for women. Furthermore, UNSCR 1325 discusses the need for 'States to put an end to impunity and to prosecute those responsible for war crimes ... including those relating to sexual and other violence against women and girls' (UNSC 2000a: Article 11), as well as the need for gender-sensitive disarmament, demobilization and reintegration programmes.

Concluding with the invitation to the Secretary-General to organize the Reports analysed in the preceding chapter, UNSCR 1325 offers a coherent and convincing account of actions that both can and should be undertaken by the member states of the United Nations in order to ameliorate 'the impact of armed conflict on women and girls' (UNSC 2000a: Article 16). Article 18 states that the Security Council '[d]ecides to remain actively seized of the matter' (Article 18), which, according to UNIFEM, 'indicates that the Security Council has recognized or elaborated the relevance of the issue to its particular mandate and responsibilities, and it remains on the agenda' (2005). Given that the issue 'remains on the agenda', it is necessary to interrogate the concepts around which it is organized, as these concepts will have further implications for the lived experiences of individuals affected.

PROBLEMATIZING UNSCR 1325: A DISCOURSE-THEORETICAL READING

As mentioned above, given my analytical strategies and theoretical framework, there are problems inherent in fixing the 'meaning' of UNSCR 1325 and assuming that this meaning is stable either historically or culturally. The politics of a United Nations organization such as UNIFEM effectively translating the Resolution and thereby attempting to assert author-ity over its meaning is problematic for the purposes of a discourse-theoretical analysis; it assumes transparency of meaning and fixity of intention in a manner that is unsustainable. But for the purposes of establishing a descriptive reading, it proved useful as a way of illustrating what the Resolution 'means' if the readership is prepared to submit to the 'heroic practice' mentioned above.

This is not to suggest that either the Resolution or the annotations and explanations offered by UNIFEM are deliberately misleading. Rather, it is to draw attention to the ways in which the Resolution is organized around particular discourses of international security and gender violence. Therefore, this section proceeds with a discourse-theoretical analysis that seeks to examine the ways in which UNSCR 1325 is organized around particular conceptualizations of gender, violence, the international and security, in much the same way as the analysis of the Secretary-General's Reports proceeded in Chapter 4. These concepts are organized into intelligible discourses of gender violence and international security, as explained in Chapter 3, and these discourses are (re)produced in the Resolution. The organization logics of these discourses contribute to the violent reproduction of both gender and the international as a spatial and conceptual domain, a claim that is explored more fully in the final section of this chapter.

GENDER

I begin this analysis with a discussion of the ways in which 'women' are represented in UNSCR 1325, rather than exploring articulations of 'gender'. 'Gender' does not feature in the text until the end of the Preamble, and the implications of this will be discussed further below. In the Preamble of UNSCR 1325, 'women and children' are positioned as 'the vast majority of those adversely affected by armed conflict' (UNSC 2000a: Preamble). In addition to the problematic representation of women as inherently associated with children,[6] this predication draws authority from the implication, evidenced in the phrase 'the vast majority', that this articulation is based on empirical research. Given the dominance of positivist, scientist accounts of social reality within both academia and policymaking, the claim to legitimacy on these grounds is understandable, but it is nonetheless difficult to sustain. For all the reasons that post-positivist research-ers have detailed, the assumptions inherent in this type of research, appealing to a legitimacy founded on a truth-claim based in the 'value-neutral facts' of numbers, are problematic.

Moreover, researchers such as Adam Jones (2000) have argued that it is also empirically verifiable that 'non-combatant men have been and continue to be the most frequent target of mass killing and genocidal slaughter, as well as a host of lesser atrocities and abuses' (2000: 186). Drawing on examples from Kosovo, Kashmir, Colombia, Rwanda and Sri Lanka, Jones constructs an argument contrary to that presented in UNSCR 1325: 'the most vulnerable and consistently targeted population group, through time and around the world today, is non-combatant men' (2000: 191). Ultimately, it should not be the case that 'women' or 'men' have their needs met because they suffer, quantifiably, more; treating gender as a variable in this way limits the ways in which it is possible to understand violence, gender and security.

While not disputing the harsh realities of the lived experiences of all of the individuals worldwide who are 'adversely affected by armed conflict', there are problems inherent in basing these demands on a sliding scale of suffering. If women are 'the vast majority of those affected by armed conflict', this invites a 'serious attempt to evaluate their suffering by comparison with men' (Jones 2002: 75). This is untenable and, in my view, counterproductive. Primarily, the idea that careful research on gendered violence could degenerate into point-scoring over whether women or men suffer more is positively worrying. My work joins in the demands for considered policy formulation and implementation that would ameliorate the situations of individuals and communities, whether they are identified as, or comprise, men or women or somewhere in-between. It is, however, premissed on the assumption that it is necessary to pay attention to the ways in which '[t]he imagery through which the protection of civilians has manifested on the U.N. agenda remains profoundly gendered' (Carpenter 2005: 327). Thus, this research investigates the ways in which violence reproduces gender, not just as an organizing conceptual category, but also as a lived identity – something that affects both 'men' and 'women'.

The positioning of women in the text of UNSCR 1325 following that discussed above allows me to identify three constructions, each of which positions the subject slightly differently. These constructions are, in the order in which they are represented in the document: women in need of protection (submission); women as informal political organizers (participation); and women as formal political actors (representation) (UNSC 2000a: Preamble).[7] Each of these articulations will be discussed below, in reverse order. Importantly, however, despite textual representation of 'gender', there is no explicit positioning of men in UNSCR 1325 – that is, the word 'men' is not used in the document. This follows what Robert Connell suggests about 'discussions of women's exclusions from power and decision making [where] men are *implicitly* present as the power holders' (2005: 1806, emphasis added). There are constructions of masculinity, both represented and absented, which structure the conceptual organization of gender within UNSCR 1325, to which I return below.

As mentioned in the previous section, Articles 1 and 3 address issues of representation (UNSC 2000a). The issue of representation is articulated as presence: 'representation of women at all decision-making levels' (Article 1). And, in this context, the more representation, the better: the Secretary-General is thus urged 'to appoint more women as special representatives' (Article 3). Rwanda is an example of a 'post-conflict' area mentioned in the Reports analysed in the previous chapter (UNSC 2004a: 55–6) that are offered as examples of good practice. In a country 'where females constitute more than 60 per cent of the post-genocide population, women won 49 per cent of parliamentary seats in the election of late 2003' (Zuckerman and Greenberg 2005: 71). However, as other scholars have noted, despite the institution of legal measures aimed at reducing the levels of sexual violence, 'data show that violence of a sexual nature in Rwanda is far from decreasing ... [and] ... access to resources remains a vital challenge ... and a real source of tension between men and women' (Gervais 2004: 307–12; see also El-Bushra 2000).

Achieving a critical mass of women as a percentage of their male counterparts in decision-making positions does not necessarily lead to manifest improvements in the lived experiences of other individuals in that context. There is a substantial body of academic literature that discusses the concept of 'critical mass' in relation to the representation of women in formal political arenas. As Sarah Childs and Mona-Lena Krook note, 'growing ranks of critics ... suggest that the time has come to examine the usefulness of this concept for understanding women's legislative impact, as higher proportions of women do not always translate into gains for women as a group' (2006: 21; see also Squires 1999: 204–16; F. Mackay 2004; Mansbridge 2003). In UNSCR 1325, the complexity of these debates is glossed over, with the Resolution subscribing to a somewhat simplistic notion of representation that sustains an essentialist reading of political agenda from biological sex.

The notion, 'given the current mechanisms of political representation, that representatives who happen to be women will be able to
represent women' is by no means universally accepted (Squires 1999:
205). UNSCR 1325 proceeds as if such a fixing of interests to identities
is not only possible but a reasonable basis for peace negotiations and
policymaking. This assumption is based on a conflation of descriptive
and substantive representation (see Squires 2005). That is, UNSCR
1325 assumes that these two dominant constructions of representation
that the feminist literature in this field addresses can be unproblematically equated. Whereas descriptive representation merely 'denotes
presence' (F. Mackay 2004: 100), substantive representation refers 'to
the congruence between representatives' actions and the interests of
the represented' (Schwindt-Bayer and Mishler 2005: 408; see also
Mansbridge 2003, 1999). The two constructions are analytically and
practically separable, and recognizing this leads to the understanding
that a purely quantitative increase in women's representation will not
necessary effect political change in formal institutions.

For the purposes of this analysis, I have made a distinction
between representations of participation and representation in
UNSCR 1325. Preceding Articles 1–4, women are represented in
the document as having an 'important role ... in the prevention
and resolution of conflicts and in peacebuilding'; this articulation
is textually prior to the positioning of women as political actors
and the need for their 'full involvement' (UNSC 2000a: Preamble).
This construction of participation is organized around the notion
of women acting as women – that is, there are objectively identifiable women who can be classified on the grounds of their shared
characteristics and whose behaviour will be conditioned in accordance
with these characteristics. In contrast to the feminist insight that
'gender-atypical work' may lead to gender-transgressive behaviours
(F. Mackay 2004: 111), UNSCR 1325 perpetuates a representation of
women that inscribes an essential link between womanhood and 'the
prevention and resolution of conflicts and ... peacebuilding' (UNSC
2000a: Preamble). Such a construction relies on the recognition of
women as nurturers (read: mothers) and supporters of peace, inherently pacifist. Sara Ruddick calls this construction the iconic figure
of the mater dolorosa, described as '[t]he representative heroine of

maternal peacefulness ... [who] as she grieves for her particular loss ... mourns war itself' (1989: 142).

A discourse that positions women as agential in the ways described above could be considered to be in tension with the third representation of women in UNSCR 1325, as in need of protection. In the context of political participation and representation, women are positioned as agents, capable of protecting others through female empowerment and maternal sacrifice. Such agency would seem to slip from the articulation of 'the protection, rights and the particular needs of women' (UNSC 2000a: Article 6). 'One of the main problems in associating women and children in international relations is that it feeds the nationalist discourse that defines women mainly as the cultural bearers of society' (Puechguirbal 2004: 11). This perspective is closely related to the maternalist discourses that see 'women', by virtue of their association with motherhood, as 'naturally' more nurturing, peaceful and protective – not, in this instance, of the body, but of the body politic. In addition to fixing 'womenandchildren' as the eternally protected, this representation also functions to define men as responsible for protecting 'their' women and children and the nation as a whole.

However, UNSCR 1325, through its articulation of 'women and peace and security' and its claiming a heritage in the UNSC Resolutions that affect civilians and children, as discussed above, positions this latter conceptualization of women as the centralized signifier in its discourses of gender. Women are part of 'women and children', 'are targeted by combatants' and therefore implicitly not combatants, women have 'special needs' and require 'protection' (UNSC 2000a: Preamble), particularly 'from gender-based violence ... rape and other forms of sexual abuse' (Article 10). Overall, women are 'linked by their gender through their vulnerability to violence' in this representation (Bahdi 2003: 46) and therefore fixed as vulnerable.

The failure to disaggregate different performances of femininity that are represented in UNSCR 1325 and the corollary differential impact on the lived experiences of various subjects diminishes the potential of the Resolution to address the issues of 'women and peace and security' to which it pertains. Woman-in-need-of-protection is the centralized signifier around which other articulations of femininity are articulated. Thus, women-as-informal-organizers and women-as-formal-actors are still, primarily, essentially women-in-need-of-protection. While sensitive research can be conducted on the basis of recognizing 'a subjectivity that gives agency to the individual while at the same time placing her within "particular discursive configurations"' (de Lauretis cited in Alcoff 1988: 425), reproducing these essentializing gender stereotypes is counterproductive and counterintuitive. As Caroline Sweetman notes, '[t]his is controversial for proponents of women's rights, since it is tempting to believe that women are intrinsically more likely than men to find non-violent means of conflict resolution' (2005: 3), but courting such controversy is necessary if it is the processes that reproduce gender difference that are under critical scrutiny, rather than proceeding with a critique that takes difference as *a priori*.

'Gender' is articulated in UNSCR 1325 as a 'perspective' (UNSC 2000a: Preamble) and also as a prefix to '-sensitive training efforts' (Article 7) and '-based violence' (Article 10). Furthermore, there are 'gender considerations' (Article 15)and 'gender dimensions' (Article 16). These constructions articulate gender as a variable, as opposed to a power relation or a discursive performance. Treating gender as a variable is premissed on the assumption that gender can be treated as an analytical device that can be measured, controlled or manipulated in social science research. For example, taking gender as a variable in the study of the impact of armed conflict would rely upon gathering data on the experiences of armed conflict and disaggregating this data by gender identity in order to allow for the construction of statements such as 'women ... account for the vast majority of those adversely affected by armed conflict' (Preamble). Associating 'gender' with 'women' in UNSC 1325, as discussed in Chapter 4, further entrenches a concept of gender as a 'women's issue'.

Articulating gender as relational has proved problematic in policy discourse. 'Although many institutions have renamed projects by changing the word 'women' to 'gender', their actions do not uniformly demonstrate a corresponding shift in behaviour or gender equality outcomes' (Staudt 2003: 49). Gender mainstreaming is seen as a mechanism for achieving this shift, 'the multi-faceted project of using gender analysis in addressing the mainstream agenda' (Ackerley 2001:

317; see also Pankhurst 2004: 33–8). This is not to assume that 'the mainstream agenda' is not already gendered but to investigate the ways in which policies have differential impacts on women and men and the relations between them. Given this acknowledgement, it is surprising that UNSCR 1325 does not mention men while addressing the issue of 'women and peace and security' – 'man' is very much the absent presence. 'He', however, is represented, embodying the subject of the United Nations Secretary-General). UNSCR 1325 thus articulates a narrative of masculinity in which the Secretary-General – 'he' – is 'urge[d] … encourage[d] … invite[d] … request[ed]' (UNSC 2000a: Articles 2–5, 16, 17) to protect the 'women' with whom the document is concerned, from the violence that is discussed in the following section.

VIOLENCE

In much the same way as the articulation of gender in UNSCR 1325 relies on a discursive link to 'women', textual priority is given to the representation of violence as conflict. Conflict is differentiated in UNSCR 1325 as 'armed conflict' (UNSC 2000a: Preamble), which suggests that there may be types of conflict that are unarmed. These latter forms of conflict are represented as outside of the remit of the Resolution, although the text also presents a notion of violence as structural, an issue to which I return below. Initially, however, it is important to problematize the concept of violence constructed as 'armed conflict', as representing violence as conflict severs the signifying links to pain, physicality and specificity of experience that 'violence' can sustain. Donna Pankhurst notes that 'no straightforward technical definition … is likely to encapsulate the complexities of contemporary conflicts in much of the world today' (2004: 9). Even with the discursive modifier 'armed', representing violence as conflict 'entails a lack of clarity about what exactly is being discussed' (2004: 9).[8] My research suggests that what 'is being discussed' is violence, as explicated in Chapter 3. Retaining the terminology of violence allows for the positioning of subjects and objects within discursive context, which in turn allows for the investigation of the specificities of those contexts in relation to violence.

Conflict is seen in UNSCR 1325 to create 'refugees and internally displaced persons' and targeting of civilians by 'combatants and

armed elements' is seen as a barrier to 'durable peace and reconciliation' (UNSC 2000a: Preamble). The agents of conflict are therefore
'combatants and armed elements', articulated in opposition to 'civilians, particularly women and children' (Preamble). This functions to
deny the possibility that civilians can be agents of 'armed conflict'.
UNSCR 1325 acknowledges (Preamble) that conflict does not necessarily respect the rule of law in its treatment of targeting of civilians
but also reproduces the division between civilian and combatant,
which functions to remove civilians from the agency of conflict:
'civilians do not have the right to participate directly in hostilities'
(Dörmann 2003: 46). Civilians, therefore, are the broader group in
need of protection, of which women are a 'particular' part. In this
construction, violence is still something that happens to women, as
discussed in Chapter 4.

Using 'conflict' to represent violence, as mentioned above, is
problematic. Not only does the language of conflict act to position
the materiality of violence assumed by UNSCR 1325 at one remove;
'there is very little discussion in much of the writing on "conflict
analysis" or "conflict resolution" of the impact of certain types of
social relations on the specific forms of violence' (Pankhurst 2004:
10). Furthermore, 'the question hardly arises as to how or why this
'conflict' situation is different from what is normal' (Pankhurst 2004:
10). As Kurtz and Turpin eloquently argue, '[t]he tendency to see
violence as the consequence of aberrant behaviour committed by
deviant individuals at the margins of society obscures the central roles
violence plays at the very foundations of the social order' (cited in
McIlwhaine 1999: 460). From a slightly different perspective, it can
be argued that 'assumptions about the nature of internal conflict
– as systemic failure and as defying rational explanation – ignore
the considerable objective (and subjective) rationality of employing
political violence' (Jackson 2001: 66). This is an issue to which I
return in the section focusing on the international.

Those who put forward arguments concerning the centrality of
violence as an organizing concept in society often 'draw on Johan
Galtung's work on "structural" violence, extending the understanding
of violence from physical to psychological hurt, which in turn includes
alienation, repression and deprivation' (cited in McIlwhaine 1999: 455).

It is evident that this conceptualization of violence also structures UNSCR 1325; the attention paid to the issues of participation and representation of women discussed above draws attention to the ways in which 'women' as a group may be alienated or deprived as well as suffering physical violence (see also Bahdi 2003: 54). However, while the Secretary-General's reports discussed in the previous chapter explicitly articulate 'cultures of violence and discrimination against women and girls' (UNSC 2002a: 5), in UCSR 1325 these 'cultures of violence' are implicit, constructed through the discourse of gender violence articulated in the Resolution. Many of the critiques levelled at the Reports in Chapter 4, however, are relevant to the discussion of the representation of violence in UNSCR 1325.

As mentioned above, violence as represented in UNSCR 1325, in particular gendered violence, happens to women: 'all parties to armed conflict [are called on] to take special measures to protect women and girls from gender-based violence, particularly rape and other forms of sexual abuse' (UNSC 2000a: Article 10). While this is unsurprising given the conflation of women and gender, it remains problematic. Fixing women as victims of violence and making women the referent object of discourses of 'gender violence' functions to reproduce a conceptualization of both gender and violence that is theoretically and practically dangerous. Furthermore, giving textual priority to the articulation of violence as 'gender-based' not only obscures the possibility that all forms of violence may contribute to the violent reproduction of gender, but also relegates 'all other forms of violence' (UNSC 2000a: Article 10) to a vague catch-all term that cannot adequately capture 'the great hardships, deprivation of adequate food, shelter, health care and education' and danger of imminent fatality experienced in situations of violence (McKay 2005: 22).

In the context of prevention of and retribution for violences experienced in 'armed conflict', UNSCR 1325 equates peace with a lack of armed conflict (UNSC 2000a: Preamble). This construction is discussed further in the section addressing the predication of security in the Resolution. 'Durable peace and reconciliation' will prevent violence, and the responsibility for achieving this peace is allocated to the United Nations Security Council (Preamble). It is therefore necessary to investigate how violence is constructed in conjunction with the international as a concept in UNSCR 1325, particularly in relation to the 'maintenance of international peace and security' (Preamble) and 'the responsibility of all States' (Article 11) to address the issue of violence, gender-ed or otherwise, as experienced by women in armed conflict.

INTERNATIONAL

In the first paragraph of UNSCR 1325, there is mention of 'the United Nations Day for Women's Rights and International Peace' (UNSC 2000a: Preamble). The discursive link between women's rights and peace is (re)produced through the articulations of gender and violence discussed above, and the representation of security that I discuss below. In this section, however, I explore the implications of forging a discursive link between the international and 'peace', as well as investigating the ways in which the conceptualization of gender evidenced in UNSCR 1325 is articulated in conjunction with a particular conceptualization of the international. In the second paragraph of the Resolution, UNSCR 1325 draws on 'the outcome document of the twenty-third Special Session of the United Nations General Assembly entitled "Women 2000: Gender Equality, Development and Peace for the Twenty-First Century"' (Preamble). Reproducing these two representations constructs the international as a domain in which securing women's rights can secure peace and further endorses the United Nations as an international institution concerned with 'gender equality'. This functions to position the international as a subject in opposition to the conflict zones of the implicitly domestic sphere. The politics of maintaining a conceptualization of violence that is somehow spatially bounded is extremely problematic.

While the 'increased representation of women at all decision-making levels in national, regional and international institutions' is called for (UNSC 2000a: Article 1), the issues of informal and formal participation and representation of women discussed above are predominantly articulated through association with the realm of the domestic, as opposed to the international. '[P]revention and resolution of conflicts and ... peace-building' happens in conflict zones (Preamble), as distinct from the domain of the international. In calling for women's 'equal participation and full involvement' (Preamble) in these processes, women are tied to the domestic. Women are expected to organize as women in the processes of nation-building, securing the boundaries of the state and sedimenting national loyalties, a conceptualization that has been thoroughly problematized by feminist scholars of women in nationalist movements.[9]

The uneasy theorizing of feminist and nationalist discourses in the context of conflict and post-conflict situations is not represented in UNSCR 1325, although it is mentioned briefly above. It is assumed that women have an 'important role' (UNSC 2000a: Preamble) to play in the construction of nationhood post-conflict and that this will somehow lead to higher valorization of women's rights in 'peacetime'. However, '[a]ll nationalist ideologies are gendered: most commonly, women are the symbol of the nation, men its agents' (Whitehead et al. 1993: 1). The responsibility of women in nationalist discourse is primarily as mothers, with a duty not only physically to reproduce the nation but also to reproduce national ideals and values.

Furthermore, in terms of retribution and reconciliation, the international (community) allows member states – or, rather, the elites in power in these states – to perpetuate the (re)production of unequal gendered relations of power. Through the articulation of circumstances where it may not be 'appropriate' to 'include a gender component' in peacekeeping operations (UNSC 2000a: Article 5) and may not be 'feasible' to exclude crimes of 'sexual and other violence against women and girls' from amnesty provisions (Article 11), UNSCR 1325 constructs a concept of the international that is the negotiator of gender equality, in opposition to the conflict-torn domestic domains that may have more pressing agendas. This concept of the international is thoroughly gendered, assuming that the power relations between individuals are so naturalized that it is possible somehow to separate gender from the bodies of the peacekeepers or the institutions of amnesty provision. Not only does this lead to the words '"Not now, later" … ring[ing] in the ears of many nationalist women' (Enloe 2000: 62) but it also supports a conventional narrative of sovereignty that itself naturalizes the gendered reproduction of the international/domestic divide.

This narrative of sovereignty has been thoroughly problematized by scholars of International Relations (see, inter alia, Weber 1995; Paul 1999; Walker 1991), in much the same way as the international/domestic divide has been challenged. Youngs, for example, writes that

> [t]he series of concepts, state-as-actor, sovereignty and anarchy, which provide the conceptual architecture for mainstream state-centric thought, affirm the importance of boundaries, but because of the *given* nature of the state they do not explore the full implications of those boundaries. (1999: 25–26, emphasis in original)

UNSCR 1325 appeals to a host of international provisions and conventions, as discussed in the section that contextualizes the Resolution, to construct a sense of legitimacy for the international (community) represented in the Resolution and the boundaries that this community inscribes onto the social world (UNSC 2000a: Preamble; Articles 9, 12). In the context of theorizing intervention, Cynthia Weber has convincingly argued that 'it is the international community that clarifies difficult interpretive questions about where the boundary of sovereign authority lies, [and] where sovereign authority resides' (1995: 16), an argument that is easily sustainable in the context of analysing UNSCR 1325.

While both 'states' and the 'Security Council' – an international institution – have responsibilities, according to UNSCR 1325 (UNSC 2000a: Preamble, Article 11), ultimate authority over 'the maintenance of international peace and security' (Preamble) resides in the Security Council, and therefore, in the international sphere. As mentioned in Chapter 4, and discussed in the context of the discourse of 'international security' in Chapter 3, this assertion of the international (community) as somehow removed from conflict and occupying a morally privileged position is inherently problematic in terms of the reproduction of gendered state identities and the international as a conceptual domain that functions to provide security. Furthermore, the conceptualization of security (re)produced in UNSCR 1325 should be investigated, to explore fully the types of security, from what and for whom, being provided.

SECURITY

Security is initially articulated in UNSCR 1325 in the context of the United Nations Security Council. Given the conceptualization of the international discussed above, and its discursive fidelity to the discourse of 'international security', positioning security in this way suggests that security is indeed something that can be achieved, rather than a discourse. Security is associated with 'peace' in the title of the Resolution and continues to be constructed in this way throughout the document (UNSC 2000a). Meanwhile, the antithesis of security is represented as 'armed conflict', so security is marked by the absence of such conflict (Preamble). This is inevitably problematic, as conflict resolution in the context of the conceptualizations of gender, violence and the international explored above can only ever provide a partial peace, a 'peace that neglects ... a large part of the community, or that supports, reconstructs, and in some cases strengthens the inequalities in the power structures' that (re)produce community (A. Mackay 2004: 107).

In addition to the inadequacy – and theoretical tautology – of defining conflict as the absence of security, and security as the absence of conflict,[10] this conceptualization fails completely to address the issues of structural violence discussed above. Over two decades ago, Enloe explored the issue of militarization and its various impacts, arguing that scholars and activists must 'put militarisation into a larger socio-economic context, rather than thinking within the conventionally narrow frameworks of foreign policy or "national security"' (1983: 207). UNSCR 1325, in addressing the '"special needs" of women and girls *during and after conflicts*' (UNSC 2000a: Preamble, emphasis added), precludes consideration of the ways in which the international system of states, according to the logic of the conventional narrative of sovereignty, allows for multiple forms of violence to structure and (re)produce the lived experiences of individuals the world over.

Furthermore, 'women' are invited to be complicit in the construction of this world order through their efforts in nation-building and conflict resolution. What Alexander Murphy refers to as 'the sovereign territorial ideal' (1996: 83) has functioned to displace questions of identity, context and the disaggregation of security discourses from studies of security, meaning that 'the manner in which the identities of nation-states themselves are (re)constituted by these processes' are absented from conventional analysis of security, sovereignty and nation-building (Varadarajan 2004: 322).[11] Peacekeeping, which UNSCR

1325 articulates as being of central significance to peace negotiations (UNSC 2000a: Preamble), has received sustained critical scrutiny on precisely these grounds: 'peacekeeping shares with colonialism the capacity to reconstruct identities. Peacekeeping not only "keeps the peace" – that is, ensures the containment of conflict – but it also configures race, gender, class and culture' (Agathangelou and Ling 2003: 141). In the context of this research, it is not even entirely appropriate to suggest that peacekeeping 'keeps the peace', subscribing as this does to a notion that peace is the absence of conflict not violence.

Conceptualizing the state as the provider of security in UNSCR 1325 reproduces these tensions, as well as reproducing 'the gendered logic of the masculine role of protector' that constructs 'a security state that wages war abroad and expects obedience and loyalty at home' (Young 2003: 2). 'Member States' are exhorted to 'ensure increased representation of women' (UNSC 2000a: Article 1), 'provide candidates to the Secretary-General' in order that 'he' might appoint more women to office (Article 3), 'train ... on the protection, rights and particular needs of women' and 'increase their voluntary financial, technical and logistical support for gender-sensitive training efforts' (Articles 6–7). Women are expected to participate. Drawing attention to the voluntary nature of support for 'gender-sensitive' initiative further entrenches a narrative of sovereignty in which 'a government ... exercises substantial authority within its own territory' (Murphy 1996: 81) and this is taken to be unproblematic – both the assumption that it occurs, and the further assumption that this is a valid mode of political organization. But as Weber asks, 'how can this community be said to exist, and how can the state be said to speak on its behalf?' (1995: 6).

Moreover, the question of what the state is assumed to provide must also be considered. Security, drawing on particular conceptualizations of gender, violence and the international represented in UNSCR 1325, is represented as the absence of conflict. In the context of 'women and peace and security', security is articulated as protection. The 'rights of women and girls' need protecting, it is necessary to 'guarantee their [women and girls'] protection' (UNSC 2000a: Preamble), and 'Member States' need 'guidelines and materials on the protection, rights and particular needs of women' (Article 6). Parties to conflict need 'to take special measures to protect women and girls from gender-based violence' (Article 10). Quite apart from the construction of women as eternal victim of violence that is by definition gendered in this articulation, the discourse of protection reaffirms a crude rendering of the state as 'man writ large and therefore implicitly endowed, conceptually at least, with the capacities of decision-making' (Youngs 1999: 25). In a hierarchical organization of 'sovereign' states, through a reworking of the discourse of 'national security' that captures this vision of state-as-man-as-actor, the discourse of 'international security' articulates a vision of security through cooperation and thus secures through this discourse of security an international system in which inequality is entrenched.

The processes of nation-building, evoked in UNSCR 1325 through the predication of 'peace-building', 'reconciliation' and 'conflict prevention and resolution' (UNSC 2000a: Preamble) as central to issues of 'women and peace and security', cannot be taken as unproblematic. Rather, it is often the case that such processes, as mentioned above, rely on and thus function to (re)produce inequality and difference, not least in the context of gender. Furthermore, 'regimes ... promote exclusionary rather than inclusionary nation building projects ... and ... some violence inevitably accompanies early stages of state making' (Ayoob 2002: 38). The point has been well made by Anna Agathangelou and Lily Ling that the security offered within a neoliberal world order by a system of nation states is by definition a situated one: 'Left unheeded are those transgressions usually characterized in terms of "third world" anger and frustration, desperation and despair ... that transpire inside the patriarchal household ... or outside the public sector' (2003: 134).

The representations of security evidenced in UNSCR 1325 contribute to the conceptual organization of the document around discourses of 'gender violence' and 'international security'. As I have argued above, it is my contention that these discourses, rather than 'describing' gender, violence, security and the international, function to reproduce identity – individual identity is (re)produced through the violence reproduction of gender, and the identities of states are (re)produced through the violent reproduction of the international. There are obvious moments of contact between these discourses, as their conceptual organization relies on understandings and interpretive contexts that make meaning of the discourses through frameworks that are situated in particular spatial and conceptual locations. That is, state identities are gendered, and gendered identities are positioned within discourses of the international.

CHALLENGING UNSCR 1325: CONCLUSIONS

In Chapter 4, I investigated the ways in which the successes and failures of UNSCR 1325 have been evaluated by the United Nations Secretary-General in the Reports of 2002 and 2004, the first of which was mandated in the Resolution itself (UNSC 2000a: Articles 16–17). This chapter has explored the discursive construction of UNSCR 1325 using a discourse-theoretical analysis. The strategy of double-reading allows for the positing of critical interjections into the dominant narrative of UNSCR 1325 and the investigation of the ways in which the document (re)produces the concepts around which it is organized. In this section I argue that it is most fruitful to consider the discourses of 'gender violence' and 'international security' that are articulated through UNSCR 1325 as discourses that permit the violent reproduction of gender and the violent reproduction of the international, both respectively and simultaneously.

UNSCR 1325 expresses the willingness of the Security Council 'to ensure that Security Council missions take into account gender considerations and the rights of women, including through consultation with local and international women's groups' (UNSC 2000a: Article 15). In the context of the first section above, in which I detail the ways in which UNSCR 1325 speaks to issues of 'women and peace and security', the articulation of such 'willingness' can be considered a nodal point where these issues come into contact. Identifying Article 15 as the articulation of a nodal point recognizes that UNSCR 1325 is organized around discourses of 'gender violence' and 'international security', into which particular conceptualizations of gender, violence, the international and security are interpellated, and that exploring the (re)production of these concepts is central to the understanding of the Resolution.

'It is amazing that the world's largest international security institution has now publicly declared that attention to gender is integral to "doing security"' (Cohn, Kinsella and Gibbings 2004: 139). My study is not aimed at discrediting the efforts made by the United Nations Security Council to ameliorate the lived experiences of 'women and girls' in conflict and post-conflict situations. Many human rights activists, feminist organizers and academics have received positively the measures called for in UNSCR 1325 (see, inter alia, Cohn et al. 2004; Rehn and Sirleaf 2002; Bahdi 2003). The descriptive reading in the first section of this chapter explores the ways in which UNSCR 1325 can be considered a 'watershed political framework' (Rehn and Sirleaf 2002: 3). However, taken in conjunction with the discourse-theoretical reading in the second section of this chapter, the pursuit of gender equality is problematized precisely because of what it represents: not the question of whether women should enjoy equal privilege with men – of course they should – but the question of how these differences are (re)produced and entrenched through even the most well-intentioned policy. This results from acknowledging that, '[a]s scholars, we need to become more knowledgeable about the worlds of advocacy and policy, and position ourselves to forge mutually advantageous relationships with feminist researchers, activists and policymakers' (True 2003: 387).

'Gender equality' is conceptualized as the advancement of women, paying scant attention to the situations in which women are active in the oppression of other women and men are similarly disadvantaged. Furthermore, 'gender equality' assumes difference, thereby obscuring the discursive mechanisms through which this difference is reproduced. One of these discursive mechanisms is violence, but this is similarly obscured through the discursive articulation of violence in UNSCR 1325 as either 'conflict' or as 'gender-based', both textually and conceptually putting the gender first. Meanwhile, the list of documents claimed as ancestry to UNSCR 1325 speaks to the conceptualization of the international represented in the Resolution. Compatible with the discourse of 'international security', the international (community) is responsible for the provision of security, which can be achieved through the elimination of violence. The tension becomes apparent when the ways in which violences, often undertaken in the name of security, function to underpin the international as a spatial and conceptual domain, are investigated.

UNSCR 1325 is a product of its discursive domain. In the previous chapter, I explored the sedimenting of the concepts around which the Resolution is organized into a frame, which is then used to critique the document, and the constitution of these concepts in a particular text. This chapter has investigated the discursive construction of the Resolution itself, and the ways in which gender violence and international security are constructed. This has allowed for an exploration of the theoretical potential of the reconceptualizations of these concepts that I offer in relations to Resolution 1325. However, to complete the analysis, it is necessary to examine the discursive terrain that UNSCR 1325 inhabits.

As mentioned above, the Resolution refers to a range of policy documents and declarations issuing from various institutions that are represented as having influenced it. In addition to these documents, there are narratives of production issuing from two distinct organizations: the United Nations system and the Non-Governmental Organization Working Group on Women, Peace and Security. The following chapter investigates the claims made by these two groups concerning the authorship of and influence over UNSCR 1325, not to establish how it 'really' got written in the way that it did, but to trace the discourses of 'gender violence' and 'international security' through their institutional contexts in an effort to establish that the Resolution could not have been written any other way.

6 | EXPLORING THE NARRATIVES

OF PRODUCTION OF UNSCR 1325

The previous two chapters investigated the ways in which the conceptualizations of (gender) violence and (international) security that are (re)produced in UNSCR 1325 impact both on the textual organization of the Resolution itself, and on the implementation of the Resolution in conflict and post-conflict situations. In this chapter the analytical focus is broader, as I explore the competing narratives of production, relating different histories of UNSCR 1325, which issue from the two sites of discursive power that influenced the construction of the Resolution. The two sites of power with which I am concerned are the United Nations Security Council (UNSC) and the Non-Governmental Organization Working Group on Women, Peace and Security (NGO WG). Both institutions claim author-ity over the Resolution and are therefore appropriate foci of analysis (see UNSC 2000a; NGO WG 2005).[1] Neither of these institutions, which for the purposes of analysis will be treated as loosely bounded entities with particular discursive terrains, is monolithic or internally consistent. However, both have distinct narratives of the history of UNSCR 1325, which will be explored in this chapter.

In this chapter I aim to draw out the discursive conditions of possibility for the construction of UNSCR 1325 through investigation of the discursive terrains of the two institutions that claim a degree of author-ity over the Resolution. By doing so, I illustrate the ways in which particular conceptualizations of gender, violence, the international and security organized and structured discussions of 'the impact of armed conflict on women and girls' previous to the production of UNSCR 1325, thus having a clear impact on the Resolution itself. Furthermore, exploring the discourses of 'gender violence' and 'international security' that were centralized in the construction of UNSCR 1325 simultaneously allows me to identify discourses that were marginalized. The next and final chapter returns to the question of the conditions of possibility constructed by UNSCR 1325 in the context of the treatment of gender violence as an issue of international security.

The analysis in this chapter is both similar to and differs from the analysis in the preceding chapters. As before, I proceed with a descriptive reading of the first site of power under investigation, the NGO WG, detailing the aims and objectives of the institution, its vision and purpose, and its membership. This leads to a discourse-theoretical reading of three key texts produced by the NGO WG in relation to UNSCR 1325. In the third section, I offer a descriptive reading of the UNSC and similarly follow this with a discourse-theoretical reading of three texts produced by the UNSC. In the case of the NGO WG, the texts are a letter to the UNSC of 23 October 2000 (NGO WG 2000a), the statement that was produced for the Arria formula meeting to discuss the possibility of a UNSC Resolution addressing 'the impact of armed conflict on women and girls' (NGO WG 2000b), and a statement made to the assembled press following the Arria formula meeting (NGO WG 2000c).[2] The key texts of the UNSC include Chapters II–VII of the Charter of the United Nations (UN 1945), the statement of the UN concerning the provisional rules that govern the actions of the UNSC (UN 1983), and a statement from the president of the Security Council on 8 March 2000 (UNSC 2000c), which was International Women's Day. I have not attempted to produce a sampling method to identify the documents I have chosen to analyse. These documents have been chosen because they are given textual priority in UNSCR 1325, as discussed in Chapter 5, and also because the institutions themselves cite them as fundamental to the production of the Resolution.

I have chosen to analyse the institutions through the texts they produce for three reasons. First, it allows me to treat the websites of the institutions, where it is possible to glean a great deal of information regarding the ways in which the institutions view themselves, as texts, and allows me to follow the links through the webpages to the documents that the institutions themselves cite as important. Second, and relatedly, the representational practices in which the institutions are engaged not only represent their visions of themselves, but also, through presence or absence, the dominant conceptualizations of (gender) violence and (international) security that organize their respective discursive terrains. Finally, given that the UNSC is self-consciously concerned with issues of security and the international, and that the NGO WG prioritizes Women, Peace and Security, following the structure of the previous two chapters and analysing both sites of power for representations of gender, violence, the international and security might obscure some interesting insights regarding the contestation over these concepts between the two institutions.

CONTEXTUALIZING THE NGO WG
ON WOMEN, PEACE AND SECURITY

In order to explore the discursive terrain of the NGO WG that claims author-ity over UNSCR 1325, it is first necessary to contextualize the Working Group as itself a product of a wider discursive terrain. The engagement of NGOs with the United Nations system has a long and complex history, and so too does the framing of particular issues that have informed the construction of UNSCR 1325. The constitution of an NGO is not under consideration here; nor will this section attempt to provide a detailed exploration of all of the issues raised in the investigation of the NGO WG. However, it is important to trace the development of the NGO WG back to the involvement of transnational NGOs in prioritizing certain issues on multiple UN agendas over the past few decades. Beginning with a discussion of the impact of NGOs on the UN system, this section will go on to explore the successes of various NGOs in pushing forward an agenda of gender mainstreaming through various mechanisms. This in turn will lead to a discussion of the watershed conference in Vienna in

1993 where violence against women was 'formally recognized by the international community as a human rights issue after unprecedented lobbying by women's groups' (O'Hare 1999: 365). These advances played a part in constructing a policy environment in which gendered violence could be considered an international issue, and, with the shift in focus to issues of human security by the UN system at the end of the Cold War (Bunch cited in Joachim 2003: 260), the NGO Working Group on Women, Peace and Security was consolidated.

As Otto notes, the UN Charter 'reveal[s] the defensive position of states towards NGOs and their insistence that the status of an NGO is peripheral to that of a state' (1996: 110). In 1968, the UN Economic and Social Council (ECOSOC) passed Resolution 1296,[3] which addressed the 'arrangements for consultation with non-governmental organizations' (ECOSOC 1968). Almost thirty years later, these arrangements were reviewed at the recommendation of a working group established by ECOSOC, leading to the approval of Resolution 1996/31[4] in 1996. Marking what Tony Hill has termed a 'second generation' of NGO–UN relations (2004), this Resolution codified a new set of arrangements between NGOs and the UN system. This led to the current situation in which 'NGOs are omnipresent in the policy and administrative process of UN organizations' and the recognition that 'the extent of their participation has progressively deepened' since the end of the Cold War (Gordenker and Weiss 1996: 43).

One of the issue areas pertinent to this investigation that was pushed to the forefront of negotiations between NGOs and the UN was gender mainstreaming. 'Delegates at the 1975 UN International Women's Year conference in Mexico City declared that all governments should establish agencies dedicated to promoting gender equality and improving the status and conditions of women' (True and Mintrom 2001: 30). This not only built on existing institutional mechanisms for the advancement of women's issues, such as the UN Division for the Advancement of Women,[5] but also represented the work undertaken by transnational networks and the building of links between various levels of political activity, from local/domestic women's organizations through to global/international policy networks and other institutions.

In response to achievements of activists involved in the push for gender mainstreaming (see, inter alia, Ackerley 2001; Staudt 2003) and the adoption of the Convention on the Elimination of All Forms of Discrimination Against Women (CEDAW) by the UN General Assembly in 1979, which was lauded as an international Bill of Rights for women, the arguments concerning the global subordination of women were used to frame interventions into the UN discourse on human rights. Drawing links between the freedoms that women should enjoy as equal citizens and the limits posed to these freedoms by the myriad forms of violence against women that occur globally, '[t]he issue of domestic violence soon became a focus point for feminist scholars' (O'Hare 1999: 364).

The Declaration on the Elimination of Violence Against Women (DEVAW), adopted in 1993, not only represented 'the culmination of a political process begun two decades earlier' (Joachim 2003: 247), but was also a pivotal document in its own right.[6] DEVAW was adopted shortly after the World Human Rights Conference in Vienna, which was also held in 1993. Jennifer Chan-Tiberghien has argued that '[t]he World Conference ... marked a paradigmatic shift ... Feminists launched a global violence against women campaign prior to the Vienna conference and managed to insert considerable gender language into its Declaration' (2004: 461). The measures contained within DEVAW build on these achievements and aim to 'ensure the elimination of violence against women in all its forms, a commitment by states in respect of their responsibilities, and a commitment by the international community at large to the elimination of violence against women' (UN 1993: Preamble).[7]

Despite a commitment to eradicating 'violence against women', the dominant conceptualization of gendered violence in the UN system is, as previously discussed, 'gender violence'. This conceptualization affected subsequent policy in such a way as to frame the issues related to 'gender violence' in terms of gender mainstreaming, such that '[i]n addressing armed or other conflicts, an active and visible policy of mainstreaming a gender perspective into all policies and programmes should be promoted so that before decisions are taken an analysis is made of the effects on women and men, respectively' (UNFCWC 1995: E.1). Drawing on the successes of CEDAW and DEVAW, and the ever-strengthening linkages between feminist theorists/activists and the UN system, the UN World Conferences on Women every five years from 1975 were increasingly well attended, leading to the 1995 Conference in Beijing, which 'was the largest UN conference up to that time. More NGOs than ever before were affiliated to the intergovernmental conference, while some 30,000 people participated in the NGO forum' (Steans 2003b: 134). The outcome document, the Beijing Platform for Action (BPFA), as mentioned in the previous chapter, is hailed as a watershed document for the securing of women's rights. As Sanam Naraghi-Anderlini and Judy El-Bushra argue,

> The BPFA is not only comprehensive but has also set clear benchmarks and a vision for improving women's lives. With 188 states as signatories, it is an influential international document on women's rights. At Beijing, the impact of armed conflict on women was noted as a specific emerging issue requiring attention. Its inclusion in the Platform for Action spurred the growth of a global women's peace movement. (2004: 13)

Thus it is possible to trace the roots of the NGO WG back through decades of feminist theorizing and activism. Following the conference in Beijing, it was argued that 'realization of the potential we viewed ... requires vigorous leadership and a willingness to engage in open and often difficult political dialogue across many differences that tend to divide women' (Bunch and Fried 1996: 204). This book details the ways in which the NGO WG on Women, Peace and Security responded to that challenge and were instrumental in the production of UNSCR 1325. During the period in which Bangladesh held the Security Council presidency, which will be discussed in more detail below, the Women and Armed Conflict caucus liaised with the Commission on the Status of Women (CSW) regarding 'obstacles to implementing the chapter of the Beijing Platform for Action ... devoted to women and armed conflict' (Hill et al. 2003: 1256). The caucus made a series of recommendations to the Security Council under the auspices of a Special Session on women, and once the negotiations with the CSW came to an end, the NGO Working Group on Women, Peace and Security was formed from the group of NGOs that were involved in the caucus (Hill et al. 2003: 1257–8).

The NGO WG, in its own words, 'was formed in May 2000 to successfully advocate for a UN Security Council Resolution on women, peace and security' (NGO WG 2005). It agreed 'to pursue two recommendations – to encourage women's participation in peace agreements and to push for the convening of a special session of the Security Council' that would eventually lead to the adoption of UNSCR 1325 (Hill et al. 2003: 1258). The strategies of the NGO WG were many and various:

> Members of the coalition lobbied and debated with every Security Council member. They created a list of experts and NGOs that would speak to the issues in the Security Council. They compiled packets of relevant documents with summaries and hand-delivered them to all Security Council members, and undertook media strategy to maximise attention on this issue. (Poehlman-Doumbouya and Hill 2001)

The NGOs involved in the NGO WG were the Women's International League for Peace and Freedom (WILPF), Amnesty International (AI), International Alert (IA), the Women's Commission for Refugee Women and Children (WCRWC) and the Hague Appeal for Peace (HAP). More detailed discussion of the membership of the NGO WG, and the productive power of the discursive terrain of the institution, is undertaken in the following section.

ANALYSING THE NGO WG ON WOMEN, PEACE AND SECURITY

Since October 2000, the membership of the NGO WG on Women, Peace and Security has increased enormously. However, for the purposes of this investigation, 'the membership' includes only those NGOs involved with the Working Group at the time that UNSCR 1325 was produced – those listed at the end of the previous section.[8] A brief investigation of the five founding members of the NGO WG illustrates the priority afforded by all five organizations to peacebuilding and the protection of human rights. The HAP explicitly links these two issue areas, stating that the organization is 'dedicated to the abolition of war and making peace a human right' (2005), as does IA, arguing that 'the denial of human rights often [leads] to internal armed conflicts which in turn undermine[s] efforts to protect individual and collective human rights and to promote sustainable development' (IA 2006). IA was founded 'in 1985 by a group of human rights advocates led by the former Secretary-General of Amnesty International ... in response to growing concerns expressed by those working in international development agencies, human rights organizations and those involved in the issues of ethnic conflict and genocide' (IA 2006), so the continuity demonstrated between IA and AI is not entirely unexpected.

As part of its mandates, the Women's Commission for Refugee Women and Children states that the organization campaigns with and on behalf of displaced 'women and children', arguing that 'their empowerment is the surest route to the greater well-being of all forcibly displaced people' (2005). This links with the emphasis put on 'sustainable human development' by IA, and also with the WILPF's goal of 'enhanc[ing] environmentally sustainable development' (2005). The performative function of organizing discourse on peace and security around the signifier of 'development' is explored more comprehensively in the final section of this chapter.[9] For the current purposes, it illustrates the comparable values propounded by each of the founding members of the NGO WG on Women, Peace and Security. Another key value is the potential of civil society activism to effect change at the state and supra-state level, suggested by Amnesty International's declaration of independence from 'any government, political ideology, economic interest or religion' (2005); WCRWC's commitment to facilitating communications from the community level to the highest offices of governments and international organizations and WILPF's aim of 'support[ing] the civil society to democratise the United Nations system' (2005). Again, the implications of this are further discussed below.

The first text I analyse in this section is the letter from the NGO WG to UN Security Council members dated 23 October 2000. In brief, the letter outlines the hopes of the NGO WG, celebrates the forthcoming Arria formula meeting, and offers to the Security Council a 'comprehensive pack of materials' (NGO WG 2000a) relating to the issue of women, peace and security. The Open Session is lauded as a 'historic event and a significant opportunity to move the agenda forward' (2000a), suggesting that there was a pre-existing agenda and that the actions of the Namibian presidency offered an opportunity to move the agenda in ways that the NGO WG would find acceptable. The pre-existing agenda is attested to not only by the body of theory and activism cited in the section above, but also in the section that follows, in which I contextualize the efforts of the UN Security Council relating to the issue of women, peace and security.

The language of the letter is appropriately formal and courteous, given that the NGO WG does not enjoy any official powers of consultation with the Security Council. Furthermore, the NGO WG states its requests in quiescent terms: 'The NGO Working Group … is hoping that the Open Session results in' certain measures and 'would like to see a commitment to follow up the outcomes of the Open Session'. In conclusion, the letter states that the Group is 'very much looking forward … [to] establishing a dialogue with you [the Security Council] on this matter' (NGO WG 2000a). Phrasing the requests in this way is testament to a recognition not only that the UN Security Council enjoys a degree of institutional power and privilege that the NGO WG does not, but also that, even if the Open Session yields spectacular results, the issue of women, peace and security will be ongoing.

The first of the NGO WG's hopes is that 'gender issues' will be 'fully mainstreamed into the actions and operations resulting from the Council's decisions' (NGO WG 2000a). While the language of 'mainstreaming' is discussed more fully in Chapter 5, the significance of asking that 'the actions and operations' of the UN Security Council be undertaken with a gendered sensitivity is great. Previous to the historic moment documented in the texts under analysis here, the UNSC 'remained tenaciously state-centred, militaristic and male-dominated' (Otto 2004: 1). Therefore, the NGO WG requesting that the Council approach issues of peace and security with an awareness of gendered differences and experiences can be read as a potentially radical demand.

The two further suggestions that the NGO WG details in its letter represent much more conventional conceptualizations of gender. The Security Council is asked 'to ensure that women play a greater role, at all levels, in peace support operations, conflict prevention and peace building' and to 'afford women and girls greater protection and assistance in situations of armed conflict' (NGO WG 2000a). These constructions relate directly to the representations of gender in UNSCR 1325, discussed in Chapter 5, where 'women' are (re)produced through the text as able to participate and represent in peace-building and conflict resolution, but also needing protection during conflict (UNSC 2000a: Preamble, Articles 1–5, 8, 10).

Considering the three results that the NGO WG hoped to achieve as a package of reform, it is clear from the analysis in the previous two chapters of this project that its hopes were, to an extent, realized. One of the Working Group's recommendations was that the Open Session be followed up 'with a report on a) women's role in peace building and b) humanitarian issues and protection of women during peacekeeping and post conflict peace support operations' (NGO WG 2000a). As is clear from my research, which began with an analysis of the Reports of the UN Secretary-General (2004a; 2002a), these follow-up reports were indeed undertaken – in fact, mandated in the UNSC Resolution that resulted from the Open Session and other negotiations. Furthermore, the Security Council was offered 'the opportunity to enter into dialogue with NGOs who are working directly with women and girls affected by armed conflict' (NGO WG 2000a), and the institution seems to have availed itself of this opportunity (Pietilä 2002: 96–8; Hill 2002: 29–30).

However, given that the heading of the letter reads 'United Nations Security Council Open Session on Women, Peace and Security', it is not entirely surprising that the subject of the discussion is women rather than gender. The reforms, with the exception of the attention called to the mainstreaming of 'gender issues', focus on 'women and girls' and the gendered issues are represented as women's issues: 'women's role in peace building', the 'protection of women' and 'women and girls affected by armed conflict' (NGO WG 2000a). This assumed translatability of women to gender is not theorized or explained within the document, and reflects a concern on the part of the NGO WG for recognition of both the 'positive role of women' and the need for their protection (2000a).

The statement read out by representatives of the NGO WG at the Arria formula meeting is faithful to these constructions of gender. The statement notes that 'women are neither simply victims, nor are they passive in the face of war. Even in the worst and most dangerous of circumstances, women have shown their courage and leadership' (NGO WG 2000b: 2). Neither the statement nor the letter discussed above represent women as perpetrators of violence. Women's agency, counterposed to the assumption of passivity that the NGO statement argues against, is fixed in these documents as benign, a construction that is highly problematic (Moser and Clark 2001; El Jack 2003).

In the statement produced for the Arria formula meeting, the link between conflict and violence is made explicit: 'women' are represented as 'women victims of violent conflict'. Moreover, 'violence against women' is articulated as 'a strategic weapon of war ... a method of ethnic cleansing and an element of genocide' (NGO WG 2000b: 1). While the construction of 'violence against women' reproduced in this document goes beyond that discussed in Chapter 3, women are still fixed in this narrative as eternal victims of violence. Even the agency discussed above is not secure. Forms of discursive and physical violence contribute to 'women's voices and their experiences [being] excluded and marginalized' from 'peace deals and high level negotiations' (NGO WG 2000b: 3). While these violences may be empirically verifiable, their reproduction in the NGO statement assigns women 'a certain type of agency and identity, namely, women are the objects of protective action and they occupy mainly the civilian space' (Väyrynen 2004: 137).

The positioning of 'women and civil society', run together in the text to form a discursive linkage, is articulated as a locus of benevolent agency (NGO WG 2000b: 4). This draws on not only the constructions of gender discussed above, but also on theorizing of state/civil society negotiations that situates civil society as a domain apart from the state and therefore unimpeded by (state) political considerations (see, inter alia, Lipschutz 1992; Baker 2000). Within this discourse, 'civil society' represents 'a bottom-up vision of civilising world order. It represents a normative theory of "human governance" which is grounded in the existence of a multiplicity of "communities of fate" and social movements, as opposed to the individualism and appeals to rational self-interest of neo-liberalism' (Held and McGrew 1998: 241).

The concept of civil society is ideologically and normatively loaded with implications of its civilized nature and its social form, and, as Jan Aart Scholte argues, 'carries connotations of civility and virtue' (2001: 19) that function to secure a place from which to speak that is located firmly on the moral high ground. Stephen Hopgood, for example, is openly sceptical concerning the emergence of 'global civil society', perceiving this theoretical construct to be, *contra* David Held and Anthony McGrew, intimately related to the triumph of a neoliberal world order (2000: 25). These contestations over the construction of civil society draw attention to just how important it is to question the representation of 'women and civil society' in the NGO statement, not least because running the two together doubles the impact of the absenting of a formal political domain.

The press statement that was released following the Arria formula meeting in part reproduces the statement made at the meeting itself (NGO WG 2000c). However, as it is a public document presented to world media, it is worthy of analytical attention in its own right. In the statement, the NGO representative describes 'women's groups and *local* organizations that *struggle* every day to prevent war' (NGO WG 2000c, emphasis added). This construction functions not only to reproduce a distinction between the international as a zone of peace and the domestic as a zone of conflict (Väyrynen 2004: 130–131), but also to reaffirm the construction of women's agency articulated in the two documents discussed previously, as connoted by the description of ongoing 'struggle'.

The direct and indirect violences against women presented in the statement to the Arria formula meeting are reproduced in the press statement, and the NGO WG condemns those who act as 'silent witnesses to these abuses', arguing that '[a] culture of silence and impunity prevails' (NGO WG 2000c). This representation draws heavily on the spatial metaphors employed in theory and activism challenging the problem of domestic violence; part of the framing of domestic violence as a public policy issue was to challenge the notion that such violence is legitimate because it occurs behind the closed doors of the private household (see, inter alia, Moore 2003; Youngs 2003). It also serves as an indictment of the 'international community', which had, thus far, not acted as vocal witness to the abuses through their failure to put the issue of women, peace and security on the agenda of the UN Security Council.

The 'culture of impunity' is stressed in the press statement (NGO WG 2000c) and functions to remind the audience that the crimes and abuses documented in the statement need not occur. If only there was an internationally binding UNSC Resolution preventing such abuses, 'the plight of women in war zones' would be ameliorated and the women would have 'the protection they need' (NGO WG 2000c). The efforts of the NGO Working Group on Women, Peace and Security are not adequately represented in this construction. The NGO WG reports that they 'asked the Security Council to ensure women have equal representation … [and] that they consider the plight of women' (2000c). These tentative terms do not adequately describe what was a historic and transformative campaign on the part of the NGO WG.

As evidenced in this section, the NGO WG has a strong claim to author-ity over the Resolution, and, through its continued political presence,[10] the Working Group has been able to transform decades of theorizing and activism into concrete achievements in the issue area of women, peace and security. However, the United Nations maintains a degree of institutional control over the Resolution, and the Security Council, as the organization through which the Resolution became binding international law, must be investigated. In the following sections I offer a contextualizing analysis of the UN Security Council, going on to read three keys texts that are cited in UNSCR 1325 as foundational to the United Nations' narrative of production of the Resolution.

CONTEXTUALIZING THE UNITED NATIONS SECURITY COUNCIL

The United Nations is unique among international organizations, given that it has near-universal membership and a wide remit of concerns and functioning bodies. Founded in San Francisco in October 1945 with 51 original members, the membership of the UN increased over the years to reach 192 member states in 2006 (UN 2008a). Aiming 'to save succeeding generations from the scourge of war', among other equally worthy goals, the United Nations was fundamentally an institution that embodied the ideals of the member-states at that time. From the ashes of the Covenant of the League of Nations,[11] founded to 'to promote international co-operation and to achieve international peace and security' (League of Nations 1924), it was hoped that the United Nations would rise to succeed where the League had failed, and the United Nations has indeed realized some remarkable goals. Adjusting the negotiation process and adhering as far as possible to a regulative democratic ideal in order to include the 140 new member-states that have joined the organization over the past decades has doubtless not been easy. As the Commission on Global Governance (CoGG) notes, '[g]iven that the United Nations system was so hobbled from the outset, it is remarkable that it accomplished so much in so many areas of international co-operation' (CoGG 1995: 231).

Exploring the ways in which the United Nations system was 'hobbled from the outset' is not the aim of this section. The aim, rather, is to explore the construction, role and conduct of the UN Security Council as one element of the UN system. Writing as early as 1966, Inis Claude commented that '[w]hile the voice of the United Nations may not be the authentic voice of mankind [*sic*], it is clearly the best available facsimile thereof' (Claude 1966: 372). Part of the legitimacy afforded to the United Nations system that Claude explores in his work draws on the performances of the UNSC. The Security Council has come to be seen as one of the most high-functioning bodies of the United Nations system and, since the end of the Cold War in particular, has 'fundamentally altered the ways in which many of us see the relationship between state and citizen the world over' (Malone 2000: 21).

As mentioned above, it is not analytically tenable to treat the United Nations as a monolithic organization. However, the foundational principles laid down in the Charter in 1945 have undoubtedly impacted on the processes and practices of organizations within the system. For example, in Article 24.1 of the Charter, 'Members [of the United Nations] confer on the Security Council primary responsibility for the maintenance of international peace and security, and agree that in carrying out its duties under this responsibility the Security Council acts on their behalf' (UN 1945: Article 24.1). Signatories of the Charter agree to be bound by the principles and procedures therein, and Resolutions passed by the UNSC have the status of international law. The Security Council, therefore, enjoys considerable institutional and legislative powers.

Since the end of the Cold War, 'the role of the Security Council not only in conferring legitimacy on certain forms of international intervention, but also in providing a mechanism for burden-sharing of expenses and risk, in an era averse to both, [has] once again prov[ed] indispensable' (Malone 2000: 40). The veto power of the five permanent members (P5) of the Security Council (China, France, the Russian Federation [formerly USSR], UK, USA) apparently dead-locked voting during the Cold War, effectively rendering the Security Council powerless in the face of threats to the international peace and security that it was charged with protecting). However, there was a 'noticeable improvement' in relations among the P5 as the 1980s drew to a close and a new decade began (Malone 2000: 21–3).

The 1990s saw a series of changes in the performance of the UNSC, not only in the number of Resolutions tabled and passed but also in the issue areas with which the UNSC concerned itself (Malone 2000: 22–3; Golberg and Hubert 2001: 223–4). The issue of human rights was given textual priority in the UN Charter in 1945: the second sentence of the Preamble announces determina-tion 'to reaffirm faith in fundamental human rights, in the dignity and worth of the human person, in the equal rights of men and women and of nations large and small' (UNSC 1945: Preamble). However, the 1990s was the decade in which the issue of human rights became central to the activities and decision-making of the UNSC (Malone 2000: 28). At the 1992 summit meeting, the first to be held at the level of heads of state and government, the Security Council recognized that 'non-military sources of instability in the economic, social, humanitarian and ecological fields have become threats to peace and security' (UNSC 1992), indicating a significant shift in the Council's agenda.

'The image of international regulation projected by the Charter ... was one of "states still jealously sovereign", but linked together now in a "myriad of relations"' (Cassese cited in Held et al. 1999: 63). However, various Resolutions adopted by the UNSC[12] mandating UN action in conflicts throughout the 1990s drew attention to the negotiability of sovereignty on the grounds of 'responsibility as a necessary additional component ... in addition to the three traditional characteristics of statehood (territory, people and authority)' (Weiss 2000: 800). This 'responsibility' was conceived of largely as a responsibility to protect the citizens of a given state, and the performance of the UNSC in the 1990s seemed to suggest that the 'international community' was willing to intervene in sovereign states when the states themselves were failing to provide adequate protection. In this way, '[t]he Council's decisions in the 1990s proved highly innovative in shaping the normative framework for international relations and stimulated several radical legal developments at the international level' (Malone 2000: 22–3).

By the time that Canada held the presidency of the UNSC in 1999, the discursive terrain of the Security Council as an institution was such that it was able to combine 'a case-by-case approach with a thematic one' and focus on 'how best to incorporate human security into the council's program of work' (Golberg and Hubert 2001: 224). As discussed in the section that contextualizes the NGO WG, framing policy issues as human security issues, blending as it does the ideological weight of human rights discourse with the strategic implications of security discourse, allowed for alternative performances of security by the UNSC. In addition, it was during the 1990s that NGO involvement with the Security Council became commonplace. 'Council members increasingly met with NGOs on their own and in groups, not only to brief them on recent developments ... but also to seek their input' (Malone 2000: 33).

At the 4,100th meeting of the UNSC in March 2000, the president of the Security Council reinforced this beneficial arrangement and applauded the role of NGOs in providing 'humanitarian assistance and alleviating the impact of humanitarian crises' (UNSC 2000c). Furthermore, the Security Council reaffirmed its commitment to a broadly conceived notion of 'humanitarian issues', stating that

> The Security Council recognizes the importance of the humanitarian dimension to the maintenance of international peace and security and to its consideration of humanitarian issues relating to the protection of all civilians and other non-combatants in situations of armed conflict. (UNSC 2000c)

Resolutions 1265 and 1296, as discussed in Chapter 4, were central to the foundations of UNSCR 1325. 'There is now general agreement among members that the safety of civilians in times of war is a central, rather than tangential, concern of the UN Security Council' (Golberg and Hubert 2001: 228). The UN Secretary-General produced Reports in 2000 addressing not only the issue of children and armed conflict (UNSC 2000d) but also the role of the UN during periods of disarmament, demobilization and reintegration (UNSC 2000e). Both of these Reports focus in part on the importance of displaying a gendered sensitivity to the issues of conflict and post-conflict reconstruction (UNSC 2000d: Articles 34–37; UNSC 2000e: Articles 7, 22, 53, 77, 93–4).

Later in 2000, the Secretary-General of the United Nations made a statement to the Security Council at the opening of a meeting on women, peace and security, arguing that the contribution of women to conflict resolution processes and peace-building was 'severely under-valued' and that women are 'often better equipped than men to prevent or resolve' conflict (UN 2000). This meeting took place in October 2000. UNSC Resolution 1325 was adopted on 31 October 2000.

ANALYSING THE UNITED NATIONS SECURITY COUNCIL

As discussed above, the UN Security Council enjoys considerable institutional privilege within the United Nations system. In part due to the historic foundations of the United Nations, '[t]he Security Council has primary responsibility under the Charter for the maintenance of international peace and security. It is so organised as to be able to function continuously, and a representative of each of its members must be present at all times at United Nations headquarters' (UN 2008b). As the Charter is cited not only in UNSCR 1325 (UNSC 2000a: Preamble) but also in the ways in which the Security Council represents itself on its homepages, the appropriate section of the Charter, Chapters II–VII, is the first of the texts I analyse in this section.

Membership of the United Nations since 1945, when the UN Charter was signed, has been dependent on recommendation from the Security Council. While the General Assembly, a nominally democratic forum in which member states each have a vote and recommendations require a two-thirds majority (UN 1945: Articles 18.1–18.2), decides on the result of an application, the application is only brought forward 'upon the recommendation of the Security Council' (Article 4.1). Similarly, membership privileges may be suspended or member states expelled according to the directives of the UNSC (Articles 5–6). Thus, although the Security Council is one of six principal organs of the United Nations systems established at its inception, the institutional power it wields is considerable.[13]

The use of the verb 'shall' throughout the Charter is suggestive of the purpose of the document: while it forms binding international law upon signing and ratification (UN 1945: Article 110), the terms of this law are expressed in the future tense. Interestingly, the functions and powers of the General Assembly (Articles 10–17) are predominantly articulated using the verb 'may', for example, '[t]he General Assembly may discuss any questions or any matters within the scope of the present Charter' (Article 10).[14] This is contrary to the explication of the functions and powers of the Security Council (Articles 24–26), which insist that 'the Security Council shall act in accordance with the Purposes and Principles of the United Nations' (Article 24.2). Furthermore, and most indicative of the privilege of the Security Council, is Article 25, which states that '[t]he Members of the United Nations agree to accept and carry out the decisions of the Security Council in accordance with the present Charter' (Article 25).

The powers of the Security Council are wide-ranging. The implications for the 'international community' of signing and ratifying a Charter that provides for the Security Council to 'adopt its own rules of procedure' (UN 1945: Article 30) and for member states to be consulted 'whenever the latter [the UNSC] considers that the interests of that Member are specially affected' (Article 31) are huge. The extreme centralization of such a variety of powers is in part what has led to the continued vocalization of calls for Security Council reform.[15] As Ted Galen Carpenter argues, 'throughout the history of the UN, the preference has clearly been for stability even when the results have been manifestly unjust.... The veto power exercised by the five permanent members of the Security Council ensures ... that they will never be subject to UN-sanctioned coercive measures' (1997: 20).

The phraseology of the UN Charter, particularly the Articles that dictate the conduct of the Security Council, demonstrates just how remarkable an achievement it was to successfully frame gendered violence as an issue of international security. According to the Charter, there are 'parties to any dispute' (UN 1945: Article 33) and '[a]ny Member of the United Nations ... *or any state*' may be 'party to a dispute' (Article 32, emphasis added). This demonstrates a state-centric conceptualization not only of conflict but also of security, and puts the problem-solving power firmly in the hands of the UN Security Council:

> The Security Council may investigate any dispute, or any situation which might lead to international friction or give rise to a dispute, in order to determine whether the continuance of the dispute or situation is likely to endanger the maintenance of international peace and security. (UN 1945: Article 34)

With this in mind, investigating the procedural rules of the UNSC is necessary to evaluate just how it became possible for the Security Council to recognize the claims made by the NGO WG as valid.

The Rules of Procedure (UN 1983), most recently amended in December 1982, provide the UNSC with guidance concerning all aspects of its functioning as a UN organization. Again, the Rules are articulated in the future tense, predominantly using the verb 'shall'. The UNSC is required to meet at least once every fourteen days, and meetings can be called by the President or 'at the request of any member of the Security Council' (UN 1983: Rules 1–2). Again, this demonstrates how much institutional capacity the Security Council has to determine the agenda of issues of international peace and security. Matters for discussion are filtered through the Secretary-General but 'approved by the President of the Security Council' (UN 1983: Rule 7), and, in conjunction with the permanent status on the Council of the P5, this effectively ensures that six representatives, five of whom are unchanging, have enormous control over the agenda.

Perhaps somewhat unsurprisingly, the gendered pronoun 'he' is mentioned in the section of the Rules governing representation and credentials:

Each member of the Security Council shall be represented at the meetings of the Security Council by an accredited representative. The credentials of a representative ... shall be communicated to the Secretary-General ... before he takes his seat on the Security Council. (UN 1983: Rule 13)

Furthermore, the president of the Security Council is articulated as male in the document, and is expected to absent himself from any discussions in which he might have a conflict of interest (UN 1983: Rule 20). The UN Secretary-General is expected to act in the capacity of Secretariat for the UNSC, although *he* too may 'authorize a deputy to act in his place at meetings of the Security Council' (Rule 21). Although such close attention to the representation of gendered subjects in the Rules may seem unwarranted, it is precisely the focus of this investigation: the representations of subjects and objects enable certain ways of thinking about and acting on these constructions.

As discussed above, membership of the United Nations organization is dependent on the recommendation of the UNSC. The recommendation is further dependent on 'the applicant [being] a peace-loving State' (UN 1983: Rule 60). This Rule effectively means that the UNSC has veto power over the possibility of expanding membership of the United Nations organization. Potentially, then, the General Assembly, functioning on a one-nation, one-vote remit, could be constructed according to the whims of the Security Council. This has important implications for the democratic credentials of the United Nations and its ability to represent 'we, the people'.

Consultation with 'the people', or, more specifically, with 'private individuals and non-governmental bodies' (UN 1983: Appendix), is also governed by the Rules. However, Appendix A addresses only the circulation of communications to members of the Security Council (Appendix). There is no provision in the Rules that governs the decision of the Security Council regarding which 'individuals and non-governmental bodies' could or should be consulted. Despite this lack of formal provision, since the end of the Cold War and subsequent shifts in the organizing discourses of the UNSC as discussed above, consultation with NGOs became increasingly common. 'NGOs ... increasingly appeared as actors in the policy process that could not be ignored and whose goodwill and support was useful, and at times even essential, to the success of government policies and Council initiatives' (Paul 2004). Eventually, in 1995, the NGO Working Group on the Security Council was founded, and it 'has become an influential forum at the United Nations' (Paul 2001).

Despite strong P5 objections, the Arria formula for meetings between the UNSC and the NGO Working Group was utilized to great effect in April 2000 when, under Canadian presidency, 'Ambassador Peter van Walsum of the Netherlands convened an Arria briefing on "Protection of Civilians in Armed Conflict" ... Five days later, the Council debated the same subject ... and eventually the related Resolution 1296 was adopted' (Paul 2004). As discussed in the preceding section, UNSCR 1296 is closely related to UNSCR 1325, and the successes of the NGO Working Group on Security evidenced in the production of Resolution 1296 opened the Arria formula to NGOs and other issue areas – notably, in this instance, the NGO Working Group on Women, Peace and Security.

However, previous even to the Arria meeting in April, the UNSC, under the presidency of Bangladesh, made a historic statement on the occasion of International Women's Day. In this statement to the attendant media, 'members of the Security Council recognize[d] that peace is inextricably linked with equality between women and men'. NGO involvement with issues under the remit of the Security Council was also celebrated in the statement, as 'members welcome[d] the review of the Fourth World Conference on Women as an essential element in achieving this goal' (UNSC 2000c). As discussed previously, the conference at Beijing involved more NGOs than any other World Conference, and was instrumental in forging the agenda for the NGO WG on Women, Peace and Security.

The conceptualization of gender in the press statement is a liberal one. The key articulations include 'equality', adequate representation, 'equal access and full participation', and political and economic empowerment (UNSC 2000c). Underpinning these constructions is a commitment to a liberal democratic ideal, and this conceptualization of gender is not incompatible with either a discourse of security that focuses on 'international' or 'human' security, nor is it incompatible with research on 'gender violence'. Both of these discourses construct a liberal individual as their subject. Although the press statement represents gendered violence as 'violence against women', this is represented as corollary to 'violation of the human rights of women' (UNSC 2000c), where human rights are themselves an articulation of liberal values.

The obligations of the 'international community' are documented in the press statement: 'all concerned' must 'refrain from human rights abuses in conflict situations' and those responsible must be prosecuted (UNSC 2000c). Although the statement constructs the subject of women as what is by now a familiar profile of peace-maker/victim, and implicit in the statement is the notion that the UNSC can and should *help* women to fulfil their potential: 'the importance of promoting an active and visible policy of mainstreaming a gender perspective into all policies and programmes while addressing armed or other conflicts' is stressed (UNSC 2000c). The disparity between the 'women' and the 'gender perspective' is never clearly articulated; indeed, it is a function of the liberal framework that gender is synonymous with sex difference.

It is, however, the final sentence referring to 'a gender perspective', which allows the greatest potential for radical reform. In the following section I draw together the arguments I have outlined in this chapter, reflecting on the implications of these arguments for the construction of UNSCR 1325 and analysing further the potentialities offered by the narratives of production explored here. The intention of this chapter is not to evaluate 'the truth' of the production of UNSCR 1325, but rather to explore the ways in which the two institutions represent their involvement with the process of production. However, as the following section indicates, the potentialities enabled by the discursive terrains of the institutions not only enabled the production of the Resolution, but also limited it in several important ways.

CHALLENGING THE NARRATIVES OF PRODUCTION: CONCLUSIONS

Reading the two narratives of production in tandem, it is possible to identify some organizational logics common to both narratives. Both narratives construct particular representations of governance, peace-building and development, and these representations are explored in turn below. In addition, I argue in this section that both narratives function to (re)produce a conventional, liberal 'Westphalian' narrative of sovereignty, largely by its representation as an absent presence. In short, by drawing out the commonalities and differences in the two narratives of production, I aim to demonstrate that, despite significant differences in institutional power and internal organization between the two sites of power under consideration, the dominant logics in the discourses of gender violence and international security issuing from these sites are compatible. It is these compatibilities that lead to both the successes and the shortcomings of UNSCR 1325 by delimiting the boundaries of possibility of the Resolution and its implementation.

The NGO WG on Women, Peace and Security is explicit, by virtue of its naming as well as its activities, about the need to engage with institutions of governance even without the institutional backing of a state. Theorizing global governance entails the rigorous consideration of core concepts of IR, including sovereignty, interdependence and democracy, to which I return below. An orthodoxy rooted in the theoretical synthesis of neorealism and neoliberalism still exists in international relations, both as academic discipline and policy practice,[16] and, in this context, global governance can be seen as the construction of international institutions that would further the efforts of powerful states to pursue their interests (see, inter alia, Mearsheimer 1995; Keohane and Martin 1995). A normatively preferable alternative is provided by James Rosenau's conception of global governance, where he suggests that 'governance refers to activities backed by shared goals ... [and] ... is a system of rule that works only if it is accepted by the majority' (1992: 4), and it is this conceptualization of global governance represented in the narrative issuing from the NGO WG. The emphasis put on collective goals and inclusivity, discussed above, by the NGO WG suggests that it seeks to intervene in mechanisms of 'global governance' – in this case, the United Nations – on behalf of a constituency that is currently un(der)represented.

However, this is by no means an unproblematic goal. Keohane suggests that the benefits of effective organs of global governance 'will accrue not only to governments but to transnational corporations and professional societies, and to some workers as well' (1995: 183). I find this view extremely difficult for many reasons, not least because it reinscribes an unsustainable division between the 'rich democracies' that are constructed as peaceful and interdependent and the 'zones of conflict' that are seen as their implicit corollary (Keohane 1995: 180), which is discussed further below, but also because it seems to suggests that constructing effective governance for the benefit of these privileged few is both politically desirable and ethically unproblematic. Although the NGO WG, through its emphasis on participation and representation, fosters an image of collective action that is opposed to the notion that the existence of a democratic deficit at either the state or the supra-state level is in any way tenable, the very simple question 'who speaks?' in this situation is an important one.[17] Deniz Kandiyoti points out that '[a]s donors, UN agencies and NGOs compete for their share in the "gender" market, often draining limited local capacity to staff their own projects in the process, there is a risk that local voices (especially non-English speaking ones) may be drowned out' (2004: 135). This is in part due to the fact that '[m]ost NGO activity at the global level is dominated by representatives from the industrialised countries' (Williams 2003: 85).

In addition to the question 'who speaks?', the question of what they are speaking to remains. The two different conceptualizations of global governance outlined above suggest that it is a complicated terrain to negotiate. The narratives issuing from the NGO WG and the UNSC seem to suggest that they share a conceptualization of 'global governance', and that the involvement of 'global civil society' in these mechanisms of governance is seen as fundamentally benign by both parties. Recognizing the NGO WG as an effective agent in the construction of world politics articulated by the United Nations Security Council legitimizes the activities of the NGO WG and also functions to cast the issues of women, peace and security in the light of 'the global' – that is, 'it is now increasingly recognized that ... processes of restructuring have a transnational dimension and that their effects on democracy ... *need to be analysed as part of the wider globalization phenomenon*' (Eschle 2002: 320, emphasis added).

If this is the case, then the particular discourse of globality, or globalization, that is (re)produced by the two institutions in question must be analysed. I argue that the discourse of globalization in this case constructs a concept of 'development' as a central signifier, and is best characterized as strongly neoliberal. Craig Murphy expresses this view succinctly: 'If there is a global polity, then certainly its dominant ideology, now, is liberalism, both economic and political' (2000: 792). This is relevant to the constitution of the concepts of gender violence and international security in this discursive context, as the concepts are brought together in these contexts such that they construct a particular notion of state-building and peace-making – otherwise known as 'development'. Mark Rupert argues that the unproblematic reproduction of this globalization discourse underpins and therefore makes possible a 'hegemonic project of liberal globalization' (2000: 42). This is closely tied to the concept of 'global governance', particularly by scholars such as Stephen Gill, who argues that '[d]isciplinary neoliberalism is institutionalized at the macro-level of power in the quasi-legal restructuring of state and international political forms ... [which] can be defined as the political project of attempting to make transnational liberalism ... the sole model for future development' (1995: 412).

At the Beijing conference, the outcome document of which was the Beijing Platform for Action, cited in UNSCR 1325 as part of its documentary heritage, 'there was no alternative voice offered in opposition to the benefits of market policies; the goal was to ensure women's participation in, and access to, the dominant structures of the market' (Chinkin 2000: 247). The participation of women in development – or 'reconstruction' – is prioritized by both institutions (NGO WG 2000a, 2000b, 2000c; UNSC 2000c). However, 'the type of social transformation agenda implicit in global neo-liberal governance, as applied to state-building, has to be interrogated from a gender perspective' (Kandiyoti 2004: 135). The image in which societies torn by conflict are to be rebuilt is decidedly conservative, drawing on concepts of state and sovereignty from the narrative issuing from the UN Security Council (UNSC 1945, 1983), despite the emphasis put on the participation, representation and protection of women (UNSC 2000c).

Problematizing the concept of development that is reproduced through the narratives of production of UNSCR 1325, and also in the Resolution itself, is necessary, particularly given that so much feminist work over recent decades has critiqued the imposition of top-down development and reconstruction programmes, citing their deleterious effects on marginalized sectors of society (see, inter alia, Runyan 2003; Marchand and Runyan 2000). The 'sustainability' of development is centralized in both narratives, but the latter is not opened to critical scrutiny. This in itself is problematic, as development signifies development (read: progression) from an undesirable starting point to a more desirable end point. 'Development', then, is thoroughly bound up with narratives of modernity and civilization:

> During the eighteenth and nineteenth centuries, development was equated with 'civilisation', which was measured by the adoption of institutions and culture.... As Western society became increasingly secular and technical, the notion of Christian 'civilisation' was replaced by a belief in modernity, particularly economic and political development. (Parpart 1995: 224)

Unquestioningly reproducing a dominant discourse of development that has its antecedents in such a belief system, and that draws discursive power from the seemingly inevitable logic of neoliberal globalization discourse, effectively proscribes the possibility of reimagining development and prescribes its unproblematized undertaking.

'International peace and security' (UNSC 2000a: Preamble), on this view, can be achieved by appropriate reconstruction and peace(state)building. This policy prescription echoes theorizing in the discipline of International Relations that argues that 'certain forms of economic and political organization are more conducive than others to peace and stability within communities; that conflict within states has an impact on the international system ... that threatens security' (Newman 2001: 248). Proponents of this thesis, often labelled a 'democratic peace thesis' (see, inter alia, Oneal et al. 1996; Russet 1993; Maoz and Russett 1993; Starr 1992), unreflectively 'presuppose the territorial state – "democracy" refers to a particular set of electoral institutions and political and civil rights within the boundaries of a sovereign state and "war" [the antonym of "peace"] refers to interstate relations' (Barkawi and Laffey 1999: 412). However, even in a piece of international legislation such as UNSCR 1325 that pays due attention to conflict at the intra-state level, the implicit assumption seems to be that resolving the conflict and implementing adequate post-conflict reconstruction programmes will benefit the 'international community', thus (re)producing the 'community' and, further, the 'international' as a functional spatial and conceptual domain.

Returning to a point raised at the beginning of this section, then, UNSCR 1325 begins to take shape not only as an important outcome document of concerted efforts on behalf of the NGO WG and prolonged discussions of the UN Security Council, but also as the discursive reproduction of discourses of (gendered) violence and (international) security, which in turn function to create and perpetuate the divide between 'rich democracies' and 'zones of conflict' (Keohane 1995: 180). Following a conventional narrative of development, the motif of peace(state)building is visible as a process of maturation, where 'zones of conflict' are assisted by the 'international community' to integrate into global mechanisms of production and consumption thereby securing not only the conflicts in question but also the reproduction of a neoliberal world order. Sovereignty is a key organizing logic in these discursive processes, and again is tied to the notion that conflict 'zones', or 'undeveloped' countries, are not sufficiently able to function as full members of the 'international community' – a kind of 'sovereignty by numbers' approach, where the numbers in question are the indices used to measure a state's incorporation into global political economic processes.[18]

The concluding chapter that follows reflects on these issues more fully. Among other concerns, I argue that it is important to recognize that the 'global polity' – or 'international community', of which the NGO WG is a part – and the globalized subject are constructed in part through the discourses under investigation here. These discourses function to (re)produce these subjects and also construct the interests of these subjects, and therefore constitute social/political order in a certain way, through the processes of predication, subject positioning and articulation that I have identified. Thus, the discourses that this project has interrogated are produced by the institutions discussed in this chapter, but are also productive of them – and, importantly, productive of a particular configuration of social/political 'reality'.

7 | CONCLUSIONS

At the outset of this study, I sought to explore the ways in which discourses of (international) security and (gender) violence were constituted, and with what effect, through the analysis of United Nations Security Council Resolution 1325. After mapping the contours of competing discourses of security and violence, in Chapter 3, I turned to Resolution 1325 and related documentation to identify the conceptualizations of security and violence that are produced by and productive of the Resolution and have become sedimented in the evaluative framework that the United Nations uses to measure the efficacy of the implementation of the Resolution. An exploration of the discursive terrain of the institutions that claim author-ity over the Resolution highlighted particular configurations of sovereignty, community, development and subjectivity that organized the production of the Resolution.

In this chapter, I draw together the strands of argument developed in the chapters above, and also reflect on the implications of the study for future policy on 'women and peace and security' and future academic research on security and violence more broadly. In the first section, I contextualize my findings from the previous chapters through a short analysis of other relevant documentation relating to Resolution 1325, including the Secretary-General's Report of October 2005, which details a 'system-wide action plan on the implementation of Security Council resolution 1325' (UNSC 2005: 3). Through this analysis, I detail the policy implications of the research I have undertaken here. The theoretical and conceptual implications are detailed in sections two and three of this chapter, in which I draw conclusions about the constitution of political community and political subjectivity. Focusing on the violent reproduction of the international and of gender allows an insight into these concepts, both of which are central to IR/ir. The final section returns to the question of UNSCR 1325 and the ways in which the document is inherently binding, both legally and philosophically, and the implications of this for the construction of social/political reality.

'HOW DOES A POLICY MEAN?'[1]

The documents that I discuss in this section are intended to give a temporal context to the conclusions I offer regarding the constitution of violence and security in Resolution 1325. Published in the years following the unanimous adoption of the Resolution, the document set comprises three statements by the President of the Security Council (UNSC 2001, 2002b, 2004b) and the 2005 Report of the Secretary-General on Women and Peace and Security. As discussed in Chapters 4, 5 and 6, Resolution 1325 and associated documents are both produced by and productive of particular conceptualizations of (international) security and (gender) violence. It is therefore somewhat unsurprising that the documents under analysis here evidence the same concepts organized in much the same way.

Over the four-year period in question, 2000–2004, the conceptual constitution of security and violence in the documents issuing from the United Nations Security Council is organized around the themes of participation, representation and integration. The presidential statements, in particular, evidence consistent articulation of the primary issue concerning 'women and peace and security' as one of 'the role of women in decision-making with regard to conflict' (UNSC 2001), 'the appointment of women as special representatives and envoys' (UNSC 2002b) and 'the equal participation of women in efforts to build sustainable peace and security' (UNSC 2004b). The concept of representation articulated in these statements, similar to that discussed in Chapter 4 with reference to Resolution 1325, relies on the notion that increasing numbers of women in decision-making roles in formal political arenas will have a positive impact on peace-building and post-conflict reconstruction.

However, this liberal notion (re)produces the subject of 'women' as a homogenous group whose interests are *essentially* peaceful and socially beneficial. There is mention of 'the vital role of women in promoting peace, particularly in preserving social order and educating for peace' (UNSC 2002b), suggesting that there is something about 'womanhood' that is intrinsically related to peace and preservation of the 'social order'. As discussed previously, this is neither empirically verifiable nor an unproblematic way in which to represent 'women' in such an important set of policy documents. This representation, however, is reproduced in the presidential statement of 2004, in which '[t]he Security Council reaffirms the important role of women in the prevention of conflict' (UNSC 2004b). Furthermore, in this later statement, the 'full participation of women' is linked to 'the incorporation of a gender perspective' (UNSC 2004b), demonstrating a conflation of 'women' and 'gender' that I have problematized more fully in the preceding chapters.

The key theme of integration is the central way in which the document set (re)produces the concept of gender as 'lazily synonymous with "women"' (Carver 1996: 18). That is, in all four documents under consideration here, mention is made of 'integration' and 'inclusion' of both 'gender' and 'women', where the two nouns are often used interchangeably. In 2001, the president of the Security Council affirmed a commitment to 'gender mainstreaming through the United Nations peacekeeping missions and on other aspects relating to women and girls', as well as the 'inclu[sion of] women in the negotiations and implementation of peace accords' (UNSC 2001). Similarly, in 2002, the president's statement notes that the Security Council 'undertakes to integrate gender perspectives into all standard operating procedures, manuals and other guidance materials' (UNSC 2002b). By 2004, 'mainstreaming', 'integration', 'inclusion' and 'incorporation' are mentioned no fewer than seven times in four paragraphs (UNSC 2004b). One of the most noteworthy aspects of these representations is the way in which participation and representation of *women* is assumed to naturally precede attention to *gender*.

'[T]he incorporation of a gender perspective in all conflict prevention work' (UNSC 2004b) and the preparation of 'a framework for the system-wide cooperation ... for the full implementation of resolution 1325' (UNSC 2005) are, indisputably, more beneficial to the constitution of social/political order than is assuming that feminist analyses have nothing to say about conflict prevention. However, for the reasons discussed in the previous chapters, I do not believe that policy organized around the articulation of concepts of gender violence and international security can ever effect the radical reforms of which it speaks. The discourses of international security and gender violence (re)present and (re)produce liberal, modernist configurations of political community and subjectivity. The 'integration' of gender is represented as synonymous with the 'integration' of women, and, furthermore, endorsing the 'integration' of gender suggests that conflict prevention policy, DDR[2] programmes, peacekeeping operations and peace(state)building processes are not always already gendered.

The 2005 Secretary-General's Report outlines twelve areas of action that structure the 'system-wide' plan. Of these twelve, one refers to 'preventing and responding to gender-based violence in armed conflict' and another simply to 'gender balance' (UNSC 2005: 10). This signifier of balance, tied as it is to the issues of participation and representation discussed above, equates the recognition of gendered politics and organizational logics with numerical equality (UNSC 2005: Annex, Section I.1). In turn, the Report concludes with a demand for '*measurable* improvement in the United Nations system's contributions to the empowerment of women in conflict areas' (UNSC 2005: 19, emphasis added). Throughout this study, I have argued that quantifiable indicators may be useful at times, but conceptual organization and the implications of that organization for the constitution of a particular social/political order cannot be so measured.

Furthermore, the conceptual organization of the Resolution and related documents has become sedimented into the evaluative framework for the implementation of the Resolution: 'Resolution 1325 (2000) and the three subsequent presidential statements on women, peace and security constitute important landmarks and provide a framework for action' (UNSC 2005: 5). This effectively leaves the United Nations system trapped within the discursive limitations of its own construction, and precludes the successful implementation of UNSCR 1325. Fidelity to the constitution of heteronormative subjectivities and neoliberal political communities, as discussed below, means that the United Nations system cannot but fail to achieve the transformations of subjectivity and community that are sought in Resolution 1325.

There is more to the state, and the corollary international domain, than security of the sovereign territory. Similarly, there is more to security than can be bound to either that which can be contained within sovereign borders or that which constitutes the 'outside'. There is more to gender than equal participation of 'men' and 'women' in formal and informal political forums. 'Integrating' gender allows for a narrative premissed on the notion that gender is not inherent in the organizational logics of the discursive terrain that constitutes social/political reality, and it does violence to the meanings that can be made of 'gender' in policy documents to bind the concept to bodies. With this in mind, I do not agree that 'ensuring that commitments to gender mainstreaming are actually implemented remains one of the most significant challenges in this area' (Bond and Sherret 2006: 2). This book has endeavoured to demonstrate that understanding the ways in which the conceptual organization of policy documents pre-/proscribe effective policy practice is a significant, and under-theorized, challenge.

In the following two sections, I expand on the analytical innovations underpinning this study, considering the ways in which theorizing the 'violent reproduction of gender' and the 'violent reproduction of the international' can allow for interventions in policy debates but also developments in academic conceptualizations of security and violence. As I have argued above, the dominant conceptualizations of 'gender violence' and 'international security' are an integral part of the problems the United Nations has identified regarding the implementation of UNSCR 1325. Part of what I seek to do here is offer different concepts with which to think effective policy, and I offer the results of my reconceptualization of (international) security and (gender) violence below.

THE VIOLENT REPRODUCTION OF THE INTERNATIONAL

One of the questions that has guided my research queried the ways in which literature on security situated within the discipline of IR conceives of its referent object. Consequently, it is interesting to explore the forms of political authority that are recognized as legitimate by the literature on security and in the documents related to UNSCR 1325. As I have argued above, the constitution of political authority evidenced in Resolution 1325 (re)produces the international as a cooperative and influential domain, positioned above the 'states' in which conflict occurs. I put 'state' in scare quotes as this is a form of political authority valorized by the Resolution through its insistence on appropriate peace-building and decision-making processes in the aftermath of armed conflict (UNSC 2000a: Preamble) but the meaning of 'state' is differentiated through the various spatial tropes deployed in the Resolution. That is, 'states' in which conflict occurs (and therefore 'states' to which the Resolution speaks) are articulated in association with predicates such as 'local' and 'indigenous' (Article 8, 15), whereas 'Member States' are called upon for 'financial, technical and logistical support' and the development of sensitive training programmes (Article 7, 6). The Security Council itself maintains 'primary responsibility' for peace and security in the international domain (Preamble).

With these concerns in mind, it is necessary to question the modalities of state-building approved in documentation associated with Resolution 1325, as this research has indicated that only peace(state)building programmes aimed at producing *appropriate* states will be discursively sanctioned. For example, the 2005 Report of the Secretary-General on Women and Peace and Security details twelve specific areas of action, of which two address peacemaking, peacebuilding and post-conflict reconstruction (UNSC 2005: 10). The image in which states are 'reconstructed', according to the Annex to the Report, again fixes the division between the international as a spatial and conceptual domain and the national level, at which 'local women's groups and civil society organizations' function (Annex B.3). The emphasis is on 'capacity-building' and the implementation of plans that facilitate 'economic and social recovery and sustainable development with particular attention to the needs of war-affected groups who are especially vulnerable' (Annex E.1). Throughout the Annex to the 2005 Report, all branches of the United Nations system, along with the World Bank and other development organizations, are tasked with 'integrating' gender into the blueprints for a successful (read: economically productive) state.

The productive power of UNSCR 1325 and associated frameworks for action to discipline political authority (re)produces the international as a domain of peace that owns the necessary knowledge to 'develop' domestic societies bounded within the confines of the territorial state. Timothy Mitchell refers to these technologies as 'disciplinary', arguing that they

> work within local domains and institutions, entering into particular social processes, breaking them down into separate functions, rearranging the parts, *increasing their efficiency and precision*, and reassembling them into *more productive* and powerful combinations. (1991: 93, emphasis added)

Within the binary logics that organize IR as a discipline, and the practices of relations international, this (re)production of the international constitutes the 'national' as a spatial domain in keeping with the accepted form of political authority recognized by IR as its object of study – the sovereign state, or, at the very least, the state that strives to be sovereign.

Fetishizing the state as a form of political authority in this way precludes the conceptualization of alternative forms of political authority that might deliver the radical reforms of social/political order that the Resolution and associated documents purport to seek. Compatible with a liberal narrative of (international) community and a neoliberal emphasis on bounded individuality and the productivity of so-constituted individuals, this configuration of political authority functions as what Matthew Sparke refers to as 'a hidden handcuffing of democracy: hidden in part because … the disciplinary effect is market mediated; but also because the reforms … slowly clos[e] down the possibilities for democratic governance' (2005: 151).[3] The state is constituted as the legitimate form of political authority, but the international is the repository of knowledge concerning the procedures and practices necessary to achieve and consolidate this authority. This is compatible with Spivak's comment that there exists an 'unspoken assumption [at] the UN that the South is not capable of governing itself' (cited in Bergeron 2001: 1000).

These concerns, regarding the ways in which social/political order is (re)produced through UNSCR 1325, lead to further questions about the centrality of the concept of sovereignty within the discipline of International Relations. Suzanne Bergeron argues that 'the abandonment of state-led national development policies and the adoption of a neoliberal, export-oriented approach ... often marks the decline of national sovereignty' (2001: 987). However, whether or not sovereignty is 'declining' or debates over what sovereignty *means* are of less interest in the context of this study (and for future research) than the ways in which sovereignty *functions* in relations international. That is, when do exercises of sovereign power constitute social/political actions that function to decrease rather than increase violence? Why is it that the myth of the sovereign state continues to hold such sway in the discipline of IR, and why are alternative forms of political authority not recognized in the international domain? These questions are beyond the scope of this book, but are central to the context within which the violent reproduction of the international makes sense within contemporary global politics.

Furthermore, while the form of the 'state' is predetermined by the ways in which the international is (re)produced through UNSCR 1325, the inhabitants of the state are similarly constituted as productive individuals. On this view, 'integrating' gender and 'empowering' women occur within a discursive terrain bounded, in the last instance, by a discourse of neoliberal development and liberal social/political order. In an analysis of World Bank policy on 'women in development', Bergeron argues that

> feminists should recognize and seize the opportunities for challenging the neoliberal and colonial logic of the World Bank opened up by its recent social turn, working within these spaces where appropriate toward the construction of their own alternative agendas. (2003: 415)

In engaging critically with the violent reproduction of the international as enabled in UNSCR 1325 and related documentation, it was never my intention to dismiss entirely the strategic gains achieved through the plans for action and implemented policies. However, it is vital to remember that the logics that organize the United Nations system and related development institutions (re)produce a social/political order that could benefit from sustained critique, for the amelioration of the lives of the 'isolated, disciplined, receptive and industrious political subject[s]' (Mitchell 1991: 93) constituted as inhabitants of the spaces I discuss here.

In short, the subjects discussed in the section below are constituted such that they inhabit state-bound spaces within an international system. The 'international' is conceived as corollary to the sovereign state, according to conventional narratives of sovereignty. Through the dominant discourse of security I discuss in this text, the international is (re)produced as the space of author-ity over the recognition and configuration of political community. In turn, the discursive horizons of possibility prescribed in UNSCR 1325 limit the appropriate form of political community to the liberal, democratic state, which functions to (re)produce the discourses of (international) security and (gender) violence under discussion here by institutionalizing efficiency, equality and empowerment.

THE VIOLENT REPRODUCTION OF GENDER

One of the major issues raised by the 'seizing of opportunity' that Bergeron endorses, as noted above, is the way in which critical discourse can be co-opted by the institution(s) under investigation. Protest rhetoric can be incorporated, bounded and made meaningful within the existing discursive terrain of the institution such that it loses the radical signification and impetus for systemic change (see, *inter alia*, Tétreault and Lipschutz 2005: 169–85; O'Brien et al. 2000: 51–66). In Chapters 5 and 6, I problematized the notion of 'gender mainstreaming', a lynchpin of UN policy on gendering armed conflict. As with any political issue, feminist theorizing is divided over gender mainstreaming, as theorists and activists question whether the strategic gains made are worth the conceptual straitjacketing in policy that conflates gender mainstreaming with the incorporation of women.[4]

Throughout this study, I have been deeply critical of the notion that gender mainstreaming is necessarily revolutionary, and in this section I argue that the emphasis put on gender mainstreaming in UNSCR 1325 is in part productive of the failure to implement the Resolution successfully since its adoption in October 2000. Emilie Hafner-Burton and Mark Pollack list six specific tools for facilitating gender mainstreaming in policy documents, arguing that '[c]eteris paribus, each of these tools should be employed as far "upstream" in the policy process as possible, so that gender issues are incorporated into the planning of policies, and not simply added on as an afterthought' (2002: 353). As I have argued in Chapter 3, 'ceteris' is rarely if ever 'paribus' in life, and this is particularly true of policy that attempts to address 'gender' issues. As gender is assumed to be synonymous with women, and women are in need of specific programmes to integrate them into the political sphere as a result of their lack of previous formal political activity, funds and support for gender mainstreaming are likely to be limited. Furthermore, the very notion of 'integrating' gender precludes the recognition that the policies and action plans are inherently gendered.

I have found the Resolution's emphasis on gender mainstreaming problematic for three reasons. Primarily, the idea that gender can be 'mainstreamed' suggests an inherent teleology of approach: the language of mainstreaming, while insistent on the need for adequate monitoring and evaluation, implies that the process can be finite; that is, it is possible to achieve, completely, the incorporation of 'basic gender concerns' (Hafner-Burton and Pollack 2002: 353). This in turn requires that attention is paid to the meaning of 'gender' within mainstreaming programmes, as it is likely that gender will be used interchangeably with 'sex' and/or 'women'. What occurs as the outcome of teleological gender mainstreaming programmes, then, is the fixing of gender as 'meaning' women and the fixing of the notion that any and all policy can be made attentive to 'gender concerns' without questioning the organizational logics of the policies that may preclude such reform.

Second, gender mainstreaming, as represented in UNSCR 1325 and subsequent action plans, is predicated on a liberal notion of equality of individuals while bracketing open political debate over what this might mean. As Mary Daly argues, 'the debate about gender inequality in society is one that took place much earlier in most countries and has not been updated or revisited in a fundamental way in the service of introducing gender mainstreaming' (2005: 440). In the context of the concerns expressed above regarding the form of political authority legitimized through UNSCR 1325, the constitution of political subjectivity along these liberal lines is also worrisome. As with much critical literature on the ways in which international organizations construct concepts such as 'good governance' and 'participatory reform',[5] in this book I have argued that the spread of liberalism, through the imposition of values taken to be unproblematic by the organizations that espouse them, evidences a particular construction of the way in which it is legitimate to live.

Finally, though relatedly, is my concern with the articulation of gender mainstreaming in policy discourse and academic writings as an implicit 'symbol of modernity': 'gender mainstreaming has become part of the accepted wisdom about what modern gender equality architecture should look like ... [which] serves to shift the orientation of and impetus for policy change away from gender inequality as a policy problem and toward the modernity of policies' (Daly 2005: 441). While I disagree with Daly regarding the ways in which 'gender inequality' constitutes a policy problem,[6] the development of 'states' as articulated in UNSCR 1325 and the Annex to the 2005 Report of the Secretary-General is very much premised on an accepted (neoliberal) vision of a modern state.

As discussed in the preceding section, the (re)production of the international as a spatial and conceptual domain constitutes the modern state as the sole form of legitimate political authority at the national level, and conceives of the most privileged of these states interacting to bring zones of conflict into line with the social/political order propagated by those states inhabiting zones of peace. These processes, and the outcome of these processes, require modern individuals to inhabit the states, which is in part the performative function of gender mainstreaming. Mainstreaming gender ensures that notional equality structures economic, social and political institutions and thereby renders all members of society able, if not willing, to participate in economic, social and political activity. The violence in this account is discursive, in the ways in which gender is articulated in UNSCR 1325, but the appropriate political subject is also constituted by violence, as violence serves an ordering function to maintain a particular conceptualization of gender. This is not to argue that gendered violence is consciously or even necessarily linked to the constitution of a neoliberal political order: rather, neoliberalism requires ordered gendered subjects and therefore benefits from the violent reproduction of gender.

Thus, gendered subjects inhabit certain spaces in the social/political order as configured by the violent reproduction of the international. These subjects are gendered not only by the violences of conflict and post-conflict peace(state)building, but also by the violences inherent in policy that seeks to differentiate subjects along gender lines, thereby constituting the differences to which it claims to attend. The violent reproduction of the international, in both a theoretical and a practical context, is dependent on the violent reproduction of gender, however these violences are manifested. Given the obsession within the discipline of International Relations with theorizing the identity of the sovereign and the practices through which the territorial integrity of the state can be defended, it is surprising that IR was so late to recognize that, '[i]f all experience is gendered, analysis of gender identities is an imperative starting point in the study of political identities and practice' (Peterson 1999: 37). Then again, International Relations fetishizes its own sovereignty as a discipline concerned with the state, and seeks to defend its borders with a vigour equal to that which it demands from its object of analysis, so the failure to take feminist analysis seriously is perhaps unsurprising after all.

The violent reproduction of the international and the violent reproduction of gender, while constituted through different, though overlapping, discourses, share common elements across the conceptualizations of international security and gender violence that I discuss here. These elements are in turn organized around specifically liberal, teleological logics of both the configuration of political community and the constitution of political subjectivity. That is, in both instances the (re)productive practices, seeking improvement on the status quo they characterize, pursue an end-state of fixed duality: in the case of the international, a domestic/international divide; and in the case of gender, differentiated but equal individuals.

Throughout this study, I have consistently problematized the assumption that gender is synonymous with women, and, moreover, that gender signifies need/want/lack. I have argued that 'mainstreaming' such a notion of gender institutionalizes this synonymity and, furthermore, reinforces liberal ideals, premissed as it is on the notion that no form of discrimination should inhibit the freedom of the individual to inhabit the social/political sphere fully. The relationship between the concept of gender and the concept of the international domain and the 'modern' state is such that the configurations of community rely on the constitution of subjectivity, as detailed above, through the discourses of violence and security I have analysed here.

I have attempted to offer new ways in which to think about the concepts of security and violence that order policy documents referring to gender and conflict such as United Nations Security Council Resolution 1325. It is admittedly only a very tentative offering with which I conclude. I emphatically do not wish to inscribe a reconceptualization that will simply reproduce the problems inherent in the concepts as they are currently configured. Any attempt at defining a concept necessarily 'fixes' that concept, at least temporarily, and in the section below I argue that it is precisely this 'fixing' that is part of the problem.

TOWARDS A FEMINIST RECONCEPTUALIZATION OF (INTERNATIONAL) SECURITY AND (GENDER) VIOLENCE

As Spike Peterson and Jacqui True comment, 'our sense of self-identity and security may seem disproportionately threatened by societal challenge to gender ordering' (1998: 17). That is, the performance of gender is immanent in the performance of security and vice versa: both concern issues of ontological cohesion. Taking this on board leads me to the conclusion that perhaps security is best conceived of as referring to ontological rather than existential identity effects. Security, if seen as performative of particular configurations of social/political order, is inherently gendered and inherently related to violence. Violence, on this view, performs an ordering function – not only in the theory/practice of security and the reproduction of the international, but also in the reproduction of gendered subjects.

Butler acknowledges that 'violence is done in the name of preserving western values' (2004: 231); that is, the ordering function that is performed through the violences investigated here, as discussed above, organizes political authority and subjectivity in an image that is in keeping with the values of the powerful, often at the expense of the marginalized. 'Clearly, the west does not author all violence, but it does, upon suffering or anticipating injury, marshal violence to preserve its borders, real or imaginary' (2004: 231). While Butler refers to the violences undertaken in the protection of the sovereign state – violence in the name of security – the preservation of borders is also recognizable in the conceptual domain of the international and in the adherence to a binary materiality of gender.

This adherence is evidenced in the desire to fix the meaning of concepts in ways that are not challenging to the current configuration of social/political order and subjectivity, and is product/productive of 'the exclusionary presuppositions and foundations that shore up discursive practices insofar as those foreclose the heterogeneity, gender, class or race of the subject' (Hanssen 2000: 215). However, the terms used to describe political action and plan future policy could be otherwise imagined. They could 'remain that which is, in the present, never fully owned, but always and only redeployed, twisted, queered from prior usage and in the direction of urgent and expanding political purposes' (Butler 1993: 228). The concepts both produced by and productive of policy could reflect an aversion to essentialism, while recognizing that strategic gains can be made through the temporary binding of identities to bodies and constraining of authority within the confines of the territorial state. This is, in short, an appeal to a politics of both/and rather than either/or.

Writing policy is reliant on the temporal and spatial fixing of identities, however briefly, and in UNSCR 1325 the identities in question were fixed in keeping with the dominant conceptualizations of (gender) violence and (international) security. The academic and non-academic understandings of these concepts were productive of, and continue to be produced by, the Resolution, and in this study I have attempted to articulate a way in which these concepts could be thought through differently. Both the state (produced through representations of security and violence) and the subject (produced through representations of gender and violence) rely on a logic of sovereignty and ontological cohesion that must be problematized if alternative visions of authority and subjectivity are to become imaginable.

International Relations as a discipline could seek to embrace the investigation of the multiple modalities of power, from the economic to the bureaucratic, from neoliberal capitalism to the juridical. Rather than defending the sovereign boundaries of the discipline from the unruly outside constituted by critical studies of development, political structures, economy and law, not to mention the analysis of social/political phenomena like those undertaken by always-already interdisciplinary feminist scholarship, IR could refuse to fix its own boundaries, and refuse to exercise sovereign power, in terms of authority, over the meanings of its objects of analysis. Future research on global politics could look very different if it weren't for the inscription of ultimately arbitrary disciplinary borderlines that function to constrain rather than facilitate understanding.

NOTES

CHAPTER I

1. All of these testimonials are taken from the 'Stories' page on Amnesty International's web portal devoted to stopping violence against women, at http://web.amnesty.org/actforwomen/stories-index-eng (accessed 25 August 2006). For a personal reflection on the politics of presenting such testimonials as the introduction to research, see my (2005) 'Loud Voices Behind the Wall: Gender Violence and the Violent Reproduction of the International'.

2. There is an enormous amount of literature on this subject. See, inter alia, Keohane 1989, and Weber's 1994 response; Zalewski 1995; Jones 1996, and Carver, Cochran and Squires's 1998 response; Sylvester 1996, 2002; Tickner 1997; Carver 2003; Steans 2003a; Agathangelou and Ling 2004.

3. Literature addressing feminist conceptualizations of security includes Peterson 1992; Tickner 1992; Broadhead 2000; Hansen 2000; Blanchard 2003; Youngs 2003; Hoogensen and Rottem 2004.

4. See, inter alia, Waltz 1979; Herz 1950; Mearsheimer 1995, 1990.

5. For example, Campbell 1998; McSweeney 1999; Bilgin 2003.

6. I use the representation of 'poststructural' rather than 'post-structural' to indicate that I consider myself to be still 'structural', building on it, rather than hyphenetically separable.

7. I employ the bracketed (re) to indicate that these practices do not conjure fully formed objects, subjects and the relationships between them within a given discursive terrain but draw on the existing knowledges about these subjects and objects in order to construct or (re)legitimize an intelligible

'reality'. It also signifies that these processes are always ongoing and never complete. I discuss representation, discourse and power in detail in Chapter 2.

8. See Nicholson 1990 for a collection of insightful and thought-provoking essays on this theme, and Zalewski 2000 for reflections on the possibilities of 'feminism after postmodernism'.

9. I have deliberately run these terms together as I perceive their rigid separation as problematic, a point to which I return in Chapter 3. I see theory as a form of practice and vice versa.

10. See Enloe 1996 for an exploration of this construction.

11. Throughout this text, I use the bracketed form '(international) security and (gender) violence' to indicate the mutability of these discourses – that is, to draw attention to the ways in which security and violence can be differently inter/nationalized and gendered. When I use the unbracketed form 'international security and gender violence', I refer specifically to the discourses that (re)produce the meaning of security and violence through particular organizational logics of the international and gender. These discourses are discussed in detail in Chapter 3.

12. In keeping with much common-sense usage of the term, the *Oxford English Dictionary* defines 'academic' as not only 'relating to education and scholarship' but also 'scholarly rather than technical or practical' and 'of only theoretical interest'.

13. I use the hyphenated 'author-ity' to draw attention to the connotations of both ownership (author) and control (authority) that the word signifies to me.

14. In the concluding chapter of this book, I argue that development and peacekeeping institutions are implicated in the production of 'appropriate' statehood, according to the dominant discourse of 'international security'. Therefore, I represent the process of peacebuilding thus.

15. Neils Andersen explores the difference between method and analytical strategy, where he argues that '[a]nalytical *strategy* [is] a way to stress the deliberate *choice* and its implications' with regard to the ways in which 'the epistemologist will construct the observations of others … to be the object of his own observations' (2003: xiii, emphasis in original). This way of conceptualizing analytical strategy is useful, as it highlights the ways in which I am embedded in my research, even as I conform to the rigours of a discipline that requires at the very least an attempt at scientific method.

16. In order to provide a sense of temporal context, Chapter 4 presents an analysis of the United Nations Secretary-General's Reports published in 2002 and 2004. Insights from subsequent reports are integrated into the concluding chapter. This is in part an analytical decision, in that the 2004 Report is much more detailed and comprehensive than the 2002 Report, but treating the two as an analytical whole allows for the interrogation of the ways in which conceptualizations of gender, violence, security and the international change over time in the Reports. However, the

decision is also practical, in that it was necessary to focus on the Reports as a temporary whole for the purposes of conducting the analysis and writing up the findings.

CHAPTER 2

1. As mentioned in the previous chapter, I employ the bracketed (re) to indicate that these practices draw on existing knowledges about these subjects and objects in order to construct or (re)legitimize an intelligible 'reality'. It also signifies that these processes are always ongoing and never complete. I discuss representation in more detail in section four. In the following section I explore in more detail the relationship between discourse and power, specifically the conceptualization of discursive practices as practices of power.

2. As discussed below, I conceive of these sets of textual mechanisms (rhetorical schemata/nodal points and predication/subject-positioning) as congruent, recognizable in the theorizing of different authors under specific names but referring to the same practices, hence I run the terms together in my discussion of them.

3. Doty is explicit about the influence that Foucault has had on her analytical strategies, but it is important to note that she also draws heavily on Derrida (1996: 6), especially in the strategic destabilizing of binary oppositions.

4. Skunk Anansie phrased this idea more succinctly when they sang 'Yes it's fucking political/ Everything's political.'

5. Tarak Barkawi uses this construction in the context of theorizing globalization as 'referring to relations of *interconnection* and *mutual constitution* in world politics' (2004: 162). This claim entails the recognition that connective relations are always already constitutive relations: 'Apparently discrete entities in world politics – such as colonies, states and national societies – are produced out of fields of mutually constitutive relations' (2004: 162) at the same time as connections between them are articulated.

6. See Weldes 2003 and Der Derian and Shapiro 1989, for further discussion of intertextuality and International Relations.

7. Roxanne Doty labels her analytical approach 'the Discursive Practices Approach' (1993: 302) as distinct from what I am calling Discourse Theoretical Analysis, but the two approaches are very similar.

8. See also Laclau and Mouffe (2001: 113) on articulation.

CHAPTER 3

1. See also Jacobs et al. 2000; Moser and Clark 2001; Giles and Hyndman 2004.

2. 'Although legend has it that Blackstone's codification of English common law in 1768 asserted that a husband had the right to "physically chastise" an errant wife provided that the stick was no thicker than his thumb

– and thus the "rule of thumb" was born – such a passage cannot be found in Blackstone' (Sommers cited in Gelles 1997: 22). However, the existence of such charming rhymes as 'The spaniel, the wife and the walnut tree, the more you beat them, the better they be' suggests that violences towards wives were commonplace and thus normalized.

3. Individual violences also play a role; substance abuse and self-harm may be more prevalent in those who are marginalized by society for displaying inappropriate behaviours. Similarly, the gendered dimensions of image-related obsessive–compulsive disorder (IROCD) have been well documented, and the pressure to achieve a particular idealized notion of femininity has had extremely destructive results in far too many instances. I object to the representation of anorexia nervosa, bulimia and compulsive overeating as 'eating disorders'. I believe that this construction has been detrimental to the efforts to alleviate and overcome the symptoms of various 'eating disorders', as it perpetuates the notion that these disorders are *about* food rather than manifested *through* food. It is important to analyse the power dimension of IROCDs and to perceive them as individual violences, sustained by the same culturally relative discourses of gender, control and the body. As long as deliberately starving yourself to death is an 'eating disorder', all you need to do to overcome it is to start eating again – an attitude which is unhelpful, misguided and unfortunately all too prevalent.

4. On 'human security', see for example UNDP 1994; Tehranian 1999; McRae 2001; Newman 2001; Paris 2001; Thomas 2001; Thomas and Tow 2002. 'Critical security studies' is exemplified by Booth 1991, 1995. See also Krause 1998; Croft and Terriff 2000; Booth 2004; Dunne and Wheeler 2004; Booth 2005; Sheehan 2005.

5. See also Roland Paris (2001: 87) and Edward Newman (2001: 240–42), both of whom offer a similar justification for treating these works as a conceptual and analytical whole.

6. It is vital to note that there is huge diversity within the bodies of theory commonly referred to as 'realist'. The representation of realism as singular and cohesive functions discursively to suggest a level of coherence that, implicitly, is lacking from alternative bodies of theory, and contributes towards the construction of a position from which the 'mainstream' can name itself thus. However, these varied theories do share certain foundational assumptions that for the purposes of this analysis enable me to treat them as minimally unitary.

7. For literature that performs this representational practice, see, inter alia, Carr 1939: 62–5; Morgenthau 1973: 9–10; Waltz 1959. The way in which IR is often taught reinscribes this mythical heritage through the organization of popular textbooks; see, inter alia, Jackson and Owens 2005: 50–51; Jackson and Sørenson 2003: 41; Viotti and Kauppi 1999: 57–61. Critical interjections to this narrative have drawn attention to the ways in which such a representation (re)produces 'the authority of

classicism' (Burchill 2001: 98; see also Steans and Pettiford 2001: 52–3; Sterling-Folker 2006: 15).

8. For representations of the former, see Morgenthau 1948: 154; 1973: 6–7. For the latter, see Waltz 1993: 76–7; Waltz 2000: 5. Keohane offers a useful overview of both strands of thinking on 'national security' (1986: 7–16).

9. For other examples of work that problematizes this particular assumption of the 'national security' literature, see inter alia Tickner 1992: 27–67; Dalby 1997; Krause and Williams 1997; Walker 1997; Blanchard 2003; Youngs 2003.

10. This is evidenced by statements such as that made by a US senator at a meeting to discuss the future of security in a post-Cold War era. When suggested that policy could be directed at reassurance rather than deterrence, 'a major shift in the organizing principles of international security' (Steinbruner 2000: 2), the senator commented: 'Well, ... you have human nature and all of history going against you there. What have you got going for you?' (Nunn cited in Steinbruner 2000: 2).

11. See Waltz 1979; Keohane 1986; Baldwin 1993: 4–5.

12. See, inter alia, Arquilla 2001; Huntington 1993; Hoffman 2002; Herz 2003.

13. A view advanced by, for example, Ayoob 1984; Jackson 1990; Jackson 2001. While these theorists remain, for the most part, faithful to the foundational assumptions of the 'national security' literature, they draw attention to the difficulties inherent in a Procrustean approach to security given the global multiplicity of processes of state-formation. For critical analyses of state-as-threat, see inter alia Agamben 1998; Niva 1999; Connelly 2004; Shapiro 2004.

14. For an excellent critique of Walt's article concerning security studies as an academic discipline, see Kolodziej 1992.

15. A recent collection edited by Ken Booth divides up the chapters according to this schema (Booth 2005).

16. See Thomas 2001: 162; Paris 2001: 89; Thomas and Tow 2002: 178; Smith 2005.

17. For just a few instances of the representational practice of listing threats in the literature on 'international security', see Booth 1995: *passim*; Newman 2001: 245; Thomas 2001: 166; Dunne and Wheeler 2004: 16.

18. See also Thomas 2001; Booth 2004, 2005; Dunne and Wheeler 2004; Alker 2005; Wyn Jones 2005; Smith 2005.

19. Regional blocs? Continents? The planet? The universe?...

CHAPTER 4

1. These concerns are broadly divisible into two strands of argument. The first relates to the 'reluctance as exists among *feminists* to discuss women and violence [that] must be seen in the light of well-founded fears that such investigations could be used to mask male violence' (Jacobsen et

al. 2000: 12, emphasis in original). The second representation of these concerns relates to the minimizing of feminist agency that occurs when the discursive space for women to act as perpetrators is curtailed (see Moser and Clark 2001).

2. 'The argument that sexuality and sexual acts, including violent ones, are not just a matter of individual preferences but are bound up with power structures in society is, of course, closely tied to feminist theory and constitutes one of its principle challenges to mainstream social science' (Jacobsen et al. 2000: 2). This is an argument that I can sustain, although I conceptualize power somewhat differently, as explained in Chapter 3. I do conceive of power as immanent in the violent reproduction of gender but I identify 'sexuality and sexual acts' as performative of gender (see Butler 1999, 1993) and thus violence manifested through 'sexuality and sexual acts' as (re)productive of the power relationships rather than conceiving of the power relationships as ahistoric and immutable.

3. See, inter alia, Youngs 1999: 104–12; Crawley 2000; Peterson 1992. Feminist scholars are not alone in their desire to problematize what could be seen as the foundational assumption of realist IR theory: the domestic/international divide. Other notable contributions to this debate include Ashley 1988; Weber 1992; Falk 1990; Walker 1990, 1993, 2002; Linklater 1996; Lake 2003; Williams 2003.

4. On the diversity of 'women' and associated debates over what constitutes a feminist political agenda, see, inter alia, hooks 1983; Alcoff 1988; Riley 1988; Fuss 1989; Di Stefano 1990; Stanley 1997; Narayan 1997; Francis 2002; Butler 2004.

5. Furthermore, the idea of the USA assisting anyone with democratic organization is rather frightening given the circumstances under which George W. Bush was initially 'elected' as president.

6. However, this construction is (re)produced through other UN agencies in statements, Reports and press statements, in which 'peace is inextricably linked to equality. Conflicts of all forms continue to cause serious obstacles to the advancement of women. If there is no security, women as well as men are unable to fully participate in the political, economic and social development at the family, community and national levels' (UNESC 2004).

CHAPTER 5

1. The full text of the Beijing Platform for Action can be accessed at www. un.org/womenwatch/daw/beijing/platform/index.html.

2. The full text of the Namibia Plan of Action can be accessed at http:// action.web.ca/home/cpcc/attach/Windhoek%20Declaration.htm.

3. The full text of the relevant Articles of the Rome Statute can be accessed at www.un.org/law/icc/statute/99_corr/2.htm.

4. Available at www.womenwarpeace.org/toolbox/Annotated_1325.pdf.

5. This is the title of UNSCR 1325 as detailed on the UN website. See www.un.org/Docs/scres/2000/sc2000.htm.
6. The discursive function and ramifications of this subject-positioning are explored in Chapter 3.
7. These distinctions are analytical, in that representation entails participation and vice versa. I disaggregate the two in order to draw attention to the different spatial and political environs assumed appropriate for each activity, and to avoid repeating 'informal representation and participation' and 'formal representation and participation' throughout.
8. It is, however, common in literature on political violence to use the terms 'violence' and 'conflict' interchangeably. See, for example, Jabri 1996; Burton 1997.
9. For feminist discussion of nations and nationalism, see, inter alia, Parker 1992; Thapar 1993; Elshtain 1995; Yuval-Davis 1997; Cockburn 1998, 2000; Pettman 1999; Cusack 2000.
10. More sophisticated theorizing of violence and conflict is offered in Jabri 1996; Schmidt and Schröder 2001; Giles and Hyndman 2004.
11. Latha Varadarajan's analysis focuses on the ways in which mainstream discourses of security fail to centralize the investigation of neoliberal economic processes, and offers a convincing account of the partiality of such approaches.

CHAPTER 6

1. In this chapter, I use 'institutions' as synonymous with 'sites of power'. The power I refer to in the latter construction is discursive, and relates to influence and author-ity over UNSCR 1325. I do not intend to signify through the use of the word 'institution' that I conceive of either the UNSC or the NGO WG as coherent or singular entities. This will be expanded on as I explore the discursive terrain of the two institutions and investigate the groups and organizations that comprise them.
2. An 'Arria formula' meeting, named after Ambassador Diego Arria of Venezuela, refers to the informal meeting of Security Council members, with or without other parties involved, to discuss issues of interest that are not deemed appropriate as agenda items for the official sessions of the Council.
3. The full text of this Resolution is available at www.globalpolicy.org/ngos/ngo-un/info/res-1296.htm.
4. The full text of this Resolution is available at http://daccessdds.un.org/doc/UNDOC/GEN/N97/775/21/IMG/N9777521.pdf?OpenElement.
5. UNDAW was established in 1946 and 'advocates the improvement of the status of women of the world and the achievement of their equality with men' (UNDAW 2007). For further information, see their website at www.un.org/womenwatch/daw/index.html.
6. DEVAW preceded the appointment of the first UN Special Rapporteur on Violence Against Women in 1994 and is recognized as foundational

to contemporary theorizing and policymaking that seeks to articulate gendered violence as an issue of security (Winter et al. 2002: 72). For a critical review of DEVAW, see my 'Loud Voices Behind the Wall: Gender Violence and the Violent Reproduction of the International' (Shepherd 2006).

7. The full text of the Declaration can be viewed at www.un.org/docu-ments/ga/res/48/a48r104.htm.

8. Given that my research into the production of UNSCR 1325 is taking place some years after the Resolution was passed, and that information, for example on the webpages of the two institutions under investigation in this chapter, has been retrospectively updated, it is important to maintain some degree of temporal specificity. It is not possible to access the NGO WG website as it was previous to the production of UNSCR 1325. Thus the texts that I analyse in this section are the texts to which there are links provided on the website, under the section header 'NGO Working Group on Women, Peace and Security', all from 2000.

9. See, inter alia, Sen 1998; Uvin 1998: 141–60; Mohanty 2002.

10. See www.peacewomen.org for an indication of the ways in which the NGO Working Group has both expanded in membership and continued to lobby for the rights of women in armed conflict from 2000 to the present day.

11. The full text of the Covenant is reproduced at www.yale.edu/lawweb/avalon/leagcov.htm.

12. See, inter alia, Resolutions pertaining to the conflicts in Iraq, Cambodia, Somalia, Bosnia, Haiti and Rwanda (Golberg and Hubert 2001: 223).

13. Article 7 of the UN Charter lists the principal organs of the United Nations: 'a General Assembly, a Security Council, an Economic and Social Council, a Trusteeship Council, an International Court of Justice and a Secretariat' (UN 1945: Article 7.1).

14. Modal verbs indicate the 'mood' of the action, indicating the level of necessity or urgency. Therefore, it is interesting that the Charter uses two different modal verbs to articulate the responsibilities of the two different institutions discussed above.

15. Karen Mingst and Margaret Karns cite a relatively comprehensive list of actors involved in the process of UN reform, ranging from the 'the Group of Eighteen High-Level Intergovernmental Experts ... established in 1985 by the General Assembly under Japanese impetus', through the Nordic UN Project, including actors from within the UN itself such as Boutros Boutros-Ghali and Kofi Annan, to '[a]d-hoc nongovernmental initiatives' such as the Commission on Global Governance mentioned above (CoGG 2000: 200–201).

16. For a cogent and sophisticated discussion of the dominance of rationalist approaches in the discipline of International Relations, see Marysia Zalewski's (1996) '"All These Theories Yet the Bodies Keep Piling Up": Theories, Theorists, Theorising'.

17. On the issue of 'democratic deficit', see Gill 1996; Murphy 2002; Moravcsik 2004; Cox and Jacobson 2005. On the issues of participation, representation and the potential for the formulation of a 'global polity', see Ougaard and Higgott (eds) 2002; Wilkinson 2002.
18. This echoes the critical interjections made by, inter alia, Cammack 2002, 2004; Ferguson and Gupta 2002; Peck and Tickell 2002; Fraser 2003.

CHAPTER 7

1. This subhead is taken from Yanow 1996.
2. Disarmament, demobilization and reintegration.
3. It should be noted that Sparke theorizes this notion in relation to the effects of free-trade agreements, although his concepts are equally applicable to the processes of peace(state)building that Resolution 1325 calls for.
4. For further discussion of these debates, see Baden and Goetz 1997; United Nations Office of the Special Adviser on Gender Issues 2002; Moser and Moser 2005; Walby 2005.
5. See, inter alia, Murphy 2001; Gill 2003: 120–38; McGrew 2002.
6. Daly argues that one of the root causes of failures to mainstream gender successfully in various policy circles is 'the malleability of gender mainstreaming as a concept' and a lack of conceptual clarity (2005: 448). Given the theoretical framework that underpins my research, and that I seek to open up possibilities to think gender (and security, violence and the international) differently, thereby contributing to such malleability, I cannot sustain this argument.

REFERENCES

Ackerley, B.A. (2001) 'Women's Human Rights Activists as Cross-Cultural Theorists', *International Feminist Journal of Politics*, vol. 3, no. 3: 311–46.

Agamben, G. (1998) *Homo Sacer: Sovereign Power and Bare Life*, trans. Daniel Heller-Roazen, Stanford, CA: Stanford University Press.

Agathangelou, A., and L.H.M. Ling (2004) 'The House of IR: From Family Power Politics to the *Poisies* of Worldism', *International Studies Review*, vol. 6, no. 1: 21–49.

Agathangelou, A., and L.H.M. Ling (2003) 'Desire Industries: Sex Trafficking, UN Peacekeeping and the Neo-Liberal World Order', *Brown Journal of World Affairs*, vol. 10, no. 1: 133–48.

AI (Amnesty International) (2005) 'About Amnesty International' http://web. amnesty.org/pages/aboutai-index-eng (accessed 14 March 2007).

AI (Amnesty International) (2004) 'Sudan: Government Responsible for Human Devastation in Darfur but Still in Denial', http://web.amnesty. org/library/index/ENGAFR540672004 (accessed 14 March 2007).

Aladjem, T. (1991) 'The Philosopher's Prism: Foucault, Feminism and Critique', *Political Theory*, vol. 19, no. 2: 277–91.

Alcoff, L. (1988) 'Cultural Feminism versus Post-Structuralism: The Identity Crisis in Feminist Theory', *Signs: Journal of Women in Culture and Society*, vol. 13, no. 3: 405–36.

Alder, C. (1997) 'Violence, Gender and Social Change' in L. O'Toole, and J. Schiffman (eds), *Gender Violence: Interdisciplinary Perspectives*, London: New York University Press, 435–42.

Alker, H. (2005) 'Emancipation in the Critical Security Studies Project', in K. Booth (ed.), *Critical Security Studies and World Politics*, London and Boulder CO: Lynne Rienner, 189–214.

Allen, B. (1996) *Rape Warfare: The Hidden Genocide in Bosnia-Herzegovina and Croatia*, Minneapolis MN: University of Minnesota Press.

Allen, G. (2000) *Intertextuality*, London: Routledge.

Andersen, N.Å. (2003) *Discursive Analytical Strategies: Understanding Foucault, Koselleck, Laclau, Luhmann*, Bristol: Policy Press.

Annan, K. (1999) 'Letters to Future Generations: Towards a Culture of Peace', www.unesco.org/opi2/lettres/TextAnglais/AnnanE.html (accessed 14 March 2007).

Arquilla, J. (2003) 'Thinking About New Security Paradigms', *Contemporary Security Policy*, vol. 24, no. 1: 209–225.

Artz, L. (2001) 'The Weather Watchers: Gender, Violence and Social Control in South Africa', http://web.uct.ac.za/depts/sjrp/publicat/weatwat.pdf (accessed 10 August 2006).

Ashley, R. K. (1988) 'Untying the Sovereign State: A Double Reading of the Anarchy Problematique', *Millennium: Journal of International Studies*, vol. 17, no. 2: 227–62.

Ayoob, M. (2002) 'Inequality and Theorizing in International Relations: The Case for Subaltern Realism', *International Studies Review*, vol. 4, no. 3: 27–48.

Ayoob, M. (1984) 'Security in the Third World: The Worm About to Turn?', *International Affairs*, vol. 60, no. 1: 41–51.

Baden, S., and A.M. Goetz (1997) 'Who Needs [Sex] When You Can Have [Gender]? Conflicting Discourses on Gender at Beijing', *Feminist Review*, vol. 56, no. 1: 3–25.

Bahdi, R. (2003) 'Security Council Resolution 1325: Practice and Prospects', *Refuge*, vol. 21, no. 2: 41–51.

Baker, G. (2000) 'Problems in the Theorisation of Global Civil Society', *Political Studies*, vol. 50, no. 5: 928–43.

Balch-Lindsay, D., and A.J. Enterline (2000) 'Killing Time: The World Politics of Civil War Duration, 1820–1992', *International Studies Quarterly*, vol. 44, no. 4: 615–42.

Baldwin, D. (1997) 'The Concept of Security', *Review of International Studies*, vol. 23, no. 1: 5–26.

Baldwin, D. (1993) 'Neoliberalism, Neorealism and World Politics' in D. Baldwin (ed.), *Neorealism and Neoliberalism: The Contemporary Debate*, New York: Columbia University Press, 3–25.

Barkawi, T. (2004) 'Connection and Constitution: Locating War and Culture in Globalization Studies', *Globalizations*, vol. 1, no. 2: 155–70.

Barkawi, T., and M. Laffey (1999) 'The Imperial Peace: Democracy, Force and Globalisation', *European Journal of International Relations*, vol. 5, no. 4: 403–34.

Bergeron, S. (2003) 'The Post-Washington Consensus and Economic Representations of Women in Development at the World Bank', *International Feminist Journal of Politics*, vol. 5, no. 3: 397–419.

Bergeron, S. (2001) 'Political Economy Discourses of Globalization and

Feminist Politics', *Signs: Journal of Women in Culture and Society*, vol. 6, no. 4: 983–1006.

Bhatta, G. (2001) 'Of Geese and Ganders: Mainstreaming Gender in the Context of Sustainable Human Development', *Journal of Gender Studies*, vol. 10, no. 1: 17–32.

Bilgin, P. (2003) 'Individual and Societal Dimensions of Security', *International Studies Review*, vol. 5, no. 2: 203–22.

Blanchard, E. (2003) 'Gender, International Relations and the Development of Feminist Security Theory', *Signs: Journal of Women in Culture and Society*, vol. 28, no. 4: 1289–312.

Bograd, M. (1988) 'Feminist Perspectives on Wife Abuse: An Introduction', 11–27 in K. Yllo and M. Bograd (eds), *Feminist Perspectives on Wife Abuse*, London: Sage.

Bond, J., and L. Sherret (2006) 'New Voice, New Perspectives: A Sight for Sore Eyes – Bringing Gender Vision to the Responsibility to Protect Framework', INSTRAW, www.un-instraw.org/en/images/stories/NewVoices/nv-bond. pdf (accessed 14 March 2007).

Booth, K. (ed.) (2005) *Critical Security Studies and World Politics*, London and Boulder CO: Lynne Rienner.

Booth, K. (2004) 'Realities of Security: Editor's Introduction', *International Relations*, vol. 18, no. 1: 5–8.

Booth, K. (1995) 'Human Wrongs and International Relations', *International Affairs*, vol. 71, no. 1: 103–26.

Booth, K. (1991) 'Security and Emancipation', *Review of International Studies*, vol. 17, no. 4: 313–26.

Broadhead, L. (2000) 'Re-packaging Notions of Security: A Skeptical Feminist Response to Recent Efforts', in S. Jacobs, R. Jacobson and J. Marchbank (eds), *States of Conflict: Gender, Violence and Resistance*, London: Zed Books, 27–44.

Brooks, A. (1997) *Postfeminisms: Feminism, Cultural Theory and Cultural Forms*, London: Routledge.

Brown, W. (2003) 'Women's Studies Unbound: Revolution, Mourning, Politics', *Parallax*, vol. 9, no. 2: 3–16.

Brown, W. (1995) *States of Injury: Power and Freedom in Late Modernity*, Princeton NJ: Princeton University Press.

Bunch, C. (1995) 'Interview with Jutta Joachim', Center for Women's Global Leadership, New Brunswick NJ, 1 November.

Bunch, C., and S. Fried (1996) 'Beijing '95: Moving Women's Human Rights from Margin to Center', *Signs: Journal of Women in Culture and Society*, vol. 22, no. 1: 200–204.

Burchill, S. (2001) 'Realism and Neo-Realism', in S. Burchill et al., *Theories of International Relations*, 2nd edn, Basingstoke: Palgrave, 70–102.

Burton, J. (1997) *Violence Explained*, Manchester: Manchester University Press.

Butler, J. (2004) *Undoing Gender*, London: Routledge.

Butler, J. (2001) 'Gender Trouble, Feminist Theory and Psychoanalytic Discourse', in L. Nicholson (ed.), *Feminism/ Postmodernism*, London: Routledge, 324–40.

Butler, J. (1999) *Gender Trouble*, rev. edn, London: Routledge.

Butler, J. (1994) 'Contingent Foundations: Feminism and the Question of Postmodernism', in S. Seidman (ed.), *The Postmodern Turn: New Perspectives on Social Theory*, Cambridge: Cambridge University Press, 153–70 (orig. 1990, presented at the Greater Philadelphia Philosophy Consortium).

Butler, J. (1993) *Bodies That Matter: On the Discursive Limits of 'Sex'*, London: Routledge.

Buzan, B. (1991) *People, States and Fear*, London: Harvester Wheatsheaf.

Buzan, B. (1984) 'Peace, Power and Security: Contending Concepts in the Study of International Relations', *Journal of Peace Research*, vol. 21, no. 2: 109–125.

Cammack, P. (2004) 'What the World Bank Means by "Poverty Reduction" and Why It Matters', *New Political Economy*, vol. 9, no. 2: 189–211.

Cammack, P. (2002) 'Attacking the Poor', *New Left Review*, vol. 13: 125–34.

Campbell, D. (1998) *Writing Security: United States Foreign Policy and the Politics of Identity*, rev. edn, Minneapolis: University of Minnesota Press.

Carpenter, R.C. (2005) '"Women, Children and Other Vulnerable Groups": Gender, Strategic Frames and the Protection of Civilians as a Transnational Issue', *International Studies Quarterly*, vol. 49, no. 2: 295–334.

Carpenter, T.G. (1997) 'The Mirage of Global Collective Security', in T.G. Carpenter (ed.), *Delusions of Grandeur: The United Nations and Global Intervention*, Washington DC: Cato Institute, 13–28.

Carr, E.H. (1939) *The Twenty Years' Crisis 1919–1939*, London: Macmillan.

Carver, T. (ed.) (2003) 'The Forum: Gender and International Relations', *International Studies Review*, vol. 5, no. 2: 287–302.

Carver, T. (1996) *Gender is Not a Synonym for Women*, London and Boulder CO: Lynne Rienner.

Carver, T., M. Cochran and J. Squires (1998) 'Gendering Jones: Feminisms, IRs, Masculinities', *Review of International Studies*, vol. 24, no. 2: 283–97.

Cassesse, A. (1986) *International Law in a Divided World*, Oxford: Clarendon.

Chan-Tiberghien, J. (2004) 'Gender Skepticism or Gender-Boom: Poststructural Feminisms, Transnational Feminisms and the World Conference Against Racism', *International Feminist Journal of Politics*, vol. 6, no. 3: 454–84.

Chandhoke, N. (2002) 'The Limits of Global Civil Society', in Centre for the Study of Global Governance, *The Global Civil Society Yearbook*, 35–53, www.lse.ac.uk/Depts/global/Publications/Yearbooks/2002/2002chapter2.pdf (accessed 14 March 2007).

Childs, S., and M.L. Krook (2006) 'Gender and Politics: The State of the Art', *Politics*, vol. 26, no. 1: 18–28.

Chinkin, C. (2000) 'Gender and International Society: Law and Policy', in R. Thakur and E. Newman (eds), *New Millennium, New Perspectives: The United Nations, Security and Governance*, New York: UN University Press, 242–60.

Claude, I.L. (1966) 'Collective Legitimization as a Political Function of the United Nations', *International Organization*, vol. 20, no. 3: 367–79.

Cockburn, C. (2004) 'The Continuum of Violence: A Gender Perspective on War and Peace', in W. Giles and J. Hyndman (eds), *Sites of Violence: Gender and Conflict Zones*, London and Berkeley: University of California Press,.

Cockburn, C. (2001) 'The Gendered Dynamic of Armed Conflict and Political Violence', in C. Moser and F. Clark (eds), *Victims, Perpetrators or Actors? Gender, Armed Conflict and Political Violence*, London: Zed Books 13–29.

Cockburn, C. (2000) 'The Anti-Essentialist Choice: Nationalism and Feminist in the Interaction between Two Women's Projects', *Nations and Nationalism*, vol. 6, no. 4: 611–29.

Cockburn, C. (1998) *The Space Between Us: Negotiating Gender and National Identities in Conflict*, London: Zed Books.

Cockburn, C., and D. Zarkov (2002) 'Introduction', in C. Cockburn and D. Zarkov (eds), *The Postwar Moment: Militaries, Masculinities and International Peacekeeping*, London: Lawrence & Wishart, 9–21.

CoGG (Commission on Global Governance) (1995) *Our Global Neighbourhood*, Oxford: Oxford University Press.

Cohn, C. (2004) 'Feminist Peacemaking', *Women's Review of Books*, vol. 11, no. 5: 8–9.

Cohn, C., H. Kinsella and S. Gibbings (2004) 'Women, Peace and Security: Resolution 1325', *International Feminist Journal of Politics*, vol. 6, no. 1: 130–40.

Connell, R.W. (2005) 'Change among the Gatekeepers: Men, Masculinities and Gender Equality in the Global Arena', *Signs: Journal of Women in Culture and Society*, vol. 30, no. 3: 1801–25.

Connelly, W. (2004) 'The Complexity of Sovereignty', in J. Edkins, V. Pin-Fat and M. Shapiro (eds), *Sovereign Lives: Power in Global Politics*, London: Routledge, 23–40.

Copelon, R. (1995) 'Gendered War Crimes: Reconceptualizing Rape in Time of War', in J. Peters and A. Wolper (eds), *Women's Rights, Human Rights: International Feminist Perspectives*, London: Routledge, 197–214.

Cox, R., and H. Jacobson (2005) 'The Framework for Inquiry', in P. Diehl (ed.), *The Politics of Global Governance: International Orgnaizations in an Inter-dependent World*, London and Boulder CO: Lynne Rienner, 111–26.

Crawley, H. (2000) 'Engendering the State in Refugee Women's Claims for Asylum', in S. Jacobs, R. Jacobson and J. Marchbank (eds), *States of Conflict: Gender, Violence and Resistance*, London: Zed Books, 87–104.

Croft, S., and T. Terriff (eds) (2000) *Critical Reflections on Security and Change*, London and Portland OR: Frank Cass.

Cusack, T. (2000) 'Janus and Gender: Women and the Nation's Backward Look', *Nations and Nationalism*, vol. 6, no. 4: 541–641.

Dalby, S. (1997) 'Contesting an Essential Concept: Reading the Dilemmas in Contemporary Security Discourse', in K. Krause and M. Williams (eds), *Critical Security Studies: Concepts and Cases*, London: UCL Press, 3–32.

Daly, M. (2005) 'Gender Mainstreaming in Theory and in Practice', *Social Politics: International Studies in Gender, State and Society*, vol. 12, no. 3: 433–50.

Das, V., and A. Kleinman (2001) 'Introduction', in V. Das et al. (eds), *Remaking a World: Violence, Social Suffering and Recovery*, London: University of California Press, 1–30.

D'Cruze, S., and A. Rao (2004) 'Violence and the Vulnerabilities of Gender', *Gender and History*, vol. 16, no. 3: 495–512.

De Lauretis, T. (1986) 'Feminist Studies/Critical Studies: Issues, Terms and Contexts', in T. de Lauretis (ed.), *Feminist Studies/Critical Studies*, Bloomington IN: Indiana University Press, 1–19.

Der Derian, J. (1992) *Antidiplomacy: Spies, Terror, Speed and War*, London: Pinter.

Der Derian, J. (1990) 'The (S)pace of International Relations: Simulation, Surveillance and Speed', *International Studies Quarterly*, vol. 34, no. 3: 295–310.

Der Derian, J. (1989) 'The Boundaries of Knowledge and Power in International Relations', in J. Der Derian and M. Shapiro (eds), *International/ Intertextual Relations: Postmodern Readings of World Politics*, Lexington MA: Lexington Books, 3–10.

Der Derian, J., and M. Shapiro (eds) (1989) *International/ Intertextual Relations: Postmodern Readings of World Politics*, Lexington MA: Lexington Books.

Derrida, J. (2000) 'Lyotard and Us', *Parallax*, vol. 6, no. 4: 28–48.

Derrida, J. (1978) *Writing and Difference*, trans. Alan Bass, London: Routledge.

Derrida, J. (1974) *Of Grammatology*, trans. Gayatri Chakravorty Spivak, London: Johns Hopkins University Press.

Desch, M.C. (1998) 'Culture Clash: Assessing the Importance of Ideas in Security Studies', *International Security*, vol. 23, no. 1: 141–70.

Di Stefano, C. (1991) *Configurations of Masculinity: A Feminist Perspective on Modern Political Theory*, New York: Cornell University Press.

Di Stefano, C. (1990) 'Dilemmas of Difference: Feminism, Modernity and Postmodernity', in L. Nicholson (ed.), *Feminism/Postmodernism*, London: Routledge, 63–82.

Digeser, P. (1992) 'The Fourth Face of Power', *Journal of Politics*, vol. 54, no. 4: 977–1007.

Dillon, M. (1996) *Politics of Security: Towards a Political Philosophy of Continental Thought*, London: Routledge.

Dobash, R.E., and R.P. Dobash (1992) *Women, Violence and Social Change*, London: Routledge.

Dörmann, K. (2003) 'The Legal Situation of 'Unlawful/Unprivileged Combatants' *International Review of the Red Cross* 849: 45–74, www.icrc. org/Web/eng/siteengo.nsf/htmlall/5LPHBV/$File/irrc_849_Dorman. pdf (accessed 14 March 2007).

Doty, R.L. (1996) *Imperial Encounters*, London: University of Minnesota Press.

Doty, R.L. (1993) 'Foreign Policy as Social Construction: A Post-Positivist Analysis of U.S. Counterinsurgency Policy in the Philippines', *International Studies Quarterly*, vol. 37, no. 3: 297–320.

Dunne, T., and N. Wheeler (2004) '"We the Peoples": Contending Discourses of Security in Human Rights Theory and Practice', *International Relations*, vol. 18, no. 1: 9–23.

ECOSOC (Economic and Social Council) (1968) 'ECOSOC Resolution 1296 (XLIV) Arrangements for Consultation with Non-Governmental Organisations', www.globalpolicy.org/ngos/ngo-un/info/res-1296.htm (accessed 14 March 2007).

Edkins, J. (2002) 'After the Subject of International Security', in A. Finlayson and J. Valentine (eds), *Politics and Post-Structuralism*, Edinburgh, Edinburgh University Press, 66–80.

Elam, D. (1994) *Feminism and Deconstruction: Ms. En Abyme*, London: Routledge.

El-Bushra, J. (2004) 'Fused in Combat: Gender Relations and Armed Conflict', in H. Afshar and D. Eade (eds), *Development, Women and War: Feminist Perspectives*, Oxford: Oxfam GB, 152–71.

El-Bushra, J. (2000) 'Transforming Conflict: Some Thoughts on a Gendered Understanding of Conflict Processes', in S. Jacobs, R. Jacobson and J. Marchbank (eds), *States of Conflict: Gender, Violence and Resistance*, London: Zed Books, 66–86.

El Jack, A. (2003) 'Gender and Armed Conflict: Overview Report', *BRIDGE Cutting Edge Pack Series*, Brighton: Institute of Development Studies.

Elshtain, J.B. (1995) *Women and War*, 2nd edn, London and Chicago: University of Chicago Press.

Enloe, C. (2000) *Bananas, Beaches and Bases*, 2nd edn, London and Berkeley: University of California Press.

Enloe, C. (1996) 'Margins, Silences and Bottom Rungs: How to Overcome the Underestimation of Power in International Relations', in K. Booth, S. Smith and M. Zalewski (eds), *International Theory: Positivism and Beyond*, Cambridge: Cambridge University Press, 186–202.

Enloe, C. (1990) 'Womenandchildren: Making Feminist Sense of the Persian Gulf Crisis', *Village Voice*, 25 September.

Enloe, C. (1983) *Does Khaki Become You? The Militarization of Women's Lives*, London: Pluto Press.

Eschle, C. (2002) 'Engendering Global Democracy', *International Feminist Journal of Politics*, vol. 4, no. 3: 315–41.

Evans, M. (1982) 'In Praise of Theory: The Case for Women's Studies', in S. Kemp and J. Squires (eds), *Feminisms*, Oxford: Oxford University Press, 17–22.

Fairclough, N. (2003) *Analysing Discourse*, Routledge, London.

Fairclough, N. (1992) *Discourse and Social Change*, Cambridge: Polity Press.

Fairclough, N., and R. Wodak (1997) 'Critical Discourse Analysis', in T.A. van Dijk (ed.), *Discourse as Social Interaction*, London: Sage, 258–84.

Falk, R. (1990) 'Evasions of Sovereignty', in R.B.J. Walker and S.H. Mend-lowitz (eds), *Contending Sovereignties: Redefining Political Communities*, London and Boulder CO: Lynne Rienner, 61–78.

Fearon, J., and D. Laitin (2003) 'Ethnicity, Insurgency and Civil War', *American Political Science Review*, vol. 97, no. 1: 75–90.

Ferguson, J., and A. Gupta (2002) 'Spatializing States: Toward an Ethnography of Neoliberal Governmentality', *American Ethnologist*, vol. 29, no. 4: 981–1002.

Foucault, M. (1984) 'What is an Author?', in P. Rabinow (ed.), *The Foucault Reader: An Introduction to Foucault's Thought*, London: Penguin, 101–20.

Foucault, M. (1980) 'Truth and Power', in C. Gorden (ed.), *Power/Knowledge: Selected Interviews and Other Writings 1972–1977 by Michel Foucault*, London: Harvester, 109–133.

Foucault, M. (1978) *The Will to Knowledge: History of Sexuality Volume I*, London: Penguin.

Foucault, M. (1972) *The Archaeology of Knowledge*, trans. A. Sheridan Smith, London: Tavistock.

Fox, V. (2002) 'Historical Perspectives on Violence against Women', *Journal of International Women's Studies*, vol. 4, no. 1: 15–34.

Francis, B. (2002) 'Relativism, Realism and Feminism: An Analysis of Some Theoretical Tensions in Research on Gender Identity', *Journal of Gender Studies*, vol. 11, no. 1: 39–54.

Fraser, N. (2003) 'From Discipline to Flexibilisation? Rereading Foucault in the Shadow of Globalization', *Constellations*, vol. 10, no. 2: 160–70.

Fuss, D. (1989) *Essentially Speaking: Feminism, Nature and Difference*, London: Routledge.

Gelles, R.J. (1997) *Intimate Violence in Families*, 3rd edn, London: Sage.

Gervais, M. (2004) 'Human Security and Reconstruction Efforts in Rwanda: Impact on the Lives of Women', in H. Afshar and D. Eade (eds), *Development, Women and War: Feminist Perspectives*, Oxford: Oxfam GB, 301–312.

Giles, W., and J. Hyndman (2004) 'Introduction: Gender and Conflict in a Global Context', in W. Giles and J. Hyndman (eds), *Sites of Violence: Gender and Conflict Zones*, London and Berkeley: University of California Press, 3–23.

Gill, S. (2003) *Power and Resistance in the New World Order*, London: Palgrave Macmillan.

Gill, S. (1996) 'Globalization, Democratization and the Politics of Indifference', in J. Mittelman (ed.), *Globalization: Critical Reflections*, London and Boulder CO: Lynne Rienner, 205–28.

Gill, S. (1995) 'Globalisation, Market Civilisation and Disciplinary Neoliberalism' *Millennium: Journal of International Studies*, vol. 24, no. 3: 399–423.

Gilpin, R. (1984a) 'The Richness of the Tradition of Political Realism', *International Organization*, vol. 38, no. 2: 287–304.

Gilpin, R. (1984b) 'The Dual Problems of Peace and National Security', *Political Science*, vol. 17, no. 1: 18–23.

Gleditsch, N.P. et al. (2002) 'Armed Conflict 1946–2001: A New Dataset', *Journal of Peace Research*, vol. 39, no. 5: 615–37.

Golberg, E., and D. Hubert (2001) 'The Security Council and the Protection of Civilians', in R. McRae and D. Hubert (eds), *Human Security and the New Diplomacy: Protecting People, Promoting Peace*, London: McGill-Queen's University Press, 223–30.

Gordenker, L., and T. Weiss (1996) 'Pluralising Global Governance: Analytical Approaches and Dimensions', in T. Weiss and L. Gordenker (eds), *NGOs, the United Nations and Global Governance*, London and Boulder CO: Lynne Rienner, 17–47.

Grant, R. (1991) 'The Sources of Gender Bias in International Relations Theory', in R. Grant and K. Newland (eds), *Gender and International Relations*, Buckingham: Open University Press/*Millennium: Journal of International Studies*, 8–26.

Grosz, E.A. (1987) 'Feminist Theory and the Challenge to Knowledge', *Women's Studies International Forum*, vol. 10, no. 5: 475–80.

Hafner-Burton, E., and M.A. Pollack (2002) 'Mainstreaming Gender in Global Governance', *European Journal of International Relations*, vol. 8, no. 3: 339–73.

Haftendorn, H. (1991) 'The Security Puzzle: Theory-building and Discipline-building in International Security', *International Studies Quarterly*, vol. 35, no. 1: 3–17.

Hall, S. (1997a) 'Cultural Identity and Diaspora', in K. Woodward (ed.), *Identity and Difference*, London: Sage, 51–59.

Hall, S. (1997b) 'The Work of Representation', in S. Hall (ed.) (1997) *Representation: Cultural Representation and Signifying Practices*, London: Sage, 13–74.

Hansen, L. (2006) *Security as Practice: Discourse Analysis and the Bosnian War*, London: Routledge.

Hansen, L. (2000) 'Gender, Nation, Rape: Bosnia and the Construction of Security', *International Feminist Journal of Politics*, vol. 3, no. 1: 55–75.

Hanssen, B. (2000) *Critique of Violence: Between Poststructuralism and Critical Theory*, London: Routledge.

HAP (Hague Appeal for Peace) (2005) 'About Us', www.haguepeace.org/index.php?action=AbtUs (accessed 14 March 2007).

Held, D., and A. McGrew (1998) 'The End of the Old Order: Globalization and the Prospects for World Order', *Review of International Studies*, vol. 24, no. 5: 219–43.

Held, D., A. McGrew, D. Goldblatt, and J. Perraton (1999) *Global Transformations: Politics, Economics and Culture*, Oxford: Blackwell.

Helliwell, C. (2000) 'It's Only a Penis: Rape, Feminism and Difference', *Signs: Journal of Women in Culture and Society*, vol. 25, no. 3: 789–816.

Herz, J. (2003) 'The Security Dilemma in International Relations: Background and Present Problems', *International Relations*, vol. 17, no. 4: 411–16.

Herz, J. (1950) 'Idealist Internationalism and the Security Dilemma', *World Politics*, vol. 2, no. 2: 157–80.

Hill, F. (2002) 'NGO Perspectives: NGOs and the Security Council', *Disarmament Forum*, vol. 1, no. 1: 27–30, www.unidir.ch/pdf/articles/pdf-art9.pdf (accessed 14 March 2007).

Hill, F., M. Aboitiz and S. Poehlman-Doumbouya (2003) 'Nongovernmental Organizations' Role in the Buildup and Implementation of Security Council Resolution 1325', *Signs: Journal of Women in Culture and Society*, vol. 28, no. 4: 1255–69.

Hill, T. (2004) 'Three Generations of UN–Civil Society Relations: A Quick Sketch', *Global Policy Forum*, www.globalpolicy.org/ngos/ngo-un/gen/2004/0404generation.htm (accessed 14 March 2007).

Hoffman, J. (2001) *Gender and Sovereignty: Feminism, the State and International Relations*, Basingstoke: Palgrave.

Hoffman, S. (2002) 'Clash of Globalizations', *Foreign Affairs*, vol. 81, no. 4.

Hoogensen, G., and S.V. Rottem (2004) 'Gender Identity and the Subject of Security', *Security Dialogue*, vol. 35, no. 2: 155–71.

hooks, b. (1982) *Ain't I a Woman*, London: Pluto Press.

Hopgood, S. (2000) 'Reading the Small Print in Global Civil Society: The Inexorable Hegemony of the Liberal Self', *Millennium: Journal of International Studies*, vol. 29, no. 1: 1–25.

Howarth, D. (2000) *Discourse*, Buckingham: Open University Press.

Howarth, D., and Y. Stavrakakis (2000) 'Introducing Discourse Theory and Political Analysis', in D. Howarth, A. Norval and Y. Stavrakakis (eds), *Discourse Theory and Political Analysis: Identities, Hegemonies and Social Change*, Manchester: Manchester University Press, 1–23.

Huntington, S. (1993) 'The Clash of Civilizations?' *Foreign Affairs*, vol. 72, no. 3: 22–49.

Huß, S. (2004) 'Backgrounder: Security Council Resolution 1325 on Women, Peace and Security', Canada: Institute for Global Issues, www.womenwarpeace.org/toolbox/1325backgrounder.pdf (accessed 14 March 2007).

IA (International Alert) (2006) 'About Us', www.international-alert.org/about_alert/index.php (accessed 14 March 2007).

Ibáñez, A.C. (2001) 'El Salvador: War and Untold Stories – Women Guerillas', 117–130 in C. Moser and F. Clark (eds) *Victims, Perpetrators or Actors? Gender, Armed Conflict and Political Violence*, London: Zed Books.

ICC (International Criminal Court) (1998) 'Rome Statute of the International Criminal Court', www.un.org/law/icc/statute/romefra.htm (accessed 14 March 2007).

Jabri, V. (1996) *Discourses on Violence: Conflict Analysis Reconsidered*, Manchester: Manchester University Press.

Jackson, R. (2001) 'The State and Internal Conflict', *Australian Journal of International Affairs*, vol. 55, no. 1: 65–81.

Jackson, R. (1990) *Quasi-States: Sovereignty, International Relations and the Third World*, Cambridge: Cambridge University Press.

Jackson, R., and P. Owens (2005) 'The Evolution of International Society', in J. Baylis and S. Smith (eds), *The Globalization of World Politics*, 3rd edn, Oxford: Oxford University Press, 45–62.

Jackson, R., and G. Sørensen (2003) *Introduction to International Relations: Theories and Approaches*, Oxford: Oxford University Press.

Jacobs, S., R. Jacobson and J. Marchbank (eds) (2000) *States of Conflict: Gender, Violence and Resistance*, London: Zed Books.

Jacobson, R., S. Jacobs and J. Marchbank (2000) 'Introduction: States of Conflict', in S. Jacobs, R. Jacobson and J. Marchbank (eds), *States of Conflict: Gender, Violence and Resistance*, London: Zed Books, 1–23.

Jaquette, J. (2003) 'Feminism and the Challenges of the "Post-Cold War" World', *International Feminist Journal of Politics*, vol. 5, no. 3: 331–54.

Jaworski, A., and N. Coupland (eds) (1999) *The Discourse Reader*, London: Routledge.

Jeffries, S. (1999) 'Queer Theory and Violence against Women', http://sisyphe. org/article.php3?id_article=1053 (accessed 30 December 2007).

Joachim, J. (2003) 'Framing Issues and Seizing Opportunities: The UN, NGOs and Women's Rights', *International Studies Quarterly*, vol. 47, no. 2: 247–74.

Jones, A. (2002) 'Gender and Genocide in Rwanda', *Journal of Genocide Research*, vol. 4, no. 1: 65–94.

Jones, A. (2000) 'Gender and Genocide', *Journal of Genocide Research*, vol. 2, no. 2: 185–211.

Jones, A. (1996) 'Does Gender Make the World Go Round? Feminist Critiques of International Relations', *Review of International Studies*, vol. 22, no. 4: 405–29.

Kalyvas, S.N. (2001) '"New" and "Old" Wars: A Valid Distinction?', *World Politics*, vol. 54, no. 1: 99–118.

Kandiyoti, D. (2004) 'Post-conflict Reconstruction, "Democratisation" and Women's Rights', *IDS Bulletin*, vol. 35, no. 4: 134–6.

Kappeler, S. (1995) *The Will to Violence: The Politics of Personal Behaviour*, Cambridge: Polity Press.

Kaufman, M. (1997) 'The Construction of Masculinity and the Triad of Men's Violence', in L. O'Toole and J. Schiffman (eds), *Gender Violence: Interdisciplinary Perspectives*, London and New York: New York University Press, 30–51.

Kelly, L. (2000) 'Wars against Women: Sexual Violence, Sexual Politics and the Militarised State', in S. Jacobs, R. Jacobson and J. Marchbank (eds), *States of Conflict: Gender, Violence and Resistance*, London: Zed Books, 45–65.

Kelly, L., S. Burton and L. Regan (1996) 'Beyond Victim or Survivor: Sexual Violence, Identity and Feminist Theory and Practice', in L. Adkins and V. Merchant (eds), *Sexualizing the Social: Power and the Organization of Sexuality*, London: Macmillan, 77–101.

Keohane, R. (1995) 'Hobbes's Dilemma and Institutional Change in World Politics: Sovereignty in International Society', in H.H. Hohn and G.

Sørensen (eds), *Whose World Order? Uneven Globalisation and the End of the Cold War*, Boulder CO: Westview, 165–86.

Keohane, R. (1989) 'International Relations Theory: Contributions of a Feminist Standpoint', *Millennium: Journal of International Studies*, vol. 18, no. 2: 245–54.

Keohane, R. (1986) 'Realism, Neorealism and the Study of World Politics', in R. Keohane (ed.), *Neorealism and Its Critics*, New York: Columbia University Press, 1–26.

Keohane, R., and L. Martin (1995) 'The Promise of Institutionalist Theory', *International Security*, vol. 20, no. 1: 39–51.

Kleinman, A. (2000) 'The Violences of Everyday Life: The Multiple Forms and Dynamics of Social Violence', in V. Das et al. (eds), *Violence and Subjectivity*, London and Berkeley: University of California Press, 226–241.

Kolodziej, E.A. (1992) 'Renaissance in Security Studies? Caveat Lector!', *International Studies Quarterly*, vol. 36, no. 4: 421–38.

Krause, K. (1998) 'Critical Theory and Security Studies: The Research Programme of "Critical Security Studies"', *Cooperation and Conflict*, vol. 33, no. 3: 298–333.

Krause, K., and M.C. Williams (1997) 'From Strategy to Security: Foundations of Critical Security Studies', in K. Krause and M.C. Williams (eds), *Critical Security Studies: Concepts and Cases*, London: UCL Press, 33–60.

Krause, K., and M.C. Williams (1996) 'Broadening the Agenda of Security Studies', *Mershon International Studies Review*, vol. 40, no. 2: 229–54.

Kupchan, C., and C. Kupchan (1995) 'The Promise of Collective Security', *International Security*, vol. 20, no. 1: 52–61.

Laclau, E., and C. Mouffe (2001) *Hegemony and Socialist Strategy: Towards a Radical Democratic Politics*, 2nd edn, London: Verso.

Lake, D. (2003) 'The New Sovereignty in International Relations', *International Studies Review*, vol. 5, no. 3: 303–23.

League of Nations (1924) 'The Covenant', www.yale.edu/lawweb/avalon/leagcov.htm (accessed 14 March 2007).

Lees, S. (1997) *Ruling Passions: Sexual Violence, Reputation and the Law*, Buckingham: Open University Press.

Leledakis, K. (2000) 'Derrida, Deconstruction and Social Theory', *European Journal of Social Theory*, vol. 3, no. 2: 175–93.

Lentin, R. (1997) *Gender and Catastrophe*, London: Zed Books.

Linklater, A. (1996) 'Citizenship and Sovereignty in the Post-Westphalian State', *European Journal of International Relations*, vol. 2, no. 1: 77–103.

Lipschutz, R.D. (1992) 'Reconstructing World Politics: The Emergence of Global Civil Society', *Millennium: Journal of International Studies*, vol. 21, no. 3: 389–420.

Littlewood, R. (1997) 'Military Rape', *Anthropology Today*, vol. 13, no. 2: 7–16.

Lovenduski, J. (2001) 'Women and Politics: Minority Representation or Critical Mass?', *Parliamentary Affairs*, vol. 54, no. 4: 743–58.

McDonald, M. (2002) 'Human Security and the Construction of Security', *Global Society*, vol. 16, no. 3: 277–95.

McGinnis, L. (2001) 'Queer-Bashing: A Sign of Individual and Cultural Illness', www.bluestarweb.on.ca/QueerBash.html (accessed 14 March 2007).

McGrew, A. (2002) 'From Global Governance to Good Governance: Theories and Prospects of Democratizing the Global Polity', in M. Ougaard and R. Higgott (eds), *Towards a Global Polity*, London: Routledge, 207–26.

McIlwhaine, C. (1999) 'Geography and Violent Crime as Development Issues', *Progress in Human Geography*, vol. 23, no. 3: 453–63.

Mackay, A. (2004) 'Training the Uniforms: Gender and Peacekeeping Operations', in H. Afshar and D. Eade (eds), *Development, Women and War: Feminist Perspectives*, Oxford: Oxfam GB, 100–108.

Mackay, F. (2004) 'Gender and Political Representation in the UK: The State of the "Discipline"', *British Journal of Politics and International Relations*, vol. 6, no. 1: 99–120.

McKay, S. (2005) 'Reconstructing Fragile Lives: Girls' Social Reintegration in Northern Uganda and Sierra Leone', in C. Sweetman (ed.), *Gender, Peacebuilding and Reconstruction*, Oxford: Oxfam GB, 19–30.

McNay, L. (1994) *Foucault: A Critical Introduction*, Cambridge: Polity Press.

McQuillan, M. (2000) 'Introduction: Five Strategies for Deconstruction', in M. McQuillan (ed.), *Deconstruction: A Reader*, Edinburgh: Edinburgh University Press, 1–43.

McRae, R. (2001) 'Human Security in a Globalised World', in R. McRae and D. Hubert (eds), *Human Security and the New Diplomacy*, London: McGill-Queen's University Press, 14–27.

McSweeney, B. (1999) *Security, Identity and Interests: A Sociology of International Relations*, Cambridge: Cambridge University Press.

Malone, D.M. (2000) 'The Security Council in the 1990s: Inconsistent, Improvisational, Indispensable?', in R. Thakur and E. Newman (eds), *New Millennium, New Perspectives: The United Nations, Security and Governance*, New York: UN University Press, 21–45.

Mansbridge, J. (2003) 'Rethinking Representation', *American Political Science Review*, vol. 97, no. 4: 515–28.

Mansbridge, J. (1999) 'Should Blacks Represent Blacks and Women Represent Women? A Contingent Yes', *Journal of Politics*, vol. 61, no. 3: 628–57.

Maoz, Z., and B. Russett (1993) 'Normative and Structural Causes of Democratic Peace, 1946–1986', *American Political Science Review*, vol. 87, no. 3: 624–38.

Marchand, M., and A.S. Runyan (eds) (2000) *Gender and Global Restructuring: Sightings, Sites, Resistance*, London: Routledge.

Marcus, S. (1992) 'Fighting Bodies, Fighting Words: A Theory and Politics of Rape Prevention', in J. Butler and J. Scott (eds), *Feminists Theorise the Political*, London: Routledge, 385–403.

Mazurana, D. (2005) 'Gender and the Causes and Consequences of Armed Conflict', in D. Mazurana, A. Raven-Roberts and J. Parpart (eds), *Gender,*

Conflict and Peacekeeping, Oxford and Lanham MD: Rowman & Littlefield, 29–42.

Mearsheimer, J.J. (1995) 'The False Promise of International Institutions', *International Security*, vol. 19, no. 3: 5–49.

Mearsheimer, J.J. (1990) 'Back to the Future: Instability in Europe after the Cold War', *International Security*, vol. 15, no. 1: 5–56.

Milliken, J. (1999) 'The Study of Discourse in International Relations: A Critique of Research Methods', *European Journal of International Relations*, vol. 5, no. 2: 225–54.

Mingst, K., and M. Karns (2000) *The United Nations in the Post-Cold War Era*, 2nd edn, Oxford and Boulder CO: Westview.

Mitchell, T. (1991) 'The Limits of the State: Beyond Statist Approaches and Their Critics', *American Political Science Review*, vol. 85, no. 1: 77–96.

Mohanty, C.T. (2002) '"Under Western Eyes" Revisited: Feminist Solidarity Through Anticapitalist Struggles', *Signs: Journal of Women in Culture and Society*, vol. 28, no. 2: 499–535.

Moi, T. (1990) 'Feminism and Postmodernism: Recent Feminist Criticism in the United States', in T. Lovell (ed.), *British Feminist Thought: A Reader*, Oxford: Blackwell, 367–76.

Moore, C. (2003) 'Women and Domestic Violence: The Public/Private Legal Dichotomy', *International Journal of Human Rights*, vol. 7, no. 4: 93–128.

Moravcsik, A. (2004) 'Is There a Democratic Deficit in World Politics? A Framework for Analysis', *Government and Opposition*, vol. 39, no. 2: 336–63.

Morgenthau, H. (1973) *Politics among Nations*, 5th edn, New York: Knopf.

Morgenthau, H. (1952) 'Another "Great Debate": The National Interest of the United States', *American Political Science Review*, vol. 46, no. 4: 961–88.

Morgenthau, H. (1948) 'World Politics in the Mid-Twentieth Century', *Review of Politics*, vol. 10, no. 2: 154–73.

Moser, C. (2001) 'The Gendered Continuum of Violence and Conflict: An Operational Framework', in C. Moser and F. Clark (eds), *Victims, Perpetrators or Actors? Gender, Armed Conflict and Political Violence*, London: Zed Books, 30–52.

Moser, C., and F. Clark (eds) (2001) *Victims, Perpetrators or Actors? Gender, Armed Conflict and Political Violence*, London: Zed Books.

Moser, C., and C. McIlwaine (2001) 'Gender and Social Capital in Contexts of Politics Violence: Community Perspectives from Colombia and Guatemala', in C. Moser and F. Clark (eds), *Victims, Perpetrators or Actors? Gender, Armed Conflict and Political Violence*, London: Zed Books, 178–200.

Moser, C., and A. Moser (2005) 'Gender Mainstreaming Since Bejing: A Review of Success and Limitations in International Institutions', *Gender and Development*, vol. 13, no. 2: 11–22.

Murphy, A.B. (1996) 'The Sovereign State System as Political-Territorial Ideal: Historical and Contemporary Considerations', in T. Biersteker and C. Weber (eds), *State Sovereignty as Social Construct*, Cambridge: Cambridge University Press, 81–120.

Murphy, C. (2002) 'Why Pay Attention to Global Governance?', in R. Wilkinson and S. Hughes (eds), *Global Governance: Critical Perspectives*, London: Routledge, xi–xvii.

Murphy, C. (2001) 'What the Third World Wants: An Interpretation of the Development and Meaning of the New International Economic Order', in P. Diehl (ed.), *The Politics of Global Governance: International Organizations in an Interdependent World*, 2nd edn, London and Boulder CO: Lynne Rienner, 261–76.

Murphy, C. (2000) 'Global Governance: Poorly Done and Poorly Understood', *International Affairs*, vol. 76, no. 4: 789–803.

Naraghi-Anderlini, S. (2000) 'The A–B–C to UN Security Council Resolution 1325 on Women, Peace and Security', www.peacewomen.org/un/sc/ABC1325.html (accessed 14 March 2007).

Naraghi-Anderlini, S., and J. El-Bushra (2004) 'The Conceptual Framework: Security, Peace, Accountability and Rights', in International Alert and Women Waging Peace, *Inclusive Security, Sustainable Peace: A Toolkit for Advocacy and Action*, London: Hunt Alternatives, 5–13.

Narayan, U. (1997) *Dislocating Cultures: Identities, Traditions and Third World Feminism*, London: Routledge.

Newman, E. (2001) 'Human Security and Constructivism' *International Studies Perspectives*, vol. 2, no. 3: 239–51.

NGO WG (NGO Working Group on Women, Peace and Security) (2005) 'NGO Working Group on Women, Peace and Security', www.peacewomen. org/un/ngo/wg.html (accessed 14 March 2007).

NGO WG (NGO Working Group on Women, Peace and Security) (2004) 'Four Years On: An Alternative Report and Progress Check on the Implementation of Security Council Resolution 1325: Findings and Recommendations for United Nations Member States and United Nations Entities from Women's Civil Society Organizations', www.peacewomen.org/un/ngo/ngopub/FourYearsOnOct04.pdf (accessed 14 March 2007).

NGO WG (NGO Working Group on Women, Peace and Security) (2000a) 'Letter to Ambassadors of the Security Council on the United Nations Security Council Open Session on Women, Peace and Security', www. peacewomen.org/un/ngo/ngoletters/excellence.html (accessed 14 March 2007).

NGO WG (NGO Working Group on Women, Peace and Security) (2000b) 'Oral Statement: The Role of Women in Achieving Peace and Maintaining International Security', www.peacewomen.org/un/sc/arria/ngost.pdf (accessed 14 March 2007).

NGO WG (NGO Working Group on Women, Peace and Security) (2000c) 'NGO Statement to the Press', www.peacewomen.org/un/sc/arria/pngo. pdf (accessed 14 March 2007).

Niarchos, C. (1995) 'Women, War and Rape: Challenges Facing the International Tribunal for the Former Yugoslavia', *Human Rights Quarterly*, vol. 17, no. 4: 649–90.

Nicholson, L. (1997) 'Introduction', in L. Nicholson (ed.), *The Second Wave: A Reader in Feminist Theory*, London: Routledge, 1–6.

Nicholson, L. (ed.) (1990) *Feminism/Postmodernism*, London: Routledge.

Niva, S. (1999) 'Contested Sovereignties and Postcolonial Insecurities in the Middle East', in J. Weldes et al. (eds), *Cultures of Insecurity: States, Communities and the Production of Danger*, Minneapolis, MN: University of Minnesota Press, 147–172.

O'Brien, R., A.M. Goetz, J.A. Scholte and M. Williams (2000) *Contesting Global Governance: Multilateral Economic Institutions and Global Social Movements*, Cambridge: Cambridge University Press.

O'Hare, U.A. (1999) 'Realizing Human Rights for Women', *Human Rights Quarterly*, vol. 21, no. 2: 364–402.

Oneal, J.R., F.H Oneal, Z. Maoz and B. Russett (1996) 'The Liberal Peace: Interdependence, Democracy and International Conflict 1950–85', *Journal of Peace Research*, vol. 33, no. 1: 11–28.

Oosterveld, V. (2005) 'Prosecution of Gender-Based Crimes in International Law', in D. Mazurana, A. Raven-Roberts and J. Parpart (eds), *Gender, Conflict and Peacekeeping*, Oxford and Lanham MD: Rowman & Littlefield, 67–82.

OPSI (Office of Public Sector Information) (2003) 'Sexual Offences Act 2003', www.opsi.gov.uk/acts/acts2003/20030042.htm (accessed 8 January 2007).

O'Toole, L., and J. Schiffman (1997a) 'Preface: Conceptualising Gender Violence', in L. O'Toole and J. Schiffman (eds), *Gender Violence: Interdisciplinary Perspectives*, London: New York University Press, xi–xiv.

O'Toole, L., and J. Schiffman (1997b) 'Gender Violence in the United States', in L. O'Toole and J. Schiffman (eds) (1997) *Gender Violence: Interdisciplinary Perspectives*, London: New York University Press, 67–73.

O'Toole, L., and J. Schiffman (1997c) 'Changing Our Minds: Towards Non-violence in Gender Relations', in L. O'Toole and J. Schiffman (eds), *Gender Violence: Interdisciplinary Perspectives*, London: New York University Press, 423–6.

O'Toole, L., and J. Schiffman (1997d) 'The Roots of Male Violence against Women', in L. O'Toole and J. Schiffman (eds), *Gender Violence: Interdisciplinary Perspectives*, London: New York University Press, 3–8.

Otto, D. (2004) 'Securing the "Gender Legitimacy" of the UN Security Council: Prising Gender From its Historical Moorings', *Legal Studies Research Paper* no. 92, www.er.uqam.ca/nobel/juris/Lamarche/Droitsdesfemmes/Documents/ssrn-id585923%5B1%5D-otto.pdf (accessed 14 March 2007).

Otto, D. (1996) 'Nongovernmental Organisations in the United Nations System: The Emerging Role of International Civil Society', *Human Rights Quarterly*, vol. 18, no. 1: 107–41.

Ougaard, M., and R. Higgott (eds) (2002) *Towards a Global Polity*, London: Routledge.

Pankhurst, D. (2004) 'The "Sex War" and Other Wars: Towards a Feminist Approach to Peacebuilding', in H. Afshar and D. Eade (eds), *Development, Women and War: Feminist Perspectives*, Oxford: Oxfam GB, 8–42.

Paris, R. (2001) 'Human Security: Paradigm Shift or Hot Air?', *International Security*, vol. 26, no. 2: 87–102.

Parker, A. (ed.) (1992) *Nationalisms and Sexualities*, London: Routledge.

Parpart, J. (1995) 'Deconstructing the Development Expert', in M. Marchand and J. Parpart (eds), *Feminism, Postmodernism, Development*, London: Routledge, 221–43.

Paul, D. (1999) 'Sovereignty, Survival, and the Westphalian Blind Alley', *Review of International Studies*, vol. 25, no. 2: 217–31.

Paul, J. (2004) 'NGOs and the Security Council', *Global Policy Forum*, www.globalpolicy.org/security/ngowkgrp/gpfpaper.htm (accessed 14 March 2007).

Paul, J. (2001) 'A Short History of the NGO Working Group on the Security Council', *Global Policy Forum*, www.globalpolicy.org/security/ngowkgrp/history.htm (accessed 14 March 2007).

PeaceWomen (2007) 'A Call for Translations of UNSC Resolution 1325 on Women, Peace and Security', www.peacewomen.org/1325inTranslation/index.html (accessed 14 March 2007).

Peck, J., and A. Tickell (2002) 'Neoliberalizing Space', *Antipode*, vol. 34, no. 3: 380–404.

Peterson, V.S. (1999) 'Sexing Political Identities/Nationalism as Heterosexism', *International Feminist Journal of Politics*, vol. 1, no. 1: 34–65.

Peterson, V.S. (1992) 'Security and Sovereign States: What is at Stake in Taking Feminism Seriously?', in V.S. Peterson (ed.), *Gendered States: Feminist (Re)visions of International Relations Theory*, London and Boulder CO: Lynne Rienner, 31–64.

Peterson, V.S., and A.S. Runyan (1999) *Global Gender Issues*, Oxford and Boulder CO: Westview.

Peterson, V.S., and J. True (1998) '"New Times" and New Conversations', in M. Zalewski and J. Parpart (eds), *The 'Man' Question in International Relations*, Oxford and Boulder CO: Westview, 14–27.

Pettman, J.J. (1999) 'Globalisation and the Gendered Politics of Citizenship', in N. Yuval-Davis and P. Werbner (eds), *Women, Citizenship and Difference*, London: Zed Books, 207–20.

Pickup, F., S. Williams and C. Sweetman (2000) *Ending Violence against Women: A Challenge for Development and Humanitarian Work*, Bournemouth: Oxfam.

Pietilä, H. (2002) 'Engendering the Global Agenda: The Story of Women and the United Nations', *Development Dossier Series*, New York: UN Non-Governmental Liaison Service.

Poehlman-Doumbouya, S., and F. Hill (2001) 'Women and Peace in the United Nations', *New Routes*, vol. 6, no. 3, www.life-peace.org/sajt/filer/pdf/New_Routes/nr200103.pdf (accessed 14 March 2007).

Puechguirbal, N. (2004) 'Women and Children: Deconstructing a Paradigm', *Seton Hall Journal of Diplomacy and International Relations*, http://diplomacy.shu.edu/journal/new/pdf/VolVNo1/1%20–%20Puechguirbal.pdf (accessed 14 March 2007).

Puechguirbal, N. (2003) 'Gender Training for Peacekeepers: Lessons from the DRC', *International Peacekeeping*, vol. 10, no. 3: 113–28.

Radford, J. (1992) 'Introduction', in J. Radford and D. Russell (eds,) *Femicide: The Politics of Women Killing*, Buckingham: Open University Press, 3–12.

Radford, J., L. Kelly and M. Hester (1996) 'Introduction', in M. Hester, L. Kelly and J. Radford (eds), *Women, Violence and Male Power: Feminist Activism, Research and Practice*, Buckingham: Open University Press, 1–16.

Ramphele, M. (2000) 'Teach Me How To Be a Man: An Exploration of the Definition of Masculinity', in V. Das et al. (eds), *Violence and Subjectivity*, London and Berkeley: University of California Press, 102–19.

Reanda, L. (1999) 'Engendering the United Nations: The Changing International Agenda', *European Journal of Women's Studies*, vol. 6, no. 1: 49–68.

Rehn, E., and E. Sirleaf (2002) *Women, War and Peace: The Independent Experts' Assessment on the Impact of Armed Conflict on Women and Women's Role in Peace-building*, New York: UNIFEM, www.reliefweb.int/rw/lib.nsf/db900SID/LGEL-5FMCM2/$FILE/unicef-WomenWarPeace.pdf?OpenElement (accessed 14 March 2007).

Riley, D. (1988) *Am I That Name? Feminism and the Category of 'Women' in History*, London: Macmillan.

Rosenau, J. (1992) 'Governance, Order and Change in World Politics', in J. Rosenau and E. Czempiel (eds), *Governance without Government: Order and Change in World Politics*, Cambridge: Cambridge University Press, 1–29.

Ruddick, S. (1989) *Maternal Thinking: Towards a Politics of Peace*, Boston, MA: Beacon Press.

Runyan, A.S. (2003) 'The Places of Women in Trading Places Revisited: Gendered Global/Regional Regimes and Internationalized Feminist Resistance', in E. Kofman and G. Youngs (eds), *Globalization: Theory and Practice*, 2nd edn, London: Continuum, 139–56.

Rupert, M. (2000) *Ideologies of Globalisation*, London: Routledge.

Russett, B. (1993) *Grasping the Democratic Peace: Principles for a Post-Cold War World*, Princeton: Princeton University Press.

Schmidt, B., and I.W. Schröder (eds) (2001) *Anthropology of Violence and Conflict*, London: Routledge.

Scholte, J.A. (2002) 'Civil Society and Governance in the Global Polity', in M. Ougaard and R. Higgott (eds), *Towards a Global Polity*, London: Routledge, 145–66.

Scholte, J.A. (2001) 'Civil Society and Democracy in Global Governance', http://www2.warwick.ac.uk/fac/soc/csgr/research/workingpapers/2001/wp6501.pdf (accessed 14 March 2007).

Schwindt-Bayer, L.A., and W. Mishler (2005) 'An Integrated Model of Women's Representation', *Journal of Politics*, vol. 67, no. 2: 407–28.

Scott, J. (1994) 'Deconstructing Equality-versus-Difference: Or, the Uses of Poststructuralist Theory for Feminism', in S. Seidman (ed.), *The Postmodern Turn: New Perspectives on Social Theory*, Cambridge: Cambridge University Press, 282–98.

Segal, L. (1987) *Is the Future Female? Troubled Thoughts on Contemporary Feminism*, London: Virago.

Sen, P. (1998) 'Development Practice and Violence against Women', *Gender and Development*, vol. 6, no. 3: 7–16.

Shapiro, M. (2004) '"The Nation-State and Violence": Wim Wenders contra Imperial Sovereignty', in J. Edkins, V. Pin-Fat and M. Shapiro (eds), *Sovereign Lives: Power in Global Politics*, London: Routledge, 101–24.

Sharoni, S. (2001) 'Rethinking Women's Struggles in Israel-Palestine and in the North of Ireland', in C. Moser and F. Clark (eds), *Victims, Perpetrators or Actors? Gender, Armed Conflict and Political Violence*, London: Zed Books, 85–98.

Shaw, M. (2001) 'The Unfinished Global Revolution: Intellectuals and the New Politics of International Relations', *Review of International Studies*, vol. 27, no. 4: 627–47.

Sheehan, M. (2005) *International Security: An Analytical Survey*, London and Boulder CO: Lynne Rienner.

Shepherd, L.J. (2005) 'Loud Voices behind the Wall: Gender Violence and the Violent Reproduction of the International', *Millennium: Journal of International Studies*, vol. 34, no. 2: 377–401.

Shepherd, L.J., and J. Weldes (2007) 'Security: The State (of) Being Free from Danger?', in H.G. Brauch et al. (eds), *Globalisation and Environmental Challenges: Reconceptualizing Security in the 21st Century* Mosbach: AFES-PRESS.

Skjelsbaek, I. (2001) 'Sexual Violence and War: Mapping Out a Complex Relationship', *European Journal of International Relations*, vol. 7, no. 2: 211–37.

Skunk Anansie (1997) 'Yes It's Fucking Political', *Stoosh*, London: One Little Indian Records.

Smith, S. (2005) 'The Contested Concept of Security', in K. Booth (ed.), *Critical Security Studies and World Politics*, London and Boulder CO: Lynne Rienner, 27–62.

Sparke, M. (2005) *In the Space of Theory: Postfoundational Geographies of the Nation-State*, London and Minneapolis: University of Minnesota Press.

Squires, J. (2005) 'Rethinking Substantive Representation', paper presented at the European Consortium of Political Research 8–10 September, available at www.essex.ac.uk/ecpr/events/generalconference/budapest/papers/symposia/1/squires.pdf (accessed 14 March 2007).

Squires, J. (1999) *Gender in Political Theory*, Cambridge: Polity Press.

Stanko, E.A. (1994) 'Challenging the Problem of Men's Individual Violence', in T. Newburn and E.A. Stanko (eds), *Just Boys Doing Business?*, London: Routledge, 32–45.

Stanko, E.A. (1985) *Intimate Intrusions: Women's Experience of Male Violence*, London: Routledge.

Stanley, L. (1997) 'Recovering Women in History from Feminist Deconstructionism', in S. Kemp and J. Squires (eds), *Feminisms*, Oxford: Oxford University Press, 274–8.

Starr, H. (1992) 'Democracy and War: Choice, Learning and Security Communities', *Journal of Peace Research*, vol. 29, no. 2: 207–13.

Staudt, K. (2003) 'Gender Mainstreaming: Conceptual Links to Institutional Machineries', in S. Rai (ed.), *Mainstreaming Gender, Democratizing the State? Institutional Mechanisms for the Advancement of Women*, Manchester: Manchester University Press on behalf of the United Nations, 40–66.

Steans, J. (2003a) 'Engaging from the Margins: Feminist Encounters with the "Mainstream" of International Relations', *British Journal of Politics and International Relations*, vol. 5, no. 3: 428–454.

Steans, J. (2003b) 'Gender Inequalities and Feminist Politics in a Global Perspective', in E. Kofman and G. Youngs (eds), *Globalization: Theory and Practice*, 2nd edn, London: Continuum, 123–38.

Steans, J., and L. Pettiford (2005) *Introduction to International Relations: Perspectives and Themes*, 2nd edn, Harlow: Pearson Longman.

Steinbruner, J.D. (2000) *Principles of Global Security*, Washington DC: Brookings Institution.

Sterling-Folker, J. (ed.) (2006) *Making Sense of International Relations Theory*, London and Boulder CO: Lynne Rienner.

Stone, A. (2005) 'Towards a Genealogical Feminism: A Reading of Judith Butler's Political Thought', *Contemporary Political Theory*, vol. 4, no. 1: 4–24.

Sunderland, J. (2004) *Gendered Discourses*, London: Palgrave.

Sutterlin, J. (2003) *The United Nations and the Maintenance of International Security: A Challenge To Be Met*, 2nd edn, London: Praeger.

Sweetman, C. (2005) 'Editorial', in C. Sweetman (ed.), *Gender, Peacebuilding and Reconstruction*, Oxford: Oxfam GB, 2–7.

Swingewood, A. (2000) *A Short History of Sociological Thought*, 3rd edn, London: Palgrave Macmillan.

Sylvester, C. (2002) *Feminist International Relations: An Unfinished Journey*, Cambridge: Cambridge University Press.

Sylvester, C. (1996) 'The Contributions of Feminist Theory to International Relations', in S. Smith, K. Booth and M. Zalewski (eds), *International Theory: Positivism and Beyond*, Cambridge: Cambridge University Press, 254–78.

Sylvester, C. (1994) *Feminist Theory and International Relations in a Postmodern Era*, Cambridge: Cambridge University Press.

Tatchell, P. (2002) 'Some People are More Equal than Others', www.petertatchell.net/hate%20crimes/moreequal.htm (accessed 14 March 2007).

Tehranian, M. (ed.) (1999) *Worlds Apart: Human Security and Global Governance*, London: I.B. Tauris.

Tétreault, M.A., and R.D. Lipschutz (2005) *Global Politics As If People Mattered*, Oxford and Lanham MD: Rowman & Littlefield.

Thapar, S. (1993) 'Women as Activists, Women as Symbols: A Study of the Indian Nationalist Movement', *Feminist Review*, vol. 44, no. 1: 81–96.

Thomas, C. (2001) 'Global Governance, Development and Human Security: Exploring the Links', *Third World Quarterly*, vol. 22, no. 2: 159–175.

Thomas, C. (2000) *Global Governance, Development and Human Security*, London: Pluto Press.

Thomas, N., and W. Tow (2002) 'The Utility of Human Security: Sovereignty and Humanitarian Intervention', *Security Dialogue*, vol. 33, no. 2: 177–92.

Tickner, J.A. (1997) 'You Just Don't Understand: Troubled Engagements Between Feminists and IR Theorists', *International Studies Quarterly*, vol. 41, no. 4: 611–32.

Tickner, J.A. (1992) *Gender in International Relations*, New York: Columbia University Press.

Tomlinson, J. (1991) *Cultural Imperialism*, Baltimore MD: Johns Hopkins University Press.

Torfing, J. (1999) *New Theories of Discourse: Laclau, Mouffe and Žižek*, Oxford: Blackwell.

True, J. (2003) 'Mainstreaming Gender in Global Public Policy' *International Feminist Journal of Politics*, vol. 5, no. 3: 368–96.

True, J., and M. Mintrom (2001) 'Transnational Networks and Policy Diffusion: The Case of Gender Mainstreaming', *International Studies Quarterly*, vol. 45, no. 1: 27–57.

Turpin, J., and L.R. Kurtz (1997) 'Introduction: Violence - The Micro–Macro Link', in J. Turpin and L.R. Kurtz (eds), *The Web of Violence: From Interpersonal to Global*, Chicago IL: University of Illinois Press, 1–27.

Ullman, R. (1983) 'Redefining Security', *International Security*, vol. 8, no. 1: 129–53.

UN (United Nations) (2008a) 'Growth in United Nations Membership, 1945–present', www.un.org/members/growth.shtml (accessed 7 January 2008).

UN (United Nations) (2008b) 'UN Security Council: Background', www.un.org/Docs/sc/unsc_background.html (accessed 7 January 2008).

UN (United Nations) (2000) 'Secretary-General Calls for Council Action to Ensure Women are Involved in Peace and Security Decisions', SG/SM/7598, www.un.org/News/Press/docs/2000/20001024.sgsm7598.doc.html (accessed 14 March 2007).

UN (United Nations) (1993) 'Declaration on the Elimination of Violence against Women', www.un.org/documents/ga/res/48/a48r104.htm (accessed 14 March 2007).

UN (United Nations) (1983) 'Provisional Rules of Procedure of the Security Council', S/96/Rev.7, www.un.org/Docs/sc/scrules.htm (accessed 14 March 2007).

UN (United Nations) (1945) 'Charter of the United Nations', www.un.org/aboutun/charter (accessed 14 March 2007).

UNDAW (United Nations Division for the Advancement of Women) (2008) 'Overview of the Convention', www.un.org/womenwatch/daw/cedaw/ (accessed 6 January 2008).

UNDAW (United Nations Division for the Advancement of Women) (2007) 'About the Division', www.un.org/womenwatch/daw/daw/ (accessed 7 January 2008).

UNDAW (United Nations Division for the Advancement of Women) (2000) 'Gender Mainstreaming', www.un.org/womenwatch/daw/csw/GMS.PDF (accessed 16 August 2006).

UNDP (United Nations Development Programme) (1994) *Human Development Report 1994: New Dimensions of Human Security*, http://hdr.undp.org/en/media/hdr_1994_en.pdf (accessed 6 January 2008).

UNESC (United Nations Economic and Social Council) (2004) 'Gender Mainstreaming in the Work of the United Nations on Peace and Security', www.un.org/womenwatch/ianwge/activities/E-2004-CRP-3.pdf (accessed 6 January 2008).

UNFWCW (United Nations Fourth World Conference on Women) (1995) 'Beijing Platform for Action', available at www.un.org/womenwatch/daw/beijing/platform/index.html (accessed 16 August 2006).

UNGA (United Nations General Assembly) (2000) 'Windhoek Declaration on the Tenth Anniversary of the United Nations Transition Assistance Group', A/55/138–S/2000/693, www.un.org/documents/ga/docs/55/a55138.pdf (accessed 14 March 2007).

UNIFEM (United Nations Development Fund for Women) (2005) 'Security Council Resolution 1325 Annotated and Explained', www.womenwarpeace.org/toolbox/Annotated_1325.pdf (accessed 14 March 2007).

UNIFEM (United Nations Development Fund for Women) (2004) 'Women, Peace and Security: UNIFEM Supporting Implementation of SC Resolution 1325', www.womenwarpeace.org/supporting1325.pdf (accessed 14 March 2007).

United Nations Office of the Special Adviser on Gender Issues (2002) 'Gender Mainstreaming: An Overview', New York: United Nations, www.un.org/womenwatch/osagi/pdf/e65237.pdf (accessed 14 March 2007]

UNSC (United Nations Security Council) (2005) 'Report of the Secretary-General on Women, Peace and Security', S/2005/636, http://daccess dds.un.org/doc/UNDOC/GEN/N05/534/82/PDF/N0553482.pdf?OpenElement (accessed 14 March 2007).

UNSC (United Nations Security Council) (2004a) 'Women, Peace and Security: Report of the Secretary-General', S/2004/814, http://daccessdds.un.org/doc/UNDOC/GEN/N04/534/14/PDF/N0453414.pdf?OpenElement (accessed 14 March 2007).

UNSC (United Nations Security Council) (2004b) 'Statement by the President of the Security Council', S/PRST/2004/40, http://daccessdds.un.org/doc/UNDOC/GEN/N04/578/09/PDF/N0457809.pdf?OpenElement (accessed 14 March 2007).

UNSC (United Nations Security Council) (2002a) 'Report of the Secretary General on Women, Peace and Security', S/2002/1154, http://daccess dds.un.org/doc/UNDOC/GEN/N02/634/68/PDF/N0263468.pdf?OpenElement (accessed 14 March 2007).

UNSC (United Nations Security Council) (2002b) 'Statement by the President of the Security Council', S/PRST/2002/32, http://daccessdds.un.org/

doc/UNDOC/GEN/N02/671/80/PDF/N0267180.pdf?OpenElement (accessed 14 March 2007).

UNSC (United Nations Security Council) (2001) 'Statement by the President of the Security Council', S/PRST/2001/31, http://daccessdds.un.org/doc/UNDOC/GEN/N01/612/25/PDF/N0161225.pdf?OpenElement (accessed 14 March 2007).

UNSC (United Nations Security Council) (2000a) 'Resolution 1325', S/RES/1325, UNSC (United Nations Security Council), 2000a, 'Resolution 1325', S/RES/1325, http://daccessdds.un.org/doc/UNDOC/GEN/N00/720/18/PDF/N0072018.pdf?OpenElement (accessed 14 March 2007).

UNSC (United Nations Security Council) (2000b) 'Resolution 1296', S/RES/1296, http://daccessdds.un.org/doc/UNDOC/GEN/N00/399/03/PDF/N0039903.pdf?OpenElement (accessed 8 November 2005).

UNSC (United Nations Security Council) (2000c) 'Peace Inextricably Linked with Equality Between Women and Men Says Security Council, in International Women's Day Statement', Press Release SC/6816, www.un.org/news/Press/docs/2000/20000308.sc6816.doc.html (accessed 14 March 2007).

UNSC (United Nations Security Council) (2000d) 'Children and Armed Conflict: Report of the Secretary-General', A/55/163–S/2000/712, http://daccessdds.un.org/doc/UNDOC/GEN/N00/529/46/PDF/N0052946.pdf?OpenElement (accessed 14 March 2007).

UNSC (United Nations Security Council) (2000e) 'The Role of United Nations Peacekeeping Personnel in Disarmament, Demobilization and Reintegration: Report of the Secretary-General' S/2000/101, http://daccessdds.un.org/doc/UNDOC/GEN/N00/291/43/PDF/N0029143.pdf?OpenElement (accessed 14 March 2007).

UNSC (United Nations Security Council) (2000f) 'Statement by the President of the Security Council' S/PRST/2000/7, http://daccessdds.un.org/doc/UNDOC/GEN/N00/340/73/PDF/N0034073.pdf?OpenElement (accessed 14 March 2007).

UNSC (United Nations Security Council) (1999) 'Resolution 1261', S/RES/1261, http://daccessdds.un.org/doc/UNDOC/GEN/N99/248/59/PDF/N9924859.pdf?OpenElement (accessed 14 March 2007).

UNSC (United Nations Security Council) (1998) 'Resolution 1208', S/RES/1208, http://daccessdds.un.org/doc/UNDOC/GEN/N98/362/90/PDF/N9836290.pdf?OpenElement (accessed 14 March 2007).

UNSC (United Nations Security Council) (1992) 'Statement by the President of the Security Council Pursuant to their 1992 Summit Meeting', www.un.org/french/docs/cs/repertoire/89–92/chapter%208/general%20issues/Item%2028%20_SC%20respons%20in%20maint%20IPS_.pdf.

Uvin, P. (1998) *Aiding Violence: The Development Enterprise in Rwanda*, Bloomfield, CT: Kumarian Press.

Van Dijk, T.A. (1997a) 'The Study of Discourse', in T.A. van Dijk (ed.) (1997) *Discourse as Structure and Process*, London: Sage, 1–34.

Van Dijk, T.A. (1997b) 'Discourse as Interaction in Society', in T.A. van Dijk (ed.), *Discourse as Social Interaction*, London: Sage, 1–37.

Varadarajan, L. (2004) 'Identity and Neoliberal (In)Security', *Review of International Studies*, vol. 30, no. 3: 319–342.

Väyrynen, T. (2004) 'Gender and UN Peace Operations: The Confines of Modernity', *International Peacekeeping*, vol. 11, no. 1: 125–42.

Viotti, P., and M. Kauppi (1999) *International Relations Theory: Realism, Pluralism, Globalism and Beyond* (3rd edn), London and Boston, MA: Allyn & Bacon.

Waever, O. (1995) 'Securitization and Desecuritization', in R.D. Lipschutz (ed.) *On Security*, Chichester: Columbia University Press, 46–86.

Walby, S. (2005) 'Gender Mainstreaming: Productive Tensions in Theory and in Practice', *Social Politics*, vol. 12, no. 3: 321–343.

Walby, S. (1992) Post-Post-Modernism? Theorising Social Complexity, in M. Barrett and A. Phillips (eds), *Destabilizing Theory: Contemporary Feminist Debates*, Cambridge: Polity Press, 31–52.

Walker, R.B.J. (2002) 'International/Inequality', *International Studies Review*, vol. 4, no. 2: 1–24.

Walker, R.B.J. (1997) 'The Subject of Security', in K. Krause and M.C Williams (eds) *Critical Security Studies: Concepts and Cases*, London: UCL Press, 61–82.

Walker, R.B.J. (1993) *Inside/Outside: International Relations as Political Theory*, Cambridge: Cambridge University Press.

Walker, R.B.J. (1991) 'State Sovereignty and the Articulation of Political Space/ Time', *Millennium: Journal of International Studies*, vol. 20, no. 3, pp. 445–61.

Walker, R.B.J. (1990) 'Sovereignty, Identity, Community: Reflections on the Horizons of Contemporary Political Practice', in R.B.J. Walker and S.H. Mendlowitz (eds), *Contending Sovereignties: Redefining Political Communities*, London and Boulder CO: Lynne Rienner, 159–86.

Walt, S. (2000) 'Fads, Fevers and Firestorms', *Foreign Policy*, no. 121: 34–42.

Walt, S. (1991) 'Renaissance in Security Studies', *International Studies Quarterly*, vol. 35, no. 2: 211–239.

Waltz, K. (2000) 'Structural Realism after the Cold War', *International Security*, vol. 25, no. 1: 5–41.

Waltz, K. (1993) 'The Emerging Structure of International Politics', *International Security*, vol. 18, no. 2: 44–79.

Waltz, K. (1979) *Theory of International Politics*, Reading MA: Addison-Wesley.

Waltz, K. (1967) 'The Politics of Peace', *International Studies Quarterly*, vol. 11, no. 3: 199–211.

Waltz, K. (1959) *Man, the State and War: A Theoretical Analysis*, New York: Columbia University Press.

WCRWC (Women's Commission for Refugee Women and Children) (2005) 'Youth Speak Out: New Voices on the Protection and Participation of

Young People Affected by Armed Conflict', www.womenscommission. org/pdf/cap_ysofinal_rev.pdf (accessed 14 March 2007).

Weber, C. (1995) *Simulating Sovereignty: Intervention, the State and Symbolic Exchange*, Cambridge: Cambridge University Press.

Weber, C. (1994) 'Good Girls, Little Girls and Bad Girls: Male Paranoia in Keohane's Critique of Feminist International Relations' *Millennium: Journal of International Studies*, vol. 23, no. 2: 337–49.

Weber, C. (1992) 'Reconsidering Statehood: Examining the Sovereignty/Intervention Boundary', *Review of International Studies*, vol. 18, no. 3: 199–216.

Weiss, T.G. (2000) 'Governance, Good Governance and Global Governance: Conceptual and Actual Challenges', *Third World Quarterly*, vol. 21, no. 5: 795–814.

Weldes, J. (ed.) (2003) *To Seek Out New Worlds: Exploring Links Between Science Fiction and World Politics*, London: Palgrave Macmillan.

Weldes, J. (1996) 'Constructing National Interest', *European Journal of International Relations*, vol. 2, no. 3: 275–318.

Weldes, J., M. Laffey, H. Gusterson and R. Duvall (1999) 'Introduction: Constructing Insecurity', in J. Weldes (eds), *Cultures of Insecurity: States, Communities and the Production of Danger*, Minneapolis, MN: University of Minnesota Press, 1–33.

Wendt, A. (1992) 'Anarchy Is What States Make of It', *International Organization*, vol. 46, no. 2: 391–425.

Whitbread, J. (2005) 'Mainstreaming Gender in Conflict Reduction: From Challenge to Opportunity', in C. Sweetman (ed.), *Gender, Peacebuilding and Reconstruction*, Oxford: Oxfam GB, 41–9.

Whitehead, A., et al. (1993) 'Editorial', *Feminist Review*, vol. 44, no. 1: 1–4.

Wilkinson, R. (2002) 'The Contours of Courtship: The WTO and Civil Society', in R. Wilkinson and S. Hughes (eds), *Global Governance: Critical Perspectives*, London: Routledge, 193–211.

Williams, J. (2003) 'Territorial Borders, International Ethics and Geography: Do Good Fences Still Make Good Neighbours?', *Geopolitics*, vol. 8, no. 2: 25–46.

Williams, S. (2004) 'Mission Impossible: Gender, Conflict and Oxfam GB', in H. Afshar and D. Eade (eds), *Development, Women and War: Feminist Perspectives*, Oxford: Oxfam GB, 315–36.

WILPF (Women's International League for Peace and Freedom) (2005) 'Welcome to the Website of the WILPF International', www.wilpf.int.ch/ (accessed 14 March 2007).

Wilson, J.Z. (2005) 'State Making, Peacemaking and the Inscription of Gendered Politics into Peace: Lessons from Angola', in D. Mazurana, A. Raven-Roberts and J. Parpart (eds), *Gender, Conflict and Peacekeeping*, Oxford and Lanham MD: Rowman & Littlefield, 242–64.

Winter, B., D. Thompson and S. Jeffreys (2002) 'The UN Approach to Harmful Traditional Practices', *International Feminist Journal of Politics*, vol. 4, no. 1: 72–94.

Wolfers, A. (1952) "National Security' as an Ambiguous Symbol', *Political Science Quarterly*, vol. 67, no. 4: 481–502.

Woodward, K. (1997) 'Concepts of Identity and Difference', in K. Woodward (ed.), *Identity and Difference*, London: Sage, 7–62.

Wyn Jones, R. (2005) 'On Emancipation: Necessity, Capacity and Concrete Utopias', in K. Booth (ed.), *Critical Security Studies and World Politics*, London and Boulder CO: Lynne Rienner, 215–36.

Yanow, D. (1996) *How Does a Policy Mean? Interpreting Policy and Organizational Actions*, Washington DC: Georgetown University Press.

Young, I.M. (2003) 'The Logic of Masculinist Protection: Reflections on the Current Security State', *Signs: Journal of Women in Culture and Society*, vol. 29, no. 1: 1–25.

Youngs, G. (2003) 'Private Pain/ Public Peace: Women's Rights as Human Rights and Amnesty International's Report on Violence against Women', *Signs: Journal of Women in Culture and Society*, vol. 28, no. 4: 1209–29.

Youngs, G. (1999) *International Relations in a Global Age: A Conceptual Challenge*, Cambridge: Polity Press.

Yuval-Davis, N. (1997) *Gender and Nation*, London: Sage.

Zalewski, M. (2000) *Feminism after Postmodernism: Theorising through Practice*, London: Routledge.

Zalewski, M. (1996) '"All These Theories Yet the Bodies Keep Piling Up": Theories, Theorists, Theorising', in S. Smith, K. Booth and M. Zalewski (eds), *International Theory: Positivism and Beyond*, Cambridge: Cambridge University Press 340–53.

Zalewski, M. (1995) 'Well, What is the Feminist Perspective on Bosnia?', *International Affairs*, vol. 71, no. 2: 339–56.

Zuckerman, E., and M. Greenberg (2005) 'The Gender Dimensions of Post-Conflict Reconstruction: An Analytical Framework for Policymakers', in C. Sweetman (ed.), *Gender, Peacebuilding and Reconstruction*, Oxford: Oxfam GB, 70–82.

INDEX